CONNECTED
in
CAIRO

PUBLIC CULTURES OF THE MIDDLE EAST AND NORTH AFRICA

Paul A. Silverstein, Susan Slyomovics, and
Ted Swedenburg, editors

CONNECTED
—in—
CAIRO

Growing up Cosmopolitan
in the
Modern Middle East

Mark Allen Peterson

Indiana University Press • *Bloomington & Indianapolis*

This book is a publication of

Indiana University Press
601 North Morton Street
Bloomington, Indiana 47404-3797 USA
www.iupress.indiana.edu

Telephone orders	800-842-6796
Fax orders	812-855-7931
Orders by e-mail	iuporder@indiana.edu

♾ The paper used in this publication meets
the minimum requirements of
the American National Standard for
Information Sciences—Permanence
of Paper for Printed Library Materials,
ANSI Z39.48-1992.

Manufactured in the United States of America

Library of Congress Cataloging-in-
Publication Data

Peterson, Mark Allen.
  Connected in Cairo : growing up cosmopoli-
tan in the modern Middle East / Mark Allen
Peterson.
     p. cm. — (Public cultures of the Middle
East and North Africa)
  Includes bibliographical references and
index.
  ISBN 978-0-253-35628-4 (alk. paper) —
ISBN 978-0-253-22311-1 (pbk. : alk. paper)
  1. Consumption (Economics)—Egypt—Cairo.
2. Cosmopolitanism—Egypt—Cairo. 3. Social
mobility—Egypt—Cairo. I. Title.
  HC830.Z9C67 2011
  306.0962'16—dc22
                                    2010043779

2 3 4 5   16 15 14 13 12 11

To Madi, Thea, and Sophie, who made Cairo home

CONTENTS

PREFACE

There is a scene in the brilliant Egyptian comedy film *Irhab wal-Kabab* (Terrorism and Barbecue) in which an old man on a crowded Cairo bus, who has been griping about all the frustrations Egyptians must put up with, is told by a young man that he sounds like a fizzing Coke bottle. The man retorts that even Coke bottles explode once in a while when you shake them up enough. That's what the Egyptian Revolution of 1958 was all about. So what, he asks the younger generation on the bus, is *their* excuse?

Many observers of the Middle East have asked the same question. Egyptian apathy was a byword. Then, on January 25, 2011, the Coke bottle finally exploded. Protesters marched into Tahrir ("Liberty") Square in unprecedented numbers. Although repeatedly forced out by police, they returned again and again, ultimately staking out a symbolic space in the center of Cairo and declaring that it belonged to the people, not the state. After 18 days, nearly 300 deaths, and over 1,000 injuries from clashes with police, *baltigiyya* (hired thugs), and counter-protesters, President Hosni Mubarak resigned, and the Supreme Council of the Armed Forces formed an interim government.

I wish I could say that the book you are holding was prescient, that it anticipates the uprising, which occurred as the book was about to go to press. It does not. I wish I could say that this book clearly points to the directions the revolution might go. It does not. It does, however, offer a description of Egyptian identity on the cusp of the revolution.

Egypt has seen a number of strikes, riots, and protests, from the Bread Riots of 1981 to the pro-Democracy marches of 2005 to the April 6 youth movement protests in 2008. Why did the protests of January 2011 succeed where so many others have failed? What made the Coke bottle, so often shaken only to fizzle out, finally explode?

One reason is that the year 2010 was a landmark year for social and political unrest in Egypt. Three events became powerful symbols of everything that was wrong with the Egyptian government. Egyptian security forces clashed with Palestinian Arabs in January, during Egypt's unpopular enforcement of the Israeli blockade against Gaza. In June, businessman and blogger Khaled Said was beaten to death by police. The fall elections were marked by blatant ballot-box stuffing and intimidation.

Social media played a crucial role in mobilizing these events as symbols among a very special group of Egyptians: the young, college-educated underemployed. Encompassing Westernized cosmopolitans, Muslim Brotherhood youth, university student organizations, and many more, these are the tech-savvy Cairenes, collectively called *shabab al-Facebook* (Facebook youth) by older generations. The internet gave these young Egyptians a view of the Gaza clashes unobtainable through state television. Disaffected government employees posted videos to YouTube taken with cell phones of fellow poll workers stuffing ballot boxes. The Facebook page *Kullina Khaled Said* (We Are All Khaled Said) became a rallying point for calls to revolution. Blogs became important sites for commenting on media, both domestic and foreign. Streams of Tweets pointed people to blogs, Facebook pages, and news sites in an ever-growing web of political resistance.

In Chapter Four, I describe a conversation with Hassan, a young man who speaks about the highly successful Egyptian film *Nasser 56*. The film created in him a nostalgia for an era he never experienced, one in which, he said, "Everyone was willing to make sacrifices, not like today." Even as he planned to leave Egypt to study and perhaps pursue a career abroad, he wished his homeland could be one worth living in, one in which citizens were willing to work together for the common good. Others I describe sought the same thing in an Islamic activism that is about changing and improving oneself and one's community, while still others turned to social media in search of an Egyptian nationalism that might transcend presidents and parties and link people together into a new public sphere.

The power of Tahrir Square was that it brought all these elements together in a single place and time. One protester compared it to Brechtian theater: singing, poetry recitals, philosophical discussions of human rights and the dignity of man(kind), and political arguments about how best to move forward, all happening simultaneously, commenting on one another to create a meaningful cacophony. Protesters pooled their skills and pitched in to organize food banks, clinics, waste management, and even the building of a small catapult to chase a sniper from a nearby location. Many protesters have noted the temporary collapse of class and sectarian distinctions that have long troubled Egypt and that provided fuel for the regime's claim that it stood between a stable society and social collapse. Without leaders, elected or otherwise, but with high energy and charismatic organizers and planners, people stepped forward and offered their skills where and when needed.

Tahrir Square exhibited a vibrant social experience of antistructure, in which the structures of everyday life of the immediate past have been disrupted or overturned, but new structures have not yet emerged to replace them. In such situations, social actors experience an intense feeling of community, social equality, solidarity, and togetherness. Protesters in Tahrir Square recognized that their situations had tremendous transformative possibilities. Indeed, it was this sense of possibility that drove the unprecedented popular struggle.

The fate of antistructure is an inexorable transformation into a new social structure that may or may not strongly resemble the old, and this seems to be occurring in Egypt as the country moves toward stability. The future of Egypt will not be decided in a few weeks, or a few months, or even a few years. Whatever happens, it seems likely that Egypt will have a government in the future that is more responsive to citizens' concerns than it has been in the past. When army units forcibly cleared Tahrir Square of protesters in the early hours of Saturday, February 26th, the Supreme Council of the Armed Forces apologized later that morning. Not only was this a dramatic change from the behavior of the ousted regime—which consistently blamed victims for the aggression meted out to them by state forces—but the act of apology itself implied a recognition that the interim government had obligations to the people it ruled.

But this new government, whatever form it takes, will be faced with significant economic dilemmas. The unresolved tension between nostalgia for Nasserist socialism and incomplete transition to neoliberal economics discussed in this book will continue to shape debates over Egypt's future. The former system fed people, guaranteed living wages, and built public infrastructure but saddled Egypt with unmanageable debt. The latter grew the economy at comfortable rates but generated few jobs and created a massive chasm between rich and poor. It is not at all unlikely that the emerging political structure will fragment between the demands of workers for immediate improvements in working conditions and the worries of the new leadership that this will lead to reduced foreign investment and a loss of global competitiveness.

Whatever the future holds, Tahrir Square will remain a powerful symbol. For the protesters, and for many of those watching and supporting them, Tahrir represented in miniature the free, cooperative nation to which they aspire. It has already become a tourist destination; it is destined to become a key reference point, one that invokes nostalgia, political agency, freedom, nationalism, and community. The power to claim this symbol will be contested between state and private actors across multiple media and in the everyday practices of a new generation of Cairenes, becoming part of the symbolic resources through which people forge their cosmopolitan identities.

MARK ALLEN PETERSON
FEBRUARY 28, 2011

ACKNOWLEDGMENTS

I went to the Middle East to teach anthropology at the American University in Cairo. That this book exists at all is due to the encouragement and support of many colleagues there, but especially Abdallah Cole, Soraya Altorki, Nick Hopkins, Rebecca Bryant, and the deeply missed Cynthia Nelson. Just as important were the contributions from the many, many undergraduates who shared their writing, their thoughts, and their experiences with me. Among those whose contributions were most helpful are (in no particular order) Sandra Abdalla, Karim Hawass, Amr Bassiouni, Mohamed Sabry Khattab, Dalal Shahin, Ahmed Mazhar El Gazzar, Ahmed Rifai, Gazbeya El Hamamsy, Hoda Ismail, Ingy Nabil Fawzy, Kara Urbanek, Mohamed Khattah, Sherine Abdel Rahman, Christine Shenouda, Hassan El-Mouelhi, Maie Shawky, Omneya Farag, Yasmine Salah El-Din, Louly Seif, Saif Nasrawy, Maha Zayan, Hoda Ismail, and Shayman Abdou. I hope that, if you find yourself lurking behind a pseudonym in these pages, or see my account of a story you shared with me, you will feel I have been both accurate and respectful.

I owe to the graduate students at AUC a debt I cannot begin to pay. Thank you, Mohamed Mosad Abdelaziz, Amira Abdel-Khalek, Sherine Hafez, Mamdouh Hakim, Maysa Ayoub, Abdel Monim El-Gak, Christy Ferguson, Yvette Isaac, Laleh Behbehanian, Marketa Sebelova, Kwasi Bempong, Hedayat Labib, Ghalia Gargani, Sherine Ramzy, Junko Toriyama, Willa Thayer, Shahinaz Khalil, James Lejukole, Ranya Abdel Sayed, Dalia El Naggar, Lisa Raiti, Tim Brown, Rama Ghazi, Anne Zaki, Deena Ibrahim, Gihan Labib, Dalia El-Noury, Caren Craigo, Iman Eissa, Noha Ali Abu Gazia, Nancy Emara, Sally El-Mahdy, and Kate Pavljuk—not only for the discussions we had and the insights you gave me in Cairo between 1998 and 2002 in and out of the classroom, but for the continued support that many of you, including some who never took a class with me, gave me over the years by e-mail and, later, through Facebook. I also thank the staff at AUC's Department of Sociology, Anthropology, Psychology, and Egyptology, especially Aida Selim, Reem Mirshak, Safaa Sedky, and Dalia Adel.

I need a special shout-out to a number of my former students whose contributions to this project continued long after I left Cairo: I thank Dalia A. A. Mustafa and Mustafa Wahdan for continued correspondence concerning the mysteries of Arabic idioms and teen behavior; Samar Ibrahim and Maysa Ayoub for hospitality and thoughtful conversation; Ivan Panovic and Shereen Abou-Hashish for collaborating with me on earlier works that led me to think deeply about class, consumption, and modernity in Egypt; Wesam Younis for friendship, thoughtful discussions, and driving me around late at night to obscure video and DVD shops; Mustafa Abdalla for hospitality and thoughtful, ironic commentary on class, power, and Egyptian films; and Shearin Abdel-Moneim for being the best graduate assistant at AUC.

In 2005, I returned to Cairo to interview entrepreneurs and businesspeople as part of the project that turned into chapter 6. I appreciate the many people who gave their time to help me understand Egyptian entrepreneurialism, including Mohammed Tawfiq of Pizza Plus; Dalia Ibrahim of Nahdet Misr; Aysha Selim and Shahira Khalil of Disney Character Voices, Inc.; Samia Sadek of Video 2000; Magda El Guindi of Al-Ahram publishing; Mones Zoheiri, editor of *Bolbol;* Sherif Bayoumi of Microsoft; Mohamed Nagui of Beano's; and the many more who preferred not to have their names mentioned in the text. I am particularly thankful to Nermine Helmi, my research assistant in Cairo, who was not only able to almost miraculously put me into busy and important people's offices on a few days' notice but who got so interested in the work that she accompanied me on almost all the interviews and offered insightful comments.

Parts of this research were funded by a faculty research support grant from the American University in Cairo. A summer faculty support grant from Miami University bought me some time for writing. Parts of chapter 1 were delivered at the workshop "New Directions in Middle East Media and Communications Technology Research" at Georgetown University's Center for Contemporary Arab Studies in April 2001. My attendance was supported by another faculty support grant from the American University in Cairo. Most of the data in chapter 5 were collected during a six-week return trip to Cairo in 2005, supported by Miami University's Philip and Elaina Hampton Fund for Faculty Initiatives, the Center for the Enhancement of Learning and Teaching, and the Center for American and World Cultures.

All translations are mine. If a translation is sometimes less clear or accurate than it should be, I can only say that it would have been worse if not for the assistance of Safaa Sedky, Jessica Winegar, Deborah Akers, and Saleh Youssef.

An earlier version of chapter 2 appeared in 2005 as "The Jinn and the Computer: Consumption and Identity in Arabic Children's Magazines," in *Childhood* 12(2): 177–200. Parts of chapter 3 appeared in 2010 as "Imsuku-hum Kulhum! Modernity and Morality in Egyptian Children's Consumption," in the *Journal of Consumer Culture* 10(2): 233–253. Portions of chapter 6 appeared in 2010 as "Agents of Hybridity: Class, Culture Brokers, and the Entrepreneurial Imagination in Cosmopolitan Cairo," in *Research in Economic Anthropology* 30: 225–256.

I would like to thank Paul Amar, Walter Armbrust, Ghada Barsoum, James Bielo, John Cinnamon, Cameron Hay-Rollins, Natalia Kasprzak, Christa Salamandra, Dalia Wahdan, and Jessica Winegar for reading versions of this manuscript and recommending changes and revisions.

Thanks are also due to Rebecca Tolen, my editor at Indiana University Press, who stuck with this manuscript for far longer than she should have needed to; editorial assistant Chandra Mevis; and copy editor Merryl Sloane, who cleaned up my stylistic excesses, moments of inattention, and errors.

Above all, thanks to Dawna, Madison, Thea, Sophie, and Jaden, who have lived with this project one way or another for eleven years, and who continually supported me, each in their own way.

NOTE ON TRANSLITERATION

This book draws primarily from oral texts in the Cairene dialect. As consistently as possible, I have followed the system adopted by the *International Journal of Middle East Studies,* except that I have omitted all diacritics except the ayn and the hamza. I have not, however, forced colloquial words into the straitjacket of modern standard Arabic. For the names of historical or contemporary persons, I have deferred to the transliterations used in standard bibliographic reference texts or to the style chosen by those persons when rendering their names in English. Similarly, when transliterating the Arabic titles of books, magazines, and brand names, I have used the conventions preferred by the companies.

CONNECTED
in
CAIRO

TOWARD AN ANTHROPOLOGY
OF CONNECTIONS

We're connected in Cairo.

Economically dependent on foreign aid, tourism, and foreign investment, Cairenes look abroad for models of development and study foreign languages in pursuit of social mobility. Meanwhile, foreign goods flood the markets. Cheap plastic toys made in China are hawked on street corners in the central urban neighborhoods of Tahrir and Dokki, electronics made in Japan are sold in high-end shops in Mohandiseen, and you can buy a Jaguar in Heliopolis if you've got the cash. Shopping centers like Giza's elegant First Mall have become spectacles of luxury and modernity, places to see and be seen. They join other translocal spaces, like McDonald's and Dreampark, where consumers can experience the global in settings whose identicality with other such settings around the world seems to put them neither in Cairo nor anywhere else in particular. A small number of upper-class elites, joined by an equally small rising middle class, some rich from their own roles in this transnational trade, others flush with petrodollars earned in the Gulf, purchase these goods, enter these hyperspaces, and send their children to expensive "American" private schools (often owned and run by Egyptians or other Arabs) to acquire modern languages and educations.

Cairo's mediascape is awash with technologically mediated interconnections. BlackBerries and iPhones have become the badges of the upper middle class. The Egyptian cinema, in spite of being the premier movie industry of the Arab world, cannot keep the local theaters filled. American films fill this gap in the high-end theaters, while Bollywood *filmis* and Hong Kong action flicks inhabit the low-end market niche. Cybercafés cluster in areas inhabited by students, expatriates, tourists, and Egyptian emigrants visiting from abroad. Satellite broadcasting has transformed viewing patterns by making an increasing amount of uncensored news

1

and entertainment programs available to the urban middle classes. Broadcast television has followed suit, changing decades-old programming patterns to meet new desires. Specialized "Arab" and "Egyptian" web portals, which promise to create "interfaces" between the "traditional" local and the (Westernized) global, are emerging. Egyptians explore websites that offer accounts of Islamic practice by engineers and others who, by virtue of their particular educations, would not be authorized to speak on these subjects in more traditional venues.

And yet not everyone in Cairo is equally connected, and not everyone is connected in the same ways. At the dawn of the twenty-first century, Egypt's mean gross domestic product (GDP) per capita was only $4,000 according to official figures, and some economists estimated it to be considerably lower. The unemployment rate was 14 percent, and 23 percent of the country lived in poverty—pegged at about $1,200 for a family of four. For tens of millions of Egyptians, the world of extraordinary luxury they see displayed on television, in films, on billboards, and on the bodies of people driving past them in Mercedes Benz cars is, and will likely always be, unattainable. For many, these lifestyles are morally suspect. For others, they are an aspiration. For most Egyptians, the morality of all these transnational connections lies somewhere between these extremes, in the "daily struggle to appropriate what they perceive as positive aspects of modernity and avoid what is considered negative" (Ghannam 2002: 133).

But this book is not a story of the poor and working classes who make up the bulk of Egyptian society, although they play a role. This is an account of the elites for whom these transnational goods and services are not luxuries but necessities, the stuff that defines who they are. The cosmopolitan class is made up of those Egyptians whose income is so far above the GDP mean that they can routinely afford to spend on a meal at McDonald's more than a café waiter makes in a day, and to frequent high-end shopping malls like CityStars, with its Mango's, Charles and Keith, and Benetton stores. The "A and B+ classes," as they are known in local marketing literature, make up only 3–6 percent of the population—but this is still some 2–4 million people, as large as the population of Kuwait or Dubai. And although this cosmopolitan class comprises only a small percentage of the Egyptian population, its significance is out of proportion to its size. To most of the international press, the state, and other agents of the neoliberal global order, the participation of Egypt's economic and educational elites in transnational flows of goods and services is a portent of the halcyon days ahead when the rising tide of global free markets will float all boats. To many Egyptians, though, these wealthy elites are less the harbingers of great days than examples of those who've sold out to "the West." Upper-class Egyptians grow up aware of both of these discourses and must negotiate their identities between them.

This book is a description of cosmopolitan Cairo, a place defined by sets of practices that are iconic, indexical, and symbolic of urbanity and modernity in Egypt. The basis of my argument is that connectedness—not only actual connectivity but displays of goods and actions that are symbolically connected to places outside Egypt—is utilized by upwardly mobile Cairenes as a form of social capital that distinguishes them from other Egyptians. Certain forms of consumption and practice are indexical of "the West" or "the global" and serve as valuable means for displaying cosmopolitan identity. At the same time, goods and practices that come from elsewhere in North Africa, or from the Gulf states, are important in establishing one's identity as an Arab and a Muslim. A tension often arises between these forms of transnational capital, for many of those who authorize Western cultural capital define it largely in opposition to Middle Eastern forms of capital—and vice versa. Class, ethnicity, patriotism, and gender are all increasingly tied, sometimes in contradictory ways, to these transnational flows.

The cosmopolitan classes do not, of course, comprise a singular entity, although they may sometimes be so characterized in the international press or by critical Marxist or Islamist writers. There are old-money families, nouveaux riches, and many subdivisions and cross-categorizations of these categories. Elite groups and persons assign labels to one another on the basis of where wealth comes from, intergenerational educational capital, and other criteria. In the following chapters, we will encounter globe-trotting teens with substantial trust funds, families that count their pounds carefully as they strategize for their children's upwardly mobile social futures, and many varieties in between. What all have in common is a particular relationship to a modernity seen as inherently rooted in a global, nonlocal realm. Members of what I'm calling the cosmopolitan class seek to incorporate this modernity into their everyday lives primarily (but not exclusively) through consumption. Yet it is primarily locally that this cosmopolitan class harvests the fruits of its transnational modernity, because participation in global flows is a circuitous route to a significant place in local class and status hierarchies.

This description of how Egyptians use transnational goods and spaces to construct identities is intended as an illustration, a contribution to theories about localization as a cultural process. By *localization,* I mean the appropriation of elements of transnational flows (including commodities but also persons, discourses, technologies, and capital) and their integration by people into their social relationships. In this process, these translocal goods, persons, and ideas are transformed by their contextualization; at the same time, the contexts themselves are transformed. On the basis of these Egyptian cases, I will argue four significant points about localization. First, localization is a cultural process that produces locality by contrasting things that are "local" with those that are from elsewhere. The local is not a preexisting given, but a concept generated in the social imagination when people perceive cultural elements as being from outside. Second, localization produces identities as people link themselves (or are linked by others) through consumption, labor, discourse, and other forms of social action to particular places—both those that are local and those that are far away. Third, localization, so understood, is inevitably a metacultural process (Urban 2001) through which people reflect on, question, interpret, reproduce, and revise their cultural categories and social actions. Because they proceed by constructing theories about connectivity and by linking the local to the distant, these metacultural processes are indexical and deictic. Finally, globalization does not just happen as a result of supernational social processes; it is always the result of specific agents situated in specific places pursuing personal goals (which are, inevitably, also social and cultural goals) through strategies involving the appropriation and recontextualization of goods, persons, capital, technologies, or ideas. Globalization, in other words, is a result of myriad localizations, and it is these localizations I will examine in this book.

MODERNITIES

The argument of this book had its genesis in a class I was teaching in 1999 at the American University in Cairo (AUC) on anthropological approaches to mass media. We were discussing one of Lila Abu-Lughod's papers on modernity and media viewing in rural Egypt (Abu-Lughod 1997). In ways their grandparents could never have imagined, the villagers Abu-Lughod describes are hedged in by state bureaucracies that determine much of their lives. They have public schooling, watch television, wear machine-woven, store-bought clothes, seek wage labor, and sell their produce to distributors who ship it to other parts of the country to be sold in supermarkets or processed into canned foods. Many live in concrete block houses built for them by the government and get their water from pipes because their own canal-irrigated family lands, close to some of the most tourist-haunted antiquities, have been rezoned to preclude their residence there.

"But you *cannot* call these people modern," protested Sabry. Sabry was the stereotypical AUC student: a young Egyptian business major, Muslim, dressed in designer jeans and a button-down shirt, well traveled, educated at private schools, and fluent in two languages but more at home writing in English than Arabic. "They wear *galabiyyas* [robes]. They have clay floors. They live with animals." He pointed particularly to the passage in the paper in which Zaynab, one of the villagers, fed to her animals packaged snacks—chips, perhaps, or Twinkies—that well-meaning tourists had given to her children. Zaynab, Abu-Lughod explains, has an "aversion to eating anything 'from outside'" (1997: 124). Real food, for Zaynab, is social; one knows where it has come from, and it is cooked by one person for another.[1] "This is not modern," Sabry finished with a flourish. Many of the other students were nodding their heads.

The distinction between my students' perspective and mine was in part that between the modernist and the postmodernist. For me, as for many social scientists, modernity was supposed to be about issues of structure and substance: technological infrastructures, political economies, increasing interpenetration of state bureaucracies, and social transformation. For my students, modernity was a matter of *style:* how you spoke, what you ate, what movies you'd seen, what you wore, where you bought it, and where you were seen wearing it. This idea that modernity is a style, a mode of performance linked to taste and education, is often linked to "the postmodern condition" (Jameson 1984), a way of looking at the world that rejects the grand, one-size-fits-all narratives of the twentieth century like Marxism, the Enlightenment, "progress," and, in this case, classic social theory, in favor of smaller practical truths that deal with the contingencies and immediacies of everyday life among particular groups of people.

The rise of the postmodern aesthetic has been closely associated with the consumption of media images. The mass media, it is argued, reduce substance to surface. Even more, mass media train the children of the managerial class, those who will inhabit administrative and leadership roles in the capitalist world system, to see the world in these ways.[2] "Postmodernism is the aesthetic of a particular class generation, the youth of the professional and managerial classes, whose cultural consumption habits are of intense concern to the culture industry" (Traube 1989: 274). There is a great deal of truth in this view. Certainly, Sabry and his cohort, the youth of Egypt's professional, managerial, and entrepreneurial classes, were shaped by media images, by advertising, by news. Sabry's interjections took place in a course on media and we were just turning from American movies to Egyptian soap operas (*musalsal*), and the students were all intimately familiar with both.

There was another reason for the students' insistence that Abu-Lughod's informant Zaynab was not modern. If modernity is a style, in Egypt it is a style to which not everyone has access. Facility with foreign languages, not only spoken languages but the languages of dress, of bodily comportment, of brand names, of technological familiarity, and of current events, rests on one's ability to afford certain schools, to shop at certain stores, and to gain access to particular technologies of connection and consumption. Modernity as style is a class issue. As such, it is a style over which people of my students' class have a monopoly. For me to posit Zaynab as modern is to strike at one of the foundations of this class system, a system that validates economic distinctions as being about the possession of skills, education, knowledge, and talent, displayed through sets of cosmopolitan styles. For me to treat these styles as irrelevant to modernity is to belittle the system of tastes and distinctions in which they and their families have invested enormous amounts of capital, time, and energy.

Transnational popular culture has become an important form of cultural capital through which the Egyptian class system replicates itself. The children of the Egyptian elites, through particular types of family structures, consumption of particular media, interactions with specific peer groups, attendance at a defined set of schools, acquisition of particular languages, consumption of particular goods, and familiarity with particular kinds of spaces, come to acquire a general character that distinguishes them from the middle and lower classes. This particularity is never merely a defined set of tastes and habits and practices; it is a general orientation toward the world, a way of understanding one's place in the world that is capable of generating new practices amid shifting social, economic, and cultural contexts. It is, moreover, a transnational orientation, not because it entails travel (although it often does) but because it looks beyond the bounds of the local—the neighborhood, the city, the nation, the Arab region—to focus on one's participation in a wider world of economic and cultural flows.

Cosmopolitanism, in other words, is conceived here as a set of practices (Bourdieu 1977, 1984) through which the Egyptian upper classes and those with upwardly mobile aspirations construct themselves as transnational elites whose unequal control over Egypt's economic and political resources is justified by their modernity, and whose modernity is in turn revealed by their cosmopolitanism: their Western educations, their easy movement across transnational borders, their consumption of transnational goods, and the general display of certain tastes in music, literature, film, clothing, and technologies that distinguish them from the masses.

This description is misleading, however, because class reproduction does not just happen to people as a consequence of social forces outside their control. It occurs through the agency of individuals and families as they struggle with the fundamental problem of how to be at once Egyptian and modern. Practices of consumption play a crucial role in the formation of a person, in conjunction with family, education, peer groups, and work. A simple description of the ways elite institutions inculcate dispositions to reproduce elite behaviors cannot sufficiently address the powerful attraction to members of the cosmopolitan class of identities that are not entirely congruent with their class positions. A fully "modern" cosmopolitan identity would seem to require a domesticated religious faith, a desultory patriotism, and an ambiguous ethnicity. Yet the desire of many members of the cosmopolitan class to be Muslim, to be Egyptian, to be Arab, to be masculine or feminine according to the local culture's codes cuts across cosmopolitan class identities. Nor is identity a matter of volition and intentional performance. As they work and travel, cosmopolitan Egyptians must deal with the identities inscribed on their bodies. The dilemmas of how to be at once cosmopolitan and Egyptian, modern and Muslim, Westernized and Arab, rich but manly, or liberated yet feminine loom large among the young Cairenes whose lives I describe in this book.

Why should transnational popular culture be a key form of capital that defines one's elite-class status? "First World cheap becomes Third World chic," an Indian journalist once told me (we were discussing the arrival of McDonald's in New Delhi in 1993), and this is certainly true of Cairo, where the commodities and spaces understood in the West as vulgarly popular—McDonald's, Pokémon, Hollywood action flicks, *Superman* comic books, and so forth—have become markers of upper-class identity. The obvious economic answer, scarcity, is certainly relevant, but it begs the question. Scarcity is significant only where there is also desire. Why should there be a marked preference for foreign goods as markers of style over locally produced high-end goods, especially when the foreign goods are held to be cheap or faddish in the places that produced them? Who brings such goods, services, and spaces into Cairo, and why? Why are some successful while others fail?

To explore these issues, I will make a specific argument about globalization and cultures, one that focuses on the cultural metadiscourses through which people represent, reflect, and reconstruct their understandings of the changing universe currently glossed under the term *globalization*. Whatever their significance in their places of origin, transnational goods draw part of their significance as cultural capital from the ways they point to their places of origin (or, in some cases, their putative places of origin). Because indexical signification rests as much on perceptions as on actual connections of causality or origin, metadiscourses have arisen that explore the significance of transnational goods and services, and their place in the moral worlds of modernity, Islam, and Egyptian nationalism. Yet precisely because transnational goods signify by pointing beyond the local, they can dislocate individuals, striking at their sense of being rooted in a particular place and ethos.

THE LOCAL AND THE GLOBAL

In making the argument that Egyptians construct themselves as particular kinds of people in part through consumption, I am conceiving of *consumption* as a cultural practice, an act through which people relate their experiences to socially learned codes. Acts of consumption, like acts of ritual, play, work, and other human activities, are means of expressing and realizing fundamental cultural principles about how the world is constituted (Douglas and Isherwood 1981). Knowing which goods are classed as "modern" and why reveals some of people's fundamental assumptions about what modernity is and its place in a larger cultural universe. Which of these commodities people choose, exchange, own, and display constructs their identities within the social fields that enable and constrain their lives: home, school, peer group, faith community, and the imagined communities represented by and through the media. People's acts of consumption are not scripted but generated; people reproduce the social order through consumption by developing particular kinds of tastes that have different kinds of consequences in various social fields (Bourdieu 1979, 1984).

These practices are complicated in Cairo, as elsewhere in the world, by the rapid changes in the political economy. Since the 1960s, Egypt has gone from a centralized socialist economy to an increasingly liberalized economy. This transformation has been accompanied by dramatic dislocations for millions of Egyptians as food subsidies, land tenure regulations, and rent controls have been changed or phased out. The globalization of the world economy into an increasingly interconnected capitalist system raises problems with any simple mapping of commodities to fixed identities. The literature on globalization emphasizes the transformations of localities that occur as multiple possible social and cultural orders come to exist simultaneously (Appadurai 1996: 49; Larkin 1997: 407; Lau 2002). This literature has emphasized the slipperiness of identity among world populations that are increasingly interconnected and aware of that interconnectedness (Hall 1990; Hannerz 1992, 1996). Globalization, in this sense, involves a breakdown of the isomorphism of people, places, and cultures on which many assumptions about socialization, enculturation, and social order are based (Giddens 1990; Gupta and Ferguson 1992). The cultural systems that give meaning to consumption are increasingly seen as mutable and shifting in response to opportunities, challenges, and transformations (Miller 1994, 1997).

There is a general agreement that "globalization" refers to an increasing number of situations in which "local events are shaped by events happening many miles away and vice versa" (Giddens 1990: 64). But it is difficult to describe just how dramatic this situation is, and what the nature of that "shaping" is. The term *globalization* has come to mean so many things to so many people that it has almost lost its utility as an analytical concept. On one hand, globalization refers to the operations of transnational or supernational agencies and agreements like the Group of Eight, the General Agreement on Tariffs and Trade, the World Bank, the World Trade Organization, the International Monetary Fund, and so forth, which operate at a genuinely global level. On the other hand, much of what goes under the name globalization is about the linking of locales. In economics and in a good deal of journalism, globalization refers to the specific process of opening markets and deregulating the worldwide movements of financial capital, an essentially political process that is prescribed as a necessary evolution by economists in countries whose elites benefit from such changes, and proscribed by others who see it as "a convenient myth which, in part, helps justify and legitimize the neo-liberal global project, that is the creation of a free market and the consolidation of Anglo-American capitalism within the world's major economic regions" (Held and McGrew 2000: 5). The advance of this neoliberal project is a crucial context for my study, for the cosmopolitan elites in whom I am interested comprise the class of Egyptians who partner with international agencies to advance globalization in Egypt and in the broader Middle East.

Attending to the ways Egyptians themselves articulate their changing lives in contemporary Cairo, I will focus on the dynamics among objective connections (i.e., actual flows of goods, people, vessels, machines, and so forth) across culturally constructed boundaries such as nations, the awareness people have of these movements, and the discourses they create to describe globalization and to situate themselves in it. The cultural dimension of globalization depends not on economic and political connectivity itself, which has always existed (Rosenberg 2000), but on "the intensification of the consciousness of the world as a whole" (Robertson 1992: 8). This shift in consciousness I take to be the integration into the cultural discourses of peoples throughout the world the recognition that their lives are increasingly affected by phenomena taking place outside their realms of experience. It is an awareness of the transnational character of goods, spaces, and images that makes cosmopolitan identities available. This awareness is expressed through complexly layered, debated, and continually changing discourses through which Egyptian publics seek to understand changing markets and social spaces and the political economies in which they are embedded.

COSMOPOLITAN DILEMMAS

If everyone in Egypt is increasingly aware of the power of transnational forces to reshape their lives, the original sociological use of the term *cosmopolitan* to distinguish between those whose orientation is parochial and those whose orientation is toward more encompassing social structures (Merton 1957: 387ff.) must be modified. Increasingly, cosmopolitanism has come to be understood as "a mode of managing meaning" (Hannerz 1990: 238) involving "the coexistence of cultures in the individual experience" (239). At once a practice and an identity, cosmopolitanism in this sense represents the capacity to live in a terrain of transition and translation, to inhabit not only the territorial landscape of Cairo but simultaneously the fluid, multi-branching topography of imagined communities, migration routes, media circulation, and financial networks across which global culture flows. At the global level, amid the networks of banks, schools, governments, nongovernmental organizations, extranational institutions, and so forth, cosmopolitanism is a style for managing difference that allows one to move easily across political, social, cultural, and economic boundaries. Locally, cosmopolitanism is about the organization of diversity (ibid.: 237) in social worlds increasingly complicated by "the challenge of multiple traditions" (Eriksen 1996: 245).

Cosmopolitanism involves the capacity to manage the coexistence and juxtaposition of different cultures and to make this capacity part of one's identity. This capacity to be open to the world has long been seen as a monopoly of elites and intellectuals, a fact reflected in the distinctions posited by Hannerz (1990) between "cosmopolitans" and "locals" and by Friedman between diasporic elites and their working-class counterparts who, he argues, are "confined in their local ghetto identity" (1997: 84). But other ethnographic work has challenged this dichotomy. "Why has cosmopolitanism as a sociopolitical appeal, or a methodology for analyzing identity, been identified with colonial elitism? How can we get beyond this?" ask Diane Singerman and Paul Amar (2006: 31). One answer can be found in a growing number of empirical accounts of working-class cosmopolitan migrants (Werbner 1999) and non-mobile groups who draw their identity from an orientation toward other peoples far away (Englund 2004). Rather than reducing the value of the concept, this work suggests that what is important is the style through which people imagine themselves as connected to distant places and cultures, and the social ends to which these styles are mobilized.

Thus, at the level of practice, both the Cairene student at AUC and the Deltan villager are equally cosmopolitan and equally indigenous. The former makes use of her economic capacity to participate in transnational flows of goods to establish her status as a member of the economic elite just as her parents and their parents have for generations; the latter uses his capacity to link what he sees on television or reads in the newspaper about the wider world to specific passages in the Qur'an or *Hadith,* or to local knowledge about unseen worlds to maintain and enhance his status as a man of perception and respectability. What is different about them is precisely what Sabry put his finger on: their style. Specifically, there is a set of tastes, linguistic codes and registers, bodily comportments, and other practices that operate at once to distinguish the Cairene upper classes from the Deltan *fallahs* (peasants) and the urban middle classes, while at the same time increasing their similarities and affinities with the managerial and moneyed classes in the wealthy nations at the core of the world system. The cosmopolitans studied in this volume are those for whom being cosmopolitan through consumption—not only of goods but of education and travel—is an essential part of their identity and class status.[3]

Certain forms of social mobility in Cairo have always involved attaining competence in the languages, styles, and modes of foreigners: Greeks, Romans, Ottomans, Britons, French.[4] Today, the cosmopolitan orientation is toward "global culture," particularly (but not exclusively) that expressed in the styles and commodities flowing from Western Europe, the United States, and, to a lesser extent, Asia. Young people like Sabry insist that their cosmopolitan social practices differentiate them from people like Zaynab, who are indigenized by their insistence on holding some of these styles at bay. That these styles are expressed through expensive commodities makes social reproduction far easier than social mobility. Those with wealth can more easily afford the commodities through which they express their cosmopolitanism. The children of the upper classes learn foreign languages at expensive private schools, mingling with the children of the expatriate community and becoming familiar with the fads of the moment. In time, they develop generative logics that allow them to unreflexively keep tabs on changing fashions and markets so as to maintain their style and the statuses that accrue to it. They attend international universities, and the credentials from these justify the social positions they inhabit by virtue of the class positions into which they were born. Terms like 'asri (contemporary or modern), madani (civilized or refined), and 'ishta (literally "cream" but idiomatically "cool") are contrasted with terms like bi'a (vulgarly popular) to distinguish the educated middle and upper classes from the poor majority.[5] However, these neat models of cosmopolitan-indigene schismogenesis are undercut by struggles over identity. Even as members of Egypt's transnational elites embrace Western styles through consumption, they often find themselves simultaneously attracted to more "rooted" notions of gender, nation, ethnos, and ethos than those they can find at the mall. Part of being cosmopolitan is having an Egyptian identity to display, a bit of local culture. Cosmopolitanism creates an ambiguous and ambivalent relationship with the local that is often expressed as a struggle or problem: how to be at once modern and Egyptian.

Cosmopolitans in Cairo, then, face at least two key dilemmas. First is the fact that cosmopolitan patterns of consumption and displays of taste that are valuable in one social field may not be valuable, and may even be liabilities, in other important social fields, such as the mosque, the military barrack, or the smoke-filled backroom of politics. Second, they face internal dilemmas about the nature of their selves as cosmopolitans and as Arabs, Muslims, or Egyptian citizens. This is not only an ethical issue about where one's loyalties lie, but may cut deeper into fundamental issues of identity and selfhood: who am I? Transcultural travelers and, especially, "third culture children," who have grown up in more than one society (Useem 1963; Haour-Knipe 1989; Cockburn 2002), frequently express this problem. In a world where even the most cosmopolitan still tend to describe themselves—and be described by others—in terms of national identities, my student Mina, who spent six years in British boarding schools, asked in a class journal, "So who am *I*, who feels British in Egypt but Egyptian in Britain?" As Englund points out, worldliness, whether it is a cosmopolitanism of impoverishment as he studied in Malawi, or a cosmopolitanism of privilege, as described here in Cairo, entails a deterritorialized mode of belonging that creates "an uneasy relation to the home that imposes itself on the subject" (2004: 293). Efforts to reterritorialize through modes of dress or a display of traditional artifacts open complex questions of authenticity.

A nuanced account of cosmopolitanism that will go beyond a class reproduction or schismogenesis model to explain why local statuses are dependent on transnational goods, and how multiple, entangled identities get constructed and reconstructed through displays of such commodities and through translocal movements, requires a semiotics of connectedness, a theory of how things connect and what these connections mean. My own efforts to understand cultural connectivity are rooted in Peircean semiotics, and particularly in his concept of indexicality, of meaning something by being connected to it. In contrast to the binary semiological theories of Saussure and Barthes, Peirce's semiotics emphasizes that meaning involves not only a signifier and a signified, but an audience and a cultural logic (interpretant) by which audiences come to understand the sign. An *index* is any relation between signifier and signified based on relations of contiguity—that is, on connectedness. Such relations can include cause and effect, origin, co-presence, pointing, proximity, collocation, anaphora, part-whole relations, and other forms of connectivity.

Indexicality is useful for studying globalization because it brings together several important elements that often get separated in globalization theories. Connectedness is real. There is nothing arbitrary or imaginary about the links we collectively call globalization. What those links mean, on the other hand, is very much a cultural construction. Particularly striking is the fact that "global modernity" implies a dichotomy between a North American/Western European "Western" style and a local or regional "authentic" Arab style regardless of the actual complexities of the transnational flows of goods and capital. Upper-class Cairenes flock to Benetton and Mango's at the elegant CityStars shopping mall to buy Western name brands without consideration of the fact that these franchises are owned by companies from the Gulf. On the other hand, Pokémon has a global and Asian "odor" (Iwabuchi 2002) but is, in fact, franchised from Nintendo North America (complete with English names), not from Japan's Nintendo. Cairenes fulfilling their socially constituted taste for Western styles do not always know or care whether commodities and consumption practices that represent cosmopolitan style according to local codes accurately map the flows of global goods.

The indexical associations between goods and other places in the world where such goods are created or consumed are crucial to their value as social and cultural capital. How then are associations of connectedness established in the rapidly changing social formations we connect with globalization? The specific meanings that connectedness will have in any social situation are governed by "indexical orders" that allow people to misrecognize in one setting facts of which they are quite cognizant in others (Silverstein 2003). The ethnographic problem is to tease out which connections apply to which commodities and practices for which people in what contexts by paying attention to the ways people work the meanings of signs through public debates that attempt to contextualize, negotiate, and articulate the meanings of indexical signs. I call these *metadeictic discourses* (Peterson 2003: 268), public discourses through which people seek to interpret and understand things and practices by linking them to near and distant places. *Deixis* refers broadly to the whole range of indexical practices by which social actors anchor the meanings of their actions to the spatiotemporal contexts in which they take place. Metadeictic discourses are public discussions about deictic meaning; they are discourses that seek to interpret and make judgments about cultural artifacts and practices by connecting them with other places.

In contemporary Cairo, many metadeictic discourses seek to tease out the nature of the interconnections that bind the global to the local and to explore what those interconnections mean to people who experience global-local interdependencies. Metadeictic discourses allow people to add moral and pragmatic dimensions to the phenomena they see before them. Are Arabic children's magazines better for children than *Archie* or *Mickey* because the former are regionally produced and the latter are foreign? Is *Mickey* a better magazine now that it is written in classical rather than colloquial Arabic? Is Pokémon Japanese or American, and what does its origin say about our children's obsession with it? Should we boycott McDonald's in Egypt because it is American (in terms of its origin), or should we support it because it is Egyptian (in that it is owned by and employs Egyptians, and buys Egyptian bread, vegetables, and other goods)? Metadeictic discourses link everyday practices with other moral, political, social, and economic concerns. The shifting connections that cosmopolitans forge with the wider world as part of creating local social relations are negotiated through these discourses.

GLOBAL CAIRO

Cairo is a good place to examine these questions because it so wonderfully captures the paradoxes and contradictions of globalization. Cairo is a global city, a node in the rising transnational service economy, a strategic site for the acceleration of capital and information flows in North Africa and the Middle East, and a space of increasing socioeconomic polarization (Sassen 2001). As well, flows of information, goods, and services have bound it into the growing web of cities becoming "global" through the networks in which they participate (Sassen 2002). Like Delhi and other emergent global cities, it is a multilayered, polysemic place marked by the juxtaposition of different images of Egypt and the West, "the local and the global, modernity and tradition, linked together by tourism, consumerism, and enhanced mobility" (Favero 2003: 553).

But Cairo is not just a global city, it is a globalizing city in which globalization is an ongoing and contingent process rather than an established stage of development. Central to this process is Cairo's expanding realm of consumerism in a land of rising poverty. "Structural adjustment," operationalized as deregulation of the Nasserist laws that controlled food, rent, and land prices, has been particularly visible in the form of land speculation, which has resulted primarily in the enrichment of property owners, an increase in social inequalities, and a rise in the poverty rates. During the structural adjustment program implemented by the IMF in Egypt, rural poverty doubled and urban poverty increased by 150 percent between 1981 and 1991 (Bayat 1997). At the time of my research (1997–2002), 23 percent of Egyptians lived below the poverty level (fixed at $1,200 per year for a family of 4.6 members). Amid this economic crisis, there has been a steady, ongoing construction of amusement parks (Mitchell 1999), beach resorts, condominiums, swimming pools, gated communities (Younis 2005), and shopping malls (Abaza 2001b), many of which sport an "Islamic" or "pharaonic" and "Western" or "modern" architectural fusion (Abaza 2006).

The concentration of wealth in the hands of a few is both marked and masked through this construction. It is masked by the growing transformation of public spaces into commodified forms that suggest a common participation in a shared modernity, what Abaza calls "the reshaping of public space to merge shopping with leisure (movie houses, billiard rooms, discotheques, ice skating rinks)" (Abaza 2001b: 107). It is marked by phenomena such as the rise of gated communities, inspired by American and Asian models. Most of all, it is marked by the forced relocation of the poor to create new spaces for the wealthy. Cairo's population density is estimated at 40,000 persons per square kilometer (Bayat 1997: 3). Like every global city, Cairo is plagued by unplanned construction, that is, by squatters and slums. There are some 400 areas of unplanned housing, with a population in excess of 7 million (al-Hiddini 1999, cited in Abaza 2001b: 108) and perhaps as great as 12 million, one-third of the city's population. Periodically, these are demolished to make way for new construction and transformations of urban space (Ghannam 2002). The World Trade Center, its attached shopping mall, and the Hilton Ramses hotel/shopping complex are cases in point; they were created by the government's selling of desirable urban land at relatively low prices to developers. The police and other mechanisms of the state were then used to remove "slum dwellers" (often the working poor and craftspeople whose families may have occupied the space for generations) so that the space could be transformed.

As in so many global cities, the neoliberal reterritorialization of the cityscape is less a process of global homogenization than "the product of very much a local hegemonic imagination—one that utilizes the discourse of 'modernization' to legitimize inequality" (Guano 2002: 182). The language of urban space becomes an idiom through which to talk about the moral characters of the people who live there. For example, *'ashwa'iyyat,* the Arabic term for slums, has taken on a whole range of moral connotations signifying disorder, backwardness, and uncivilized behavior. It is associated with immoral behavior, such as illicit sexual relations and *'urfi* (unwitnessed) marriage (Abaza 2001a). By associating the term, on one hand, with gendered concepts of honor and shame and, on the other, with sociological conceptions of urban criminality, powerful ideologies of disenfranchisement are generated. In turn, these concepts are drawn on by the upper classes to constitute their own enfranchisement through practices of differentiation. Cairo is a site in which people with very different backgrounds, educations, and life trajectories encounter transnational flows of goods, ideas, and technologies, and incorporate them into their social relations in contexts of coercion, inequality, and, sometimes, conflict.

CONNECTING IN CAIRO

This book is based on five years of fieldwork in Cairo from August 1997 through May 2002, during which I was teaching anthropology at the American University in Cairo. A generation ago, Gilsenan wrote of seeking a place in Cairo "small enough" for ethnographic fieldwork (1982). While I never found a place that would encapsulate cosmopolitan Cairo, I did find many small places that offered glimpses of upper-class Cairene life: bookstores, private schools, universities, coffee shops, upscale businesses, and local offices of multinational corporations. Unlike classical ethnographic fieldwork, which is often rooted in an isomorphism of people, place, and culture, my account is expressed in a series of case studies (Epstein 1967; van Velsen 1967), each of which took me to different places and among different people.

I did not go to Cairo to do research; I went to teach. The research began on a modest scale in my second year, and increased as my Arabic improved and as I was encouraged by my students and colleagues that the work I was doing was interesting and worth pursuing. Each of the transnational projects I examine here—Arabic children's magazines, Pokémon, private "language" schools, restaurant and café franchises—served as a "rich point" (Agar 1994: 100) through which I gained insights into the lives of those I taught, worked with, and lived among. Trying to understand these projects led me to more systematic data gathering. My data are derived from a number of sources: participant observation, novels, newspapers, movies, magazines, conversations, maps, sales figures, and interviews with consumers and with the entrepreneurs and businesspeople selling them goods and services. For each project, I will offer both a "thick description" (Geertz 1973) and "thick contextualization" (Ortner 1995) that will allow the reader to share my glimpses of how people make culture with transnational goods in local places.

My use of case studies is no doubt influenced by my other set of professional practices, those of a journalist developed as a part of the Washington press corps during two three-year stints. As when I was a journalist, there were stories I wanted to tell: the story of Pokémon, the story of McDonald's, the story of the American University in Cairo. Embedded in these institutional stories were stories of people: the story of Yasseen and his computer; the story of Hosni, whose son took first prize in the school preparatory exam; the story of Dr. Reem and her Pokémon party. At the same time, I have been keenly aware of the risks of what Clifford Geertz has characterized as "hit and run ethnography" in which "middle distance, walk-through research" produces "thoroughly ephemeral accounts" (Geertz 1998: 72). This was a real danger when I began this project. When I started, for example, I thought I would be doing a study of "hybridity," a trendy topic in cultural theories about globalization and localization. Yet as I discussed examples of what seemed to me clearly hybrid phenomena with my students and friends in Egypt, I discovered that, for many of them, these places and objects were not hybrid at all, but touchstones of modernity. I was confronted with the question posed by Jonathan Friedman: "Hybrid for whom?" (2002b: 23). Answering this question forced me out of a voyeuristic, journalistic role of seeing things and thinking about them in theoretically informed ways into the traditional ethnographer's role of seeing things and seeking to describe the contexts that make them meaningful to the people in whose lives they are embedded. This led me to begin thinking about signs of modernity, the global, and the local in terms of such classical anthropological problems as the relationship between systems of symbols, social organization, and, because so many of my examples involve consumption, exchange.

The other important aspect of my ethnographic encounters that helped me to avoid what began as a more two-dimensional approach to globalization was the deeply dialogical nature of the project as it unfolded over time. In speaking of it as dialogical, I am not seeking to embrace the "messianic" (Crapanzano 1992: 188) or utopian overtones of some explicitly dialogical anthropologies nor to give equal weight to the voices of one or two significant research partners from the local community (Dwyer 1987). Rather, I am trying to explain that this work took shape as an ongoing series of interactions with literally hundreds of Egyptians with whom I shared my experiences, described my observations, and explained my analyses. I listened to their comments, criticisms, suggestions, accusations, and contradictions, and returned to my fieldwork informed by these dialogues, not just once but again and again over several years as my analysis evolved.

These dialogues began with such mundane things as classroom discussions and my readings of student assignments. In a unit on kinship, I'd ask students to write a short essay on how a particular *musalsal* (soap opera) posed a problem of kin relations and how it was resolved. In other units, I might ask them to note particular issues of ethnicity in popular Egyptian films, or to reflect on particular consumer goods as examples of the ways material culture shapes and is shaped by social relations. As I read their essays, not just at first but semester after semester, I was struck by themes of modernity, authenticity, and globalization that I would not have noted. I began to talk about these themes in class, and allowed students to affirm, disagree with, and refine my arguments. Many students became interested in or excited by the tentative models of Egyptian modernity I was proposing, and they took me to art galleries, *'ahawi* (traditional coffee houses), coffee shops, jazz clubs, restaurants, shopping malls, and other sites they felt provided support or contradiction for my speculations. This process was dialectical; as I used examples drawn from these experiences to refine my arguments and shared them with subsequent classes of students, some of the later students would in turn propose additional or alternative examples or counterexamples. For example, when I told a class in 2000 about my visits in 1998–1999 to *'ahawi* with a group of five male students, and offered an account of them as rituals of masculinity, a group of female students insisted I come with them to a Beano's coffee shop and examine it as a ritual of their femininity.

Sharing control means being open to the contingent, evolving, possible interpretations and explanations offered by my interlocutors, but it does not mean "letting the natives do the analysis," as my mentor Phyllis Chock once advised me. Thus, when the students took me to Beano's, I saw an example of gender performance but also began to see the relationship between traditional *'ahawi* and international-style coffee shops as in tension with one another. As I developed this notion, I shared it with still other classes of students and incorporated their insights. Still later, Jessica Winegar, who was conducting an ethnography of Cairo's art worlds (2006), pointed out how thoroughly gender and class intersected in my data.

My fieldwork was not merely a projection of my classes, nor are my data merely anecdotal. Once the broad outlines of the project had begun to take shape, and I had begun to narrow my analysis to a handful of particularly illustrative cases, I moved beyond chance encounters and brief observations to more systematic fieldwork, involving detailed ethnographic description, participant observation, and semi-structured interviews. I went to key sites like McDonald's and Cilantro, counted people, mapped spatial arrangements, participated in activities with habitual consumers, and interviewed customers, employees, managers, and, eventually, particularly on a return visit in the summer of 2005, company owners. As I met these people, I included some of them, too, in the process of sharing, listening, and refining my arguments.

The internet allowed me to continue these dialogues even after I left Egypt to return to the United States in 2002. Over the years, I have pestered former students and other interlocutors with questions as I reviewed my field logs and interview transcripts. Thanks to some listservs, I've received answers not only from former students but from interested people who never met me. Some of my former graduate students have been particularly involved, reading entire drafts of chapters and commenting, critiquing my arguments, and offering suggestions and observations. All these people have been shaped in various ways by the processes described in this book; all have exerted their own agency to shape their life trajectories in different ways. And the evolution of this book has coincided with the evolution of their lives, including their educations, careers, and families.

I have tried throughout this book to make transparent my ethnography and my relationships with the many people, especially students at

AUC, who have made the work possible. Throughout the text, my attention to the phenomena I discuss is guided by, and in dialogue with, the cosmopolitan men and women who were my students, my colleagues, and my family's friends. I cannot emphasize strongly enough that I could never have written this book, or even thought deeply about these issues, without the interest, engagement, and contributions of my colleagues, students, and friends. Many of the chapters had their genesis in incidents like the discussion with Sabry, in mentoring relationships, and in my participation in weddings and other life activities with friends. I first encountered Pokémon on a trip home to the United States, but it was graduate students with young children who directed me to the public debates about Pokémon in the Middle East. Some described these with ironic detachment, others were passionately concerned. Through them, I was led to conduct fieldwork at two schools. Every chapter derives in some way from conversations—and arguments—with Egyptian friends and students.

I am not the only researcher to find Cairo a compelling place to study issues of the intersections of transnational flows of goods and peoples, global-local relations, intercultural identities, political economies, traditions, modernities, and authenticities. Ethnographers of modern Cairo previously touched on many of these issues (e.g., Gaffney 1994, Inhorn 1995, van Nieuwkerk 1995, Singerman 1995, Wikan 1996, Hoodfar 1997, Cole and Altorki 1998, Starrett 1998, Toth 1999, El-Aswad 2002, El Kholy 2003), but the twenty-first century has seen an outpouring of work that uses Cairo as a site for exploring these issues. In this century, work on modernity, class, and neoliberal globalization has moved to the center, not only among anthropologists (Armbrust 2000, Ghannam 2002, Mitchell 2002, Inhorn 2003, Abu-Lughod 2005, Winegar 2006, Wynn 2009) but among historians (Gordon 2002), sociologists (Abaza 2006), ethnomusicologists (Danielson 1998), and others. The historical development of the intersections of class, consumption, and education has been carefully articulated in some accounts, especially those by Russell (2004) and Shechter (2006).

This research has led to the emergence of the self-styled "Cairo school" of urban studies, a loose network of critical scholarship focusing on "urban social movements, state forms, public policy, elite domination and subaltern politics" (Singerman and Amar 2006: 18). The critical nature of the work of the new Cairo school is rooted in a self-conscious recognition of the role that the social sciences—especially ethnography, demography, and human geography—have played historically in efforts to objectify, modernize, and govern Egypt through colonial, socialist, and neoliberal regimes (El-Shakry 2007).

My work runs parallel to, but is not part of, the work of the Cairo school. It differs in two important ways. First, I use *cosmopolitanism* here in a very restricted way, tied to class and related to the ways Cairenes themselves use the term, rather than the "cosmopolitanism from below" approach of the Cairo school (Singerman and Amar 2006: 33). My use of the term in this book is restricted to those practices, especially the practices of consumption, through which the Egyptian upper classes and those with upwardly mobile aspirations construct themselves as transnational elites whose unequal control over Egypt's economic and political resources is justified by their modernity, and whose modernity is in turn revealed by their cosmopolitanism: their Western educations, their easy movement across transnational borders, their consumption of transnational goods, and the general display of tastes in music, literature, film, clothing, and technologies that distinguishes them from the masses. This is consistent with the way most Egyptians would understand themselves and others as "cosmopolitan."

The second way in which my work diverges somewhat from that of the Cairo school is that because I lived and worked with Cairene elites I am more sympathetic to them. In their introductory essay in *Cairo Cosmopolitan,* Singerman and Amar describe Egypt's elites as "Cairo-based capitalists who call themselves liberals or globalizers or democratizers . . . even as they insist on repression, the extension of the emergency law and police-state practices in the public sphere" (2006: 9). And they quote Mona El-Ghobashy's caricature of young Cairene elites as "technologically savvy, US-educated and American accented, and properly deferential to private sector dominance and the laws of the market," and the claim that "when it comes to protecting citizens from arbitrary state power their silence is palpable" (2005: 9). The notion that the elites are utterly alienated from the rest of the Egyptian populace is itself a cultural belief held by Egyptians, and I am uncomfortable with uncritically accepting and reifying the cultural forms I seek to analyze. While many of the nationalist gestures and discourses of Arab solidarity ring false, or at least superficial, I think the evidence is strong that there are degrees of alienation, not a gulf, and that cosmopolitanism itself is a continuum of practices and identities. Accounts of utterly aloof and alienated Westernized elites oversimplify and essentialize the complexities of growing up as part of Egypt's cosmopolitan elite, which I try to make explicit here.

Yet, my work in no way contradicts the critical position taken by this emerging scholarly literature toward the effects of the neoliberal policies in Egypt, nor the extent to which the actions of the present regime systematically disenfranchise millions of citizens. The young cosmopolitan Cairenes I describe are not unaware or uncritical of most of the issues raised by the Cairo school, and yet they, like the citizens of the lower and middle classes, often feel constrained and powerless to make change. Elites in Egypt have considerable power but not, most of them feel, the power to change the social order which grants them their influence and affluence.

GROWING UP COSMOPOLITAN

My discussion begins with families and the social futures that children imagine for themselves and that are imagined for them by their parents. One of the fundamental problems facing middle-class Egyptian parents is how to ensure that their children are simultaneously modern and Egyptian. Chapter 2 examines a series of Arabic children's magazines and describes the ways in which they construct children as simultaneously modern and Arab. Regional children's magazines like *Alaa Eldin, Bolbol, Majid, Samir,* and *Al Arabi Alsaghir* offer Egyptian children and their families strikingly similar models of the modern Arab child as someone who is simultaneously familiar with the history of Islamic heroes, computer-literate and knowledgeable about technology, and familiar with worldwide popular children's culture from Pokémon to Harry Potter. Above all, these magazines position children as consumers. Buying the magazine offers, through both advertising and articles, a world of other things to imagine buying, from technological gadgets to trips to theme parks. Through such media, children may enter into an imagined world of other children like themselves playing with Pokémon in such places as America, Spain, and Japan.

Children are never only passive recipients of such identities, of course. They actively consume commodities and use them to construct identities in interaction with one another and within contexts generated by the larger society, contexts which may shift even as a result of the children's behavior. Thus, even as they consume these representations of a seamless regional class of modern Arab consumers, household incomes and spending preferences, school choices and tastes in foods are already beginning to divide children into different consumer classes. Chapter 3 explores how children at Cairo's elite private schools engaged with Pokémon, and the moral panics that followed. At first, Pokémon served Cairenes in upper-class schools as a cosmopolitan credential. As popularity waxed among the upwardly aspirational middle classes, public debates emerged over the risks of Pokémon to children's educational, psychological, and moral development. Lurking behind the rumors and hyperbole of the debate were significant questions about the means and ends of globalization, which were framed through idioms of religious morality.

As upper-class Egyptians grow up and go to college, questions of identity become more complex and their articulation of these questions more sophisticated. In particular, the problem of authenticity emerges as central to the construction of cosmopolitan identities. Chapter 4 describes teenagers and young adults seeking to find the limits of their own Westernization. For many, this quest is made particularly salient by their decision to apply to universities abroad or to attend the American University in Cairo, a place that represents to many Egyptians the best and worst aspects of Westernized modernity. The search for authenticity often involves reflexive, interpretive assessments of their own and others' behaviors, evaluated against their leisure experiences, consumption practices, travels, family expectations, peer values, and other social relations. Some seek an assured authenticity in nationalism or in a deeper Islamic piety. Yet even these often prove elusive as authoritative voices differ on which practices constitute an "authentic" nationalism or "true" Muslim piety.

Similar dilemmas of authenticity arise in regard to masculinity and femininity. Chapter 5 explores some of the ways class and gender are interwoven into constructions of local and cosmopolitan Egyptian identities. Class identities involve not only the display of cosmopolitan consumer tastes but the exclusion of middle- and lower-class people from the sites of such class performances. Gender identities are constructed not only through particular bodily comportments but through controlling the publics who will evaluate those performances. These two strands come together in the new translocal spaces of leisure occupied by cosmopolitan consumers: franchise restaurants, shopping malls, and so forth. Chapter 5 focuses on Euroamerican-style coffee houses and their contrast with the traditional *'ahwa.* The arrival of expensive, upscale Euroamerican-style coffee shops has allowed upper-middle- and upper-class Cairenes to create new spaces in which to enact cosmopolitanism. The *'ahwa* is central to Cairene public life, but it is part of the traditionally exclusive masculinity of public life. The new coffee shops offer spaces where men and women can gather together, a space neither completely private nor completely public, neither wholly foreign nor wholly local. While cosmopolitan women construct themselves as modern and liberal by feminizing this new space from which the lower classes are excluded, many young upper-class men turn to the *'ahwa* to reassert their masculinities.

Overattention to consumption can lead us away from a focus on the ways in which the goods that cosmopolitans acquire and the spaces in which cosmopolitans live have come to be in Cairo at all. For the public spaces in which modern, cosmopolitan identities can be tried out are not generated by abstract processes of globalization; they are *made* by entrepreneurs who imagine markets, offer themselves as local partners, and put up often considerable amounts of capital. Processes of globalization and localization, of hybridization, are managed by culture brokers, entrepreneurs, managers, and marketers, who are themselves cosmopolitans. Focusing particularly on McDonald's Egypt, but with attention to several other forms of entrepreneurial and marketing practices, as well as the agency of the state, chapter 6 explores how local agents of globalization actively engage in the production and distribution of the transnational commodities and services consumed by Egypt's elite, and examines the ways in which the cosmopolitan class imagines itself and expresses itself through marketing and distribution.

The notion that the cosmopolitan class reproduces itself through the goods and places that cosmopolitans themselves create, in partnership with transnational agencies like multinational corporations, would seem to frame the transnational elite as a closed system. But such systems are by no means immune to events, which can colonize the mediascape, the financial world, and other transnational flows. The epilogue returns to questions about the ways an anthropology of connections can broaden our understandings of the processes we gloss as globalization and localization, and of the social relations and identities produced through these processes.

2

I think *Majid* is important because it helps children think about the world outside their home and school . . . and also I think it teaches children to enjoy a good read. I think this is important for children, and I worry that the new generation, the computer generation, is missing this.

—MARWA,
twenty-five-year-old Egyptian
journalist, unmarried, no children

These magazines . . . they make children want things, and then you are embarrassed if you cannot give them. But how can we give our children all of these things?

—AMIN,
thirty-year-old Egyptian chemist and
pharmacist, married, father of four

MAKING KIDS MODERN:
AGENCY AND IDENTITY IN ARABIC
CHILDREN'S MAGAZINES

On a warm day in October 2001, I watched two preadolescent boys walking down the street. I was sitting outside an apartment building in the affluent suburb of Maʿadi, sipping tea and waiting for my host, the apartment complex's security guard, to return from a telephone call. The boys caught my eye as a study in contrasts. One was dressed in the cheap blue pants, pale grey shirt, and black shoes that were the uniform at Unity College, a nearby private school originally founded to educate the children of British colonials and those "natives" who could afford it, now best known in the community for renting out its vast athletic fields to expatriate amateur sports teams. The other boy, dressed in jeans, a T-shirt emblazoned "Metallica," and Nike tennis shoes, had just walked down from the gates of the American School in Cairo (ASC), an expensive private school educating the children of American and other expatriates, as well as Egyptians who can afford its hefty fees. The two boys were less than three feet apart yet they took no notice of one another, each apparently in his own world, looking around for his own friends. Their paths diverged at the end of the street when they came to a *midan,* a circular intersection where several streets meet. The Unity boy crossed the street and continued on, pausing in front of Bakra Stationery to page through some magazines displayed along the sidewalk. The ASC boy turned right as he crossed the *midan.* At this point, my observations were interrupted by my host, so I cannot be sure, but I believe he entered the doors of the First Page stationery store. I am, at any rate, going to suppose he did, because the reason this snippet of observation entered my fieldnotes at all is that it offers a useful illustration of the intersections of dress, education, consumption, and media in the making of class difference.

At this time, Unity College was a decaying relic whose primary assets were its name, with its rich historical associations, and several large athletic fields, whose rental to expatriate community groups supplied a large portion of the school's funds for maintenance. In 2000, fees were a modest EGP 2,000 per year (US$435), only boys were admitted, instruction was in Arabic, and prayer was compulsory. The ASC, by contrast, was a thriving and highly prestigious school with facilities other institutions could only envy. Fees were in U.S. dollars—$10,450 per year—which paid for a co-educational American curriculum taught in English by a U.S.-accredited faculty under an American principal. Salaries were among the highest paid by any Egyptian school.[1] The vast economic gulf between the two students was displayed not only in their clothing but in the style of their consumption. First Page is an elegant marble and glass shop occupying the basement and ground floor of a three-story residential building.[2] A wooden rack outside offers the major local newspapers (*Al-Ahram, Akbar al Yom, Egyptian Gazette,* and *Al-Ahram Weekly*) as well as the *International Herald Tribune, Der Zeitung,* and the occasional French or Spanish newspaper. Inside, except for a small section offering a few shelves each of Arabic, French, German, Korean, and Spanish books, the entire store is given over to English texts. To the right as he entered the store, the boy I was observing would have seen an entire room of children's books. To his left would have been a rack twice the size of the one outside, offering a plethora of English magazines. The bottom two shelves are entirely for children's magazines: *Archie Digest,* a half-dozen American comic books (including *Action, Amazing Spider-Man,* and *X-Men*), and several gaming magazines. The average price at the time was EGP 15 (US$3.50), but because of import fees some ran as high as EGP 45 (US$10).

The selection perused by the Unity College boy would have been quite different. A vast array of Arabic magazines and newspapers spreads out in front of Bakra Stationery, covering the lawn and spilling onto the sidewalk. These periodicals are not entirely from Egypt.[3] Many are from UAE, Kuwait, Qatar, Saudi Arabia, and other Arabic-speaking countries. Of particular interest to the Unity College boy would have been the colorful comics and children's magazines. The comics are mostly Arabic translations of foreign comics: *Miki* (*Mickey Mouse*), *Tom and Jerry, Super Miki, Miki Geib* (pocket size), and *Superman* are the most popular, in that order. A stack of *Markhah ar-Ru'b* (*Cry of Terror,* the Arabic translations of R. L. Stine's U.S. bestselling *Goosebumps* series) separates the comics from a row of children's magazines: *Bolbol, Majid, Alaa Eldin,* and *Al Arabi Alsaghir.* All the comics and magazines cost between one and three pounds (US$0.21–0.63). In many cases, the prices of magazines imported from elsewhere in the region are reduced from what they cost in their countries of publication, reflecting the economic differences between Egypt and the oil-rich Gulf states. Most young consumers do not seem to know this, nor do they care when I explain. In this context, if it is in Arabic, it is "local." What is important are the pictures, the stories, and the advertisements.

Commodified media—local and foreign—play a significant role in the making of cosmopolitan identities. Media encourage children to see themselves as consumers, and media are themselves one of the primary commodities children consume (Moore and Moschis 1983). Magazines, television, and other media offer a host of powerful images that serve as symbolic reservoirs for children growing up in global Cairo. Yet media are by no means determinant in the formation of personhood. Children come to understand social power, hierarchy, gender, and other cultural categories by weighing what they learn from media against what they are learning within a set of other social fields equally crucial in their lives: homes, neighborhoods, peer groups, and schools. The manner in which youths learn from media is a dynamic and recursive process in which "guiding motivations" from peer, institutional, and family cultures help them to define social futures, which are then further refined and reimagined through media imagery and narrative (Fisherkeller 1997).

Arabic children's magazines offer one field in which we can examine how consumption links childhood and modernity in the social imaginations of children and their parents as they construct social futures. Regional children's magazines like *Bolbol, Majid, Alaa Eldin,* and *Al Arabi Alsaghir* offer Egyptian children and their families strikingly similar models of the modern Arab child as someone who simultaneously is familiar with Arab history, folktales, and stories of caliphs and sultans; is computer literate and knowledgeable about technology; and is familiar with worldwide popular children's icons from Pokémon to Harry Potter. Above all, these magazines construct children as consumers. Buying the magazine offers, through both advertising and articles, a world of other things to imagine buying, including technological gadgets and trips to theme parks.

Through such media, Egyptian children may enter into an imagined community (Anderson 1991) of other children like themselves playing and consuming, both elsewhere in the Middle East and in the wider worlds of America, Europe, and Japan. Yet, there is a profound irony here. The majority of Egyptian children who read them, like the boy from Unity College, cannot afford the lifestyle they portray. And those who can afford this lifestyle, like the Egyptian boy attending ASC, choose very different media and commodities. Children's media not only construct children as consumers but different media construct them as different kinds of consumers, and to consume different kinds of media is to construct different kinds of social futures. It is not simply through the consumption of media images, but rather through these divergences of taste, habit, and consumption that class distinctions are produced.

BEING, BECOMING, AND CONSUMING

Childhood is simultaneously a life stage, through which individual social actors pass, and a cultural category, a set of discourses that seeks both to define childhood and to articulate the behaviors, activities, and values that should be associated with it (Cook 2002). Children are social actors engaged in the normal human problem of making sense of the world and their place in it. One of the things that makes childhood a particularly complex cultural construction is that children are seen, by themselves, by their parents, and by the society at large, as being in a state of becoming. A great deal of time and energy is spent articulating children's possible social futures, that web of social roles, identities, and activities that children, their parents, educators, public officials, and others imagine for children— both individual children and children collectively—as they make the transition to adulthood. What children will become is a moral discourse that permeates Egyptian society. This discourse is especially salient when it attempts to articulate the meaning of childhood in a rapidly changing world. Ewen (1976) argued that the reshaping of consumption among immigrant families in the United States in the early decades of the twentieth century was in part achieved through a reshaping of parent-child relations. Youth became associated with modern and age with "old-fashioned." Variants of this process are taking place throughout the globe in culturally shaped, local ways. Far from homogenizing culture, the influx of goods, images, ideas, and people from elsewhere in the world—labeled globalization—has created a bewildering variety of new choices. In the face of these new possibilities, the child has become a crucial "site, or . . . [a] relocation of discourses concerning stability, integration, and the social bond" (Jenks 1996: 106).

Because they live in the present but represent the future, children are faced with a twofold challenge in their social interactions. Through play, family relations, peer socialization, work, media, and education, they must negotiate not only who they are but who they are going to become. It is important to recognize, however, that parents as well as children are engaged in this process. Parents imagine particular kinds of social futures for their children. In Egypt, where social mobility is usually a generational project, parents imagine social futures for their children that are better than their own present, and one of the ways they seek to realize these futures is through shaping their children's consumption. While parents enjoy buying their children the things they ask for, when they can, the satisfaction they derive from their children's delight is mitigated by other concerns: Is it morally good for them? Is it educational? Can we afford all these new things they want?

The tool I employ for explicating the relations among globalization, consumption, identities, and social futures is the concept of the *social imagination* as the domain in which people produce cultural orders and in which cultural orders produce people (Appadurai 1996). Arjun Appadurai argues that, beginning in the late twentieth century, the social imagination has taken on a crucial new character. First, the imagination is no longer confined to limited spaces but extends throughout the social process. In a world of interconnectedness, there are no identities, no roles, no courses of action for which alternatives cannot be imagined. Second, the social imagination is not limited to realms of fantasy and expressive culture as escapes into impossibilities. Rather, it has become an expression of new possibilities, including those of children's social futures. As ideas flow between and among media, financial, political, and social worlds, the imagination becomes a platform for social action. Finally, Appadurai argues that the social imagination is always collective rather than individual. The production and consumption of ideas are not individual acts but social and cultural acts, whose stimuli are increasingly coming from across borders.

Appadurai directs us to the media as crucial vehicles for the circulation of ideas and as resources for the social imagination. While many media texts continue to represent nationalist ideologies (Dissanayake 1994; Abu-Lughod 2005), alternative readings are always possible, and the range and depth of these readings increase as texts circulate further and further from their sites of production (Peterson 2003). As audiences shift their social positions—physically, by changing locales, but also through social mobility within a particular locale or because their world changes around them—media provide them with resources to imagine new possible forms of action and new social futures. This approach emphasizes the agency of actors in social change as well as in social reproduction.

Appadurai's use of the term *imagination* is adapted from Benedict Anderson's (1991) concept of the *imagined community*. Anderson used the term to describe nations as collectivities of persons, the majority of whom will never meet or interact, but who nonetheless imagine themselves as sharing a deep comradeship that cuts across other divisions (of race, religion, class, language, caste) to form a whole greater than the sum of its parts. Subsequent scholars have extended the notion of imagined communities to other social formations with similar characteristics. Here, I write of a regional Arab imagined community. The emphasis on a regional identity is motivated in part by the desires of magazine publishers to sell their products across the Arabic-reading world, but it also resonates with historic discourses of Arabic nationalism, which still have some currency in the popular imagination.

DOUBLED COMMODITIES

Anderson sees the rise of mass media—beginning with "print capitalism"—as essential to the emergence of imagined communities because of the opportunities it offers for persons to imagine others like themselves whom they have not, and probably never will, meet. Mass media cannot, of course, create imagined communities; only collectivities of readers can do that. Rather, magazines and other media offer what Mato (1998) has called a *proposed community*: an articulation of a group image which emphasizes the importance of certain common characteristics over others that might constitute references of difference—and which thus invites readers to posit themselves as part of an "us" rather than "them." Magazines are a particularly interesting form of media for this discussion because unlike the relatively structured and coherent narratives of a film or television show, magazines are a jumble of different genres and texts whose coherence is constructed in part by the consumer. Edward Cave, founder in 1731 of the first "magazine," chose the term to emphasize that, like a military storehouse, the periodical contained a wide variety of materials. The analogy between the magazine, which draws many unlike texts together into a single hybrid master text, and the nation, which draws many different persons and communities together into a single hybrid community, is exemplified by the motto of Cave's *Gentleman's Magazine: E Pluribus Unum*, "one out of many," which was subsequently borrowed for the motto of the newly created United States (Okker 2003: 1).

The cultural work that magazines do extends beyond their diverse yet unified content to the functions they serve as commodities. Magazines are always simultaneously both cultural products whose contents are understood according to particular interpretive frameworks, and commodities which derive meaning from their place within a world of goods:

> As *cultural products,* they circulate in a cultural economy of collective meanings, providing recipes, patterns, narratives, and models of and/or for the reader. As *commodities,* they are products of the print industry and crucial sites for advertising and sale of commodities. . . . Magazines are thus deeply involved in capitalist production and consumption at national, regional and global levels. (Moeran 2004: 260, emphases in original)

Furthermore, as goods, magazines are double commodities. Producers of magazines must simultaneously sell their contents to consumers and their consumers to advertisers. Magazines accomplish this double task by constructing through their contents an ideal audience that actual consumers will want to be part of and that advertisers will consider likely to purchase the kinds of goods advertised. In the children's magazines sold in Egypt, this has meant constructing an ideal audience that is affluent, equally comfortable with regional and Western styles of dress and behavior, and familiar with a range of goods from candies to electronics. The price of the magazines, one to two pounds, is expensive enough to set limits on the range of children who can make the magazine part of their social imagination, but inexpensive enough to embrace a wide audience who will have aspirations for the computers, electronic games, automobiles, cell phones, and other goods depicted, but whose actual possession of such goods is likely to remain limited.

CONSUMPTION IN CAIRO

When Hosni picked me up in Ma'adi to take me downtown to the university, I could barely enter the car for fear of ripping the dozens of newspaper clippings taped to the walls and windows. His son had achieved the highest score in the nation on the *i'dadiyya 'amma,* the national examination between primary and secondary school. There are three national examinations: the *ibtida'yya,* or primary exam, administered to children after they have completed six years of school; the *i'dadiyya,* or preparatory exam, administered after nine years of school; and the *thanawiyya,* or secondary exam, administered after twelve years. Tension arises at each level and becomes more intense with each exam. Good primary scores can determine access to a good preparatory school; good prep scores to a good high school; and good secondary exams to valued schools (medicine, engineering) in the university. Among lower- and middle-class families like Hosni's, in which a private school education is out of the question, good *i'dadiyya* scores are especially important because they determine whether a student can continue on to high school or to a commercial institute. A high school diploma is supposed to qualify students for clerical work in an office or bank. A commercial institute trains students in typing, business arithmetic, and other skills that might enable them to work in a shop. Those who do not qualify for one of these must leave school with a *diblum* (diploma), which promises only "'*shughl basit bi-marattab basit*' (simple work for simple pay)" (Starrett 1998: 116). No certificate, not even a university degree, is a guarantee of a job, of course. The anxiety with which parents approach the exams and the joy or disappointment with which they greet the results are tied to their hopes and aspirations for their children. So it was with Hosni. He bubbled over with excitement as he mapped out his son's social future. His son was going to be a doctor, he said. The boy's role model was an Egyptian doctor he had read about in a magazine. This doctor had gone abroad and "made a fortune" as a surgeon, but he came back each year to perform surgical operations free for the poor. As narrated by Hosni, this was the very kind of role model one would expect to find profiled in an Arabic children's magazine, fusing a modern identity that involves education, wealth, and displacement from the local with a moral concern for the poor but honest local people of one's roots.

The role model seemed less distant to the family now that Hosni's son was himself featured in newspapers and magazines, held up as a role model to other Egyptian youths: the boy who is bettering himself and his country through education. But the best thing about the publicity, Hosni said, was that the family had met the Egyptian minister of education, and he'd promised to take over the boy's school fees. "Then you'll be able to take some time off," I joked. I didn't know Hosni well; this was only the third time we'd met. But at our second meeting, we had a glass of tea and conversation, and I knew he had a son and two daughters and that he worked three jobs to pay school fees totaling, in his worst year, more than EGP 1,400. But in answer to my joke, he shook his head and smiled: "Now I am working for the computer." The computer, he explained to me, was going to be his son's edge in the next phase, as he struggled to learn enough to pass the *thanawiyya 'amma* with a high enough score to get into the prestigious School of Medicine.

As Hosni's priorities suggest, consumption in Cairo is largely a family activity. Children are generally expected to live in the parental home until marriage. The education and marriage of children are often the most significant economic challenges that families face. And they are related: one of the functions of a good—and hence expensive—education is to improve the child's chances of a good marriage, while a good marriage is often described as one that will be able to ensure a good education for its children (Abu-Hashish and Peterson 1999). The display of commodities—including good private schools, tutors, and adjunct learning programs—plays a significant role in family economies, as does their exchange. Gifts mark most important life passages, and the capacity to earn the cash needed to buy these commodities is important to a father's masculinity and to the general status of the family in the community. Most families develop complex networks of debts and obligations as they work to meet these social needs (see, e.g., Hoodfar 1997; Singerman 1995).

Some studies of consumption have emphasized the home as a crucial site for the development and reproduction of social relations both generally (Miller 2001) and in the Middle East (Pollard 2003; Russell 2003). These studies emphasize the ways in which the institutions of state and market and the ideologies of modernity, nationalism, and globalization interact dialectically with family life. Russell argues that the emergence of the "urban bourgeois household helped to create both a modern Egypt and an Egyptian national identity" (2003: 38) so that Egyptians have viewed "changes in household arrangements as heralding political and economic centralization and modernization" (15) at least since the reign of Muham-mad Ali in the early nineteenth century. Understanding consumption in the social imagination of Cairene children and their families thus requires situating the home in the economic macro context within whose histori-cally structured financial constraints the social imagination operates.

Most middle-class Egyptian families are caught between nostalgia for the socialist past under Gamal Abdel Nasser's regime—when high school and university degrees were guarantees of government jobs and when the prices of staple commodities like cooking oil, kerosene, lentils, rice, sugar, and flour were artificially low—and the promise of rapid, but uneven and unequal, economic growth in the current liberalization and privatization of the economy. This shift from a welfare to a market orientation, first announced by Nasser's successor, Anwar Sadat, in 1974, is often called the *infitah,* or "open door" policy. But in spite of the gradual structural adjust-ments that did away with food subsidies and rent controls, Egypt has been slow to attract either multinational corporations or Arab capitalists on a large scale. The level of production remains low, imports far outstrip ex-ports, and Egypt's debt continues to mount, leading to continued inflation (World Bank 1998).[4] International goods from computers to McDonald's restaurants have arrived, but these remain out of reach of most consum-ers. At the time of my research, inflation was high, nearly 5 percent, and although the economy was growing at a respectable 3.2 percent, the wealth being generated was very unequally distributed.

In the wake of these economic changes, public programs like free health care and education suffered considerably, stimulating the establishment of private, for-profit alternatives. Of particular significance is the commodification of the schools. The free, national schools established during the Nasserist revolution of the 1950s, with instruction in Arabic, are almost universally agreed to be in the midst of an "educational crisis" (*mushkilat at-ta'lim*) caused by untrained teachers, obsolete schooling practices, and overcrowded classrooms. This has stimulated the development of a hierarchy of increasingly expensive private schools. At the top of this hierarchy are the "international schools" like ASC, partially staffed by foreign teachers and administrators, offering instruction in European languages and curricula based on American, British, French, or German models.[5] Less expensive, but still out of reach of most Egyptians, is a range of private "language schools," owned and staffed primarily by Egyptians, but offering instruction in various foreign languages. These language schools often have two tracks, one preparing students for the national exam, the *thanawiyya 'amma,* and the other fulfilling the requirements for an international baccalaureate. Privatization extends even into the free, public schools, where poorly paid teachers offer private tutoring for a fee, often in public school buildings. Many teachers make the bulk of their incomes through such lessons, and parents often fear that to refuse to pay for private tutoring means their children will be less competitive than their peers. The tension between the promise of school as a means of social mobility and the increasing cost of schooling that might actually prepare children for success in the new economy frames most discussions of childhood.

The economic distinctions between the schools are transformed into class distinctions. Education in foreign languages, the ability to adopt appropriate Western dress, familiarity with technologies, and an appreciation of Western tastes—and the brand names through which these are codified—rapidly have become class markers. These competencies are no mere status symbols; they have real economic consequences for the middle class. Competence in displaying the appropriate symbolic capital is readily transferable into economic capital: the ability to distinguish clearly between the /b/ and /p/ phonemes, for example, or competence in properly accessorizing a Western dress, can mean the difference between a salary of EGP 50 and one of EGP 500 per month. Barsoum (1999, 2004) describes how employment agents for Egyptian and multinational corpo-rations seize on subtle distinctions in the ways young women speak, the clothes they wear, and the ways they accessorize them to evaluate their character. A fashionably dressed woman with an American or European accent, who takes for granted the signs of wealth on display in the offices of a large company is *wilad an-nas*—literally, "child of the people" but used idiomatically to refer to children of privilege. Possession of academic degrees or specialized computer and secretarial training offers no competi-tive advantage for those who speak English with an Egyptian accent or wear the wrong shoes for their dress. In Barsoum's account, young women of the lower classes who have struggled and sacrificed to get a college de-gree but failed to accumulate the requisite symbolic capital are unable to find better work than as a shopkeeper's assistant.

These historic economic transformations have structured contempo-rary attitudes toward consumption. The seductions of goods and promises of new opportunities offered by the liberalization of markets vie with the realities of chronic unemployment, low wages, and nostalgia for the se-curity of the socialist past. Nowhere are these dilemmas more acute than among the middle classes, who must carefully calculate their consumption of an expanding universe of goods in a world of economic constraints. On one hand, the shift from webs of exchange to the consumption of mass market goods, many manufactured abroad, is widely recognized as a sign of Egypt's modernity and of increasing opportunities. Yet the choices of what to consume—Egyptian brands or transnational brands, imports or goods from local franchises, and so forth—derive from and evoke very different forms of social experience. To consume is problematic precisely because one's choices define and limit one. In the expanding world of goods, the choice is never simply between a "traditional" *galabiyya* and a "modern" business suit; there is a bewildering variety of possibilities, tastes, and styles. This is consonant with the growing literature on con-sumption which suggests that, as the available ranges of commodities and media images grows, the variety of identities people can imagine for themselves through consumption also increases (Wilk 1990; Miller 1995). It is to this middle-class audience, represented here by Hosni's son and the Unity College boy, concerned with goods, identities, education, and social mobility, that Arabic children's magazines are addressed.

CHILDREN'S MAGAZINES IN EGYPT

Magazines abound at Cairo's newsstands, markets, and kiosks, and they are sometimes hawked by roaming vendors in the street. Among them are many children's magazines, published in Cairo, Kuwait City, Abu Dhabi, and elsewhere and circulated throughout the region. The most popular children's magazines in the Arabic world are comic books. The most popular title is *Miki,* an Arabic translation of the perennial Disney comic, which claims a weekly distribution of 150,000 issues in Cairo alone. Another foreign comic that has been around for many years is *Tom and Jerry.* Relative newcomers are *Superman* and *Batman* in Arabic translations of the American comics. Other popular comic books include *Mini,* another Disney product, and *Archie Digest,* distributed only in the original English. With the exception of *Archie Digest,* the foreign comics are localized through editing. Computer technologies make it possible to manipulate the interior artwork, so that not only text in balloons but drawn sound effects, entrance and exit signs, marquees, newspaper headlines, and other textual aspects of the artwork are re-rendered in Arabic script. In addition, each contains a two- to four-page spread of letters and artwork submitted by readers, as well as games and puzzles.

The second major newsstand genre for children is what I will call the *regional children's magazine.* These are magazines in the original sense of the word, containing between two covers a wide variety of different materials: comics, stories, news, science, history, product reviews, games, puzzles, jokes, and more. These magazines are published in a number of different places, including Egypt, Kuwait, Saudi Arabia, Tunisia, and the United Arab Emirates, and distributed throughout the region. These magazines accordingly represent broad, regional identities rather than focusing on national symbols. The five magazines I will examine here are *Samir, Majid, Alaa Eldin, Al Arabi Alsaghir,* and *Bolbol.*

Samir is Egypt's oldest existing Arabic children's magazine. Established in 1955, it was originally a comic book in the tradition of the Belgian *Tintin* and *Spirou.* Samir and his friends faced gangsters, thieves, and murderers with the same aplomb as his Belgian inspirations. Today, *Samir* is a glossy magazine claiming an Egyptian circulation that rivals *Miki.* Issues run an average of forty-two pages. Of these, ten pages are devoted to funny comics and eight to an adventure comic. The remaining pages are devoted to games, puzzles, jokes, computer site reviews, news, science articles, and photographs and stories about readers. All the articles are accompanied by color photographs and artwork. The comics and most of the artwork are locally produced, but some of the art and photographs come from purchased collections. Advertising is limited to the inside covers and consists mostly of ads for consumable sweets.

Majid, published weekly in Kuwait by Emirates Media, Inc., is probably the most popular children's magazine in the Gulf region, with a total circulation of about 150,000 per week.[6] Founded in 1979, it is famous for its comics, which take up about one-third of its seventy to eighty pages. The magazine advertises itself with pictures of seventeen recurring cartoon characters, including Majid himself, a black-haired young boy in a *thub* and *kiffiya* (the traditional Arab men's robe and head covering) who has no strip of his own but appears throughout the magazine introducing its features. Majid is said by his editor to be named after the fifteenth-century navigator and scholar Ahmad ibn Majid (Douglas and Malti-Douglas 1994: 151), but most readers only know him as the magazine's cartoon namesake. The comics are a blend of regionally produced strips by Egyptian, Gulf, and Syrian artists and foreign cartoons, including the United Feature Syndicate's *Nancy and Sluggo* (called *Lovable Muzah and Terrible Rushdu* in its Arabic incarnation) and King Features' *Henry* (known in Arabic as *Shumlul*, "Little One").[7]

In addition to comics, *Majid* includes an editorial; short stories; articles on history, science, and technology; photo news about the region and the world; website reviews; and puzzles, games, and jokes. A large amount of space is given over to interactive features such as letters, photos of readers, art contests, news items about readers, pen pals, and e-mail pals. All these features are crowded together, giving the magazine a busy look. *Majid* has few ads in Egypt. The percentage of ads compared to text in the issues I examined in 2003 ranged from 4 percent to none. Most ads are for inexpensive consumable goods like SunTop juices or Nestle's Nesquik chocolate milk, which children might be expected to buy at kiosks on their way to or from school. The other major advertising category is electronic goods, such as Asder toy computers.

Alaa Eldin (*Aladdin*) claims a circulation across the region of 86,000 weekly, three-quarters of which is in Egypt, where the magazine is printed by publishing giant Al-Ahram, which also publishes Egypt's leading daily newspaper and its most influential English weekly. This children's magazine is shorter than most of the others, rarely exceeding sixty pages. About one-fifth of the pages are comic strips, and they are fewer in number (the panels are printed larger than in most other children's magazines); all the comics are local productions. Alaa Eldin himself is portrayed as a boy with unruly black hair, wearing jeans, tennis shoes, a button-down shirt, and a vest. One regular strip involves him and a friend of his, a *jinn* named Morgan.

Like *Majid, Alaa Eldin* includes short stories, articles, puzzles, games, jokes, letters, and photos sent in by readers. *Alaa Eldin* relies much more heavily on photography than the others, and less on cartoons and other drawings. As with the comic strips, there is less overall content, and it is laid out with larger fonts and photographs, for a less busy look.[8]

From a marketing and consumer viewpoint, *Alaa Eldin* is the trendiest of the region's children's magazines, often featuring product tie-ins. During 2001–2002, such tie-ins included pencils, crayons, a cassette tape of Golden Books children's songs, a Flash video featuring an animated film about Sinbad, and a board game sponsored by Enjoy dairy. Although these are labeled as "gifts" from the publisher, many newsstands and stationers charge extra for issues containing such gifts. (I was charged seven extra pounds for the Sinbad video and five pounds for the cassette tape.) An Al-Ahram executive told me that they send out letters reminding vendors that this practice is illegal, but the problem remains. Since the profit margin for vendors is slight, and enforcement is almost impossible, selling the enclosed video for more than the price of the magazine ensures a tidy profit. Excluding product tie-ins, *Alaa Eldin*'s ad ratio averages 5 percent, only slightly higher than *Majid*'s. As with the others, ads are divided between consumable goods, like Covertina candies and Enjoy flavored milks, and electronic goods, including Flash videos.[9]

Al Arabi Alsaghir (*Little Arab*), published by the Ministry of Information in Kuwait, claims a readership of about 50,000 per month. Begun in 1959 as a children's supplement to the ministry's *Al Arabi* magazine, it has been a separate and independent magazine since its February 1986 issue. A typical issue of *Al Arabi Alsaghir* runs eighty to ninety pages, of which about one-quarter are comics. All the comics appear to be locally produced, but several show the influence of *Tintin* and Japanese anime. There are no ads in *Al Arabi Alsaghir*, as it is a government publication, but many of the articles are about consumer products, especially electronics.

Bolbol is a local Egyptian product, but it appears to have less reach than *Alaa Eldin* and *Samir* outside of Egypt. Within Egypt, it claims a circulation of about 35,000 per week. Published by the Dar Akhbar El Yom newspaper chain, *Bolbol* is larger than the normal magazine format (9"×12" as opposed to the standard 8"×11"). It is also the shortest of the magazines, running an average of fifty pages, of which about 30 percent are comics. Of these, nearly all are translations of foreign comics, syndicated by the Belgian comic publisher Dargaud. *Bolbol* has exclusive Arabic rights to many of these.

Bolbol is probably the brightest and busiest of all the children's magazines. Articles and stories are short, large photographs are everywhere, and colorful clip art is squeezed in wherever possible. *Bolbol* emphasizes its educational role. Most issues carry a page of illustrated vocabulary in English, French, or German, the lexicons of the prestigious language schools. Gifts are usually school supplies—pencils, erasers, sharpeners— or educational games. The magazine's local flavor is readily apparent from the ads. In addition to the usual consumables (e.g., Blox bubble gum) and electronic goods (e.g., Innovations Arabic-language PDA), there are small ads for local toy stores and language schools. Some ads even list the names, addresses, and phone numbers of stores in the Cairo area carrying the goods they promote.

SELLING COMMUNITY

Arabic children's magazines function not only to entertain but to stimulate children's social imaginations along particular pathways. Marwa, a twenty-five-year-old journalist, described for me some of the ways in which reading *Majid* may stimulate an imagined sense of community. Born in Egypt, Marwa grew up in Kuwait, where her father worked as a dentist, but returned to Egypt for her education. She writes for a number of newspapers and magazines in Egypt and throughout the region. Over a cup of tea in a café in the Garden City suburb of Cairo in 2002, we talked about the place *Majid* once played in her life.

MARWA: I first started reading *Majid* when I was seven, I think, maybe eight. It was the first journal I ever put my hands on. I remember it came out Wednesdays, and the whole day had this special flavor because I knew my dad would get it for me on his way home from work. This made my whole day. It made my whole week, even, because I used to read it over and over.

MARK: All these contests and letters and things . . . did you ever participate?

MARWA: All the time. I never wrote letters, or . . .

MARK: Did you ever send in a picture?

MARWA: No, but I participated in the competitions and I even joined the pen pals club. But the pictures . . . I used to look at them and think . . . about these kids, they were from Tunis and Saudia and Al-Yemen and Al-Maghreb, and Egypt, where I was from but I didn't remember it very well, and we were all reading the same, all reading *Majid*.

Marwa's account of *Majid* focuses not on the content of the stories she read, but on the *experience* of reading the magazine.[10] Anticipation of the magazine played a part in its significance, as did the fact that consuming *Majid* involved a weekly ritual of receiving the magazine as a gift from her father. The photographs generated reflections on identity. She saw children from places far away portrayed as part of a common community of readers that included her. The labels on the photographs drew her attention to her own displacement as an Egyptian girl in Kuwait. Marwa also extended her experience of the magazine through contests and writing to pen pals, accepting *Majid*'s invitation to actively make herself part of its prospective community.

This form of indexical play, in which one uses a magazine's many signifiers as vehicles for imaginatively connecting with others displaced in time and space, depends on characteristics designed into the magazines. The publishers of *Al Arabi Alsaghir, Bolbol, Alaa Eldin, Samir,* and *Majid* are actively engaged in the process of creating an imagined community of transnational kids by encouraging readers to encounter and imagine one another within and through the pages of the magazine. Techniques include making members of the community visually present to one another, offering stories about readers' lives, and encouraging interactions, both mediated through the magazine and direct from reader to reader.

All of these publications publish large numbers of photographs of their readers, which are sent in by the readers or their parents. The photographs, individually and collectively, invite readers to imagine themselves as part of the community indexed by these images. A typical issue of *Majid* runs 50–60 thumbnail photographs of readers, each neatly labeled with the name of the child and the country of origin. *Alaa Eldin* runs upward of 175 pictures in a typical issue. In addition to three pages devoted exclusively to photographs, *Alaa Eldin* runs rows of photos along the margins of pages otherwise devoted to jokes or brief articles. Just in case people miss the point, the magazine's eponymous Alaa Eldin's own cartoon picture is prominently featured among the photographs on one of the pages. In *Bolbol*, the number of pictures can approach 200, most arranged in full-page spreads of seven columns by seven rows. *Bolbol*, moreover, encourages former readers to keep in touch by sending in photographs of their graduations, their weddings, and their babies. These photographs portray readers across a range of ages, with a variety of pigmentations and features. Some boys wear Islamic headgear of various kinds, others have a variety of hairstyles. Some girls wear the *higab*, the woman's head scarf, but most are uncovered. A few have short, carefully styled haircuts. The overall effect is to demonstrate a community that encompasses a variety of children throughout the Gulf and North Africa, cutting across divisions of religious practice and ethnicity. To drive the message home, cartoon characters are used to emphasize the readerships' extension across the ethnic differences of the region. On one of *Al Arabi Alsaghir*'s letters pages, there appears a row of fourteen cartoon portraits of children in a variety of regional garb, while on one of *Majid*'s letters pages, Majid's image appears nine times, each face identical but with different pigmentation and clad in a different regional dress. Readers may not wear such dress, but they certainly recognize it as indexical of their part of the Middle East. One of the most interesting forms of this self-referential community building occurs in *Samir*. In both the humorous and the adventure comics, the main characters themselves are shown reading *Samir*; often, the cover is that of the very issue in which the comic appears. Readers are not only invited to imagine themselves in the storyworld of the cartoon characters, but the world in-habited by those characters is shown to be that of *Samir* readers. Through consumption of *Samir*, readers are connected both to other readers whose photos appear and to the characters whose adventures they enjoy.

If an imagined community is inspired by these batteries of names and faces of persons with whom one shares the reading experience, it is confirmed or anchored by news of their lives. Several pages are devoted in every issue of these magazines to news events attended by or about the readers: students who placed high in their national exams, the opening of a new school museum, winners of contests, and so forth. *Majid* offers a section titled "*Majid* Correspondents" (*Mandubu Majid*) that may run up to three pages of photographs and articles submitted by its readers. Medi-ated communication between consumers and producers thus becomes remediated communication between consumers.

The imagined community becomes an interactive community through correspondence between members, a correspondence strongly encouraged by the magazines' producers. This includes letters between consumers and producers, as well as between readers. *Majid* and *Bolbol* offer full-page, pre-addressed, tear-out letter forms that can be filled out, folded, and dropped in the mail. Every one of the five magazines offers a pen pal club, some with dozens of members listed in every issue.[11] Only *Majid* offers an e-mail pen pal column, and it rarely features more than four persons, reflecting once again the gap between the representation of computers as common goods and the relative rarity of computers among the magazines' Egyptian readers. The magazines also regularly offer art and writing com-petitions, photo caption contests, and similar features.

INTEGRATION THROUGH JUXTAPOSITION

Imagined communities, says Anderson, are to be understood "not by their falsity/genuineness, but by the style in which they are to be imagined" (1991: 6). If the experience of community is created through mediated interactions, the style of the community is shaped by the magazine's con-tents. The style of imagination shaped by the words and images of *Samir*, *Al Arabi Alsaghir*, *Bolbol*, *Alaa Eldin*, and *Majid* constructs a particular ideology of regional identity that is simultaneously Arab, Islamic, and part of a larger global community of consumption.

Regional identity is constructed through a series of tropes that minimize internal differences between peoples of the Middle East.[12] Part of this involves selectivity on the part of the magazines' editors: regional news is selected over foreign news, especially in relation to politics and sports. As with the reader photographs, the representation of multiple styles of clothing and headdress is a powerful signifier. In some comic strips, clothing distinctions are used to differentiate class identities—the naïve but honest provincial in his *galabiyya* versus the clever but unscrupulous banker in his Western business suit—but for the most part, the juxtaposition seems to imply that all forms of dress are equally valid. This is graphically represented in strips like *Amunah Almaziyunah* (*Amunah the Amazing*), in which Amunah's father wears a *thub* and *kiffiya*, her mother a modest dress and colorful *higab*, and her brother a *galabiyya*—but Amunah wears polka-dotted dresses and bows in her hair.[13]

Another important aspect of the imagined world of these texts is their naturalization of Islam. Although many of the countries in which these magazines circulate have large Christian minorities, there are few unambiguously Christian names among the readers.[14] Articles emphasize Islamic history, and several magazines have regular columns on Islam: *Majid*'s is four pages and is marked by a pastel orange and yellow cartoon mosque with pink minarets. Even where specific features about Islam are absent, Islam is the unmarked normative cultural backdrop to most narratives.

A third significant form of regional identification is produced by the magazines' politicization of the Palestinian situation. Some of these features are simple-language versions of themes and issues that appear in the mainstream press—a free insert in the April 4, 2002, issue of *Alaa Eldin*, sponsored by Flash, carried an illustrated article comparing Ariel Sharon to Adolf Hitler—but the majority focus on the children of Palestine. The regional news section of *Al Arabi Alsaghir* frequently carries news of the Al-Aqsa intifada. A January 2001 issue carried a large photograph of the Dome of the Rock inset with two smaller photos: one of a young boy hurling a rock, another of a stretcher carrying the now wounded boy away from the mosque. The brief accompanying story reminded readers of the cruelty of Israel to children. Here, as in most representations of Palestine in the region's children's magazines, the emphasis is on the children in the conflict—especially the contrast between adult Israeli soldiers and Palestinian children. Arabic children's magazines construct a particular Arab-centered view of the world by integrating local, regional, and international issues and by "relating adult politics to the realities of children's lives" (Douglas and Malti-Douglas 1994: 156).[15] This practice varies widely from editor to editor, and so changes over time, even within the same magazines.

A great deal of the power of these regional images derives from their juxtaposition with two other sets of images: that of the world of consumer goods and that of a transnational world of commodities. The importance of consumption in the imagination of the modern Egyptian child is not limited to advertising; advertisements are but one of the ways consumption is embedded in the storyworlds that magazines conjure up for their readers. Although there is relatively little advertising in these publications, advertising nonetheless plays a significant role in the ways *Alaa Eldin, Al Arabi Alsaghir, Bolbol, Samir,* and *Majid* represent for middle-class readers a world of goods. One of the most interesting aspects is that, unlike the text of the magazines, which is almost entirely in Arabic, almost all of the advertising is bilingual in Arabic and English. English, increasingly the language of social mobility in Egypt, is also the language of brand-name goods. Brand names in both Arabic and English are signs of modernity and quality—and also price. Amin, the father of Ismail, a student at the Modern Language School in the middle-class suburb of Maʻadi Gadida, expressed his disgruntlement with his son's need to buy Lay's chips, which sell for fifteen piasters more than local brands like Chipsy. While the price difference may seem miniscule to many upscale Egyptians (fifteen piasters at that time was about three cents), those who are making considerable sacrifices to send their children to expensive language schools find the 30 percent price difference between international brands and cheap local snack foods irritating. Yet Amin said he knew that if he didn't give Ismail the extra money for the brand-name chips, the boy would use his lunch money to buy them, and skip lunch altogether.

Lay's is a status snack, not so much because it is more expensive but because, like the photographs in the magazines, it simultaneously indexes a wider world "out there" and a community of consumers. Whereas everyone in Egypt eats Chipsy, Lay's is for those who want to identify themselves with an international brand. Noha, a journalist writing for Egypt's upscale English-language lifestyle and business magazines, balked at this description, insisting that she preferred Lay's because they taste better. While this may be true, the fact that Noha attended ASC and the American University in Cairo indicates that she belongs to the class for which Lay's are *supposed* to taste better. The manufacturer is well aware of these distinctions and has constructed its marketing and distribution of the products around it. Once company officials realized that the international brand would never become nationally dominant, Lay's Egypt bought out Chipsy, and now specifically markets and distributes the two brands to their separate demographics. A Lay's marketing official told me in 2005 that Lay's chips were only being distributed in stores in upper-class areas like Heliopolis, Zamalek, and Ma'adi, and then only in "modern" supermarkets, not in kiosks or small shops, further accentuating the class associations of the brand. Amin's resistance to his son's insistence on Lay's comes from a growing uneasy recognition that the language-school education he is buying for his son entails much more than academic skills and facility in English. There is a real economic concern here. Those few piasters add up, and choosing the more expensive brand may be the beginning of a slippery slope of expenditures that may lead to tastes and dispositions Amin worries that his son has little hope of satisfying.

But these concerns are also linked to issues of identity. In emphasizing to me that *he* grew up eating Chipsy *and* that it is the cheaper brand, Amin is expressing his concern that his son is differentiating himself from values Amin holds, which is expressed in part through brands. Identity, as the term implies, involves mapping oneself, through forms of social action including consumption, to some group or category. Ismail's school offers him access to a proposed community different than that to which his father belongs. In making himself more like his schoolmates through patterns of consumption, Ismail is making himself less like his father.

Advertisements are only one way Arabic children's magazines emphasize the importance of familiarity with the world of goods. The Kuwaiti government publication *Al Arabi Alsaghir* accepts no advertising, but it nonetheless keeps its readers informed about the latest international children's commodities. It has offered features on Pokémon, scuba-diving sites and equipment, model trains, Game Boys, and other consumer electronics; published a translation/redaction of the first *Harry Potter* book; and featured photographs of amusement parks. One comic strip in *Majid* featured a woodcutter who, growing increasingly wealthy through wishes granted by a friendly *jinn*, decides he is best off being what he was in the first place, but such lessons are countered by illustrations elsewhere in the issue of genies rising from magic lamps to give computers and other electronic goods to delighted children.[16] Unlike the woodcutter, the children who read these magazines know exactly what commodities they need to transform themselves. The magazines themselves are guides. Characters in the stories routinely show familiarity with a range of goods and their uses. Education is a key theme in these magazines, but education is tied to social mobility, which is increasingly marked by the acquisition of transnational commodities.

The use of English in brand-name goods; the articles profiling IBM, Nintendo, and other international manufacturers of electronic goods; the description of international bestselling *Harry Potter* books—all emphasize another crucial element in the construction of a social world expressed through consumer goods: the globalization of valuable goods. These magazines allow children to imagine themselves, through consumption, to be linked to the larger international world of children. And if internationally syndicated cartoons like *Nancy and Sluggo* are regionalized by linguistically erasing all signs of their foreign origin, local commodities like Enjoy milk are internationalized by branding them in both Arabic and English. Nestle's Nesquik is an international brand; Enjoy is not. But by imitating the dual-language marketing of the international brands, Enjoy positions itself as a competitor worthy of being consumed by discriminating middle-class children.

My point here is that through juxtapositions of regional solidarity, Islamic religiosity, and commodification, Arabic children's magazines construct a hybrid subject who is at once fully "modern" and fully "Arab." The ideal subject posited by these magazines is Arabic-speaking but worldly literate; cosmopolitan but regional; and equally comfortable with Western and regional styles of dress and personal display. These magazines tie together two sets of values. The first is a set of Islamic moral values, which are treated as endemic to the Arab region (rather than linked to the entire global Islamic community, the *ummah*). The second is a set of global consumer values. Rather than separating and clarifying these sets of values, as much contemporary religious literature seeks to do (Eickelman and Anderson 1997), these magazines juxtapose and combine them.

COMPUTERS IN EVERY HOME

What is unfortunate is that the Unity College boy thumbing through these magazines on the sidewalk in Ma'adi is unlikely to ever be able to achieve the expression of modernity constructed by these juxtapositions of local moral and global consumer values. He may be able to afford to buy Nesquik over Enjoy, and Lay's over Chipsy. He may buy *Harry Potter* and *Goosebumps* books in the Arabic translations put out by Nahdet Misr, the educational publishing firm, which also brings out *Superman* and *Batman* comics, all in elegant modern standard Arabic. But only a handful of boys at his school have electronic games, and those are mostly gifts from relatives working in the Gulf. Computers, he knows only from his school's library, where access is jealously guarded. But he can dream, and the magazines will help him.

An editorial in the October 31, 2001, issue of *Majid* is titled "A Computer in Every Home." In the accompanying illustration, an anthropomorphic computer monitor and equally humanized computer tower walk hand in hand with a boy in a *thub* and *kiffiya,* leading him toward a rising sun. This image of computers leading the Arab child into the dawn of a new day might serve as a summarizing symbol of all the images of computers that fill the pages of these magazines. Personal computers are one of the most ubiquitous images in Arabic children's magazines, second only to cars. In *Alaa Eldin* and *Samir,* an average of five photographs or drawings of computers or computer parts appears in each issue; in *Al Arabi Alsaghir,* six; in *Bolbol,* eight; and in *Majid,* fifteen. Each magazine offers features on websites for kids, and *Alaa Eldin* has gone so far as to offer lessons in programming. This is especially interesting because computers are beyond the reach of so many of the readers. In 2001, when the GDP was estimated at EGP 19,000 (US$4,000), a top-of-the-line imported Apple Macintosh desktop might cost as much as EGP 20,875 (US$4,350), although a locally assembled personal computer with a generic motherboard and processor might be had for as little as EGP 3,500 (US$750). Nationwide, there was only one computer for every 100 persons, and since most of these were owned by corporations and schools, many reports emphasize that fewer than 1 percent of Egypt's 68 million people own computers (Burkhart and Older 2003). Advertisers do not bother to market computers in the pages of children's magazines, but they do market to children's desires for them. One company, Innovations, offers an Arabic-language personal data assistant for teens, and another, Asder, advertises toy "computers," which are actually electronic quiz devices which the ads claim will make children ready for real computers and will help them with their exams.

Computers are a tantalizing good whose values are widely touted, but they are out of reach of most people. To appreciate the fantasy of the personal computer, one need only make a simple (albeit perhaps simplistic) comparison: if a computer cost an American the same percentage of the U.S. per capita GDP as Egyptians paid, personal computers in the United States would have been priced in 2001 between $8,500 and $38,000, putting them as far outside the range of U.S. middle-class consumption as they were in Egypt at the time of my study. Given the unlikelihood of readers being able to buy a personal computer, it is useful to unpack the item's significance and ask why this technology, more than other commodities that might be more readily affordable by the middle-class readers of *Samir, Bolbol,* or *Alaa Eldin,* serves as a symbol of the future of the Arab child. While it is impossible to predict the meanings children make out of all these computer images, one can certainly describe a range of possible meanings encoded into the text by producers, which have become part of the repertoire children draw on in making sense of themselves as modern Arab children.

The significance of the computer as a symbol in Arabic children's magazines rests on a twofold transformative capacity. First, the computer has the power to conflate the worlds of work, education, and play, three domains of great importance in the social imaginations of children. Second, computers have the capacity to connect users to the wider world while at the same time, through the use of Arabic-language platforms and Arabic websites, to regionalize that larger world. Computers are hybrids: although recognized as a "Western" technology, their software can be Arabicized, and indeed, most children first encounter actual (as opposed to imagined) computers in the classroom, where they use Arabic-language operating systems.

The spheres of work, play, and education are crucial to the discursive construction of audience in children's magazines. Representations of work in the adult world are central to the construction of imagined social futures, and computers figure largely in the portrayals of that world. In a single episode of *Majid's* comic strip *Fariq Albahath Algana'y* (*Department of Criminal Investigation*), the policewoman hero is seen using a computer, holding a CD-ROM, and explaining or learning about some new technology bearing on her current case. That computers are educational is emphasized in any number of features, including a news item about a girl who won a programming award and a photo of a classroom with a computer in the background. Between one-quarter and one-third of all websites reviewed in the magazines are educational sites. Most representations of computers, though, emphasize their capacity for play. The majority of websites reviewed are sites that offer games. In addition, in *Majid's* three-page section of games and puzzles, each is drawn within a frame representing a computer screen.

Although communication is a primary activity among children who do have access to computers—my daughters regularly keep in touch with some of their Egyptian friends by e-mail, social networking sites, and instant messaging—such uses of the computer are less commonly depicted than play, work, or educational uses. Representations of computer-mediated communication tend to focus on Arabic portals, web tools for exploring the Arabic strands of the worldwide web. This capacity for computers to localize the global through language, and through networks of hyperlinks that connect sites where tropes of regional identity like those expressed in the pages of Arabic children's magazines are likely to be repeated, is central to their magazine representations.

ENACTING CONSUMPTION

To describe the prospective identities encoded in these magazines is not to describe their Egyptian readers. Children who consume magazines do not necessarily consume the worlds constructed by the texts wholesale, as hegemonies. If we are to take consumption seriously as a social practice, we must recognize that the use of consumption in the construction of identities is a matter of bricolage, the selective appropriation and assembly of different elements to construct everyday life. Attention to human agency, the capacity to act on dominant discourses rather than merely being acted upon (Butler 1990), requires us to examine how people negotiate these registers. I will look at two upper-middle-class Egyptian readers of children's magazines and the ways their consumption, identities, and social futures are generated within the fields of school, family, and market.

Yasseen collects Pokémon cards. He was first exposed to Pokémon in an article about the Nintendo Game Boy in *Al Arabi Alsaghir* in 2001. The article didn't really register, he said, until weeks later, when he found a small plastic disk, called a *tazu*, in his Lay's potato chips. The *tazu*, used to play a game also called *tazu*, features the word "Pokémon" rendered in Arabic script on one side, with a likeness of one of the game's monsters on the other. Returning to the magazine, Yasseen was able to learn enough about Pokémon to locate Pokémon websites on the family computer. Eventually, a friend showed him the English-language collector's cards, and he was hooked. The cards, imported from the United States, are expensive by local standards, running EGP 20 (US$4.15) for a packet of ten cards. He surfs the web almost daily, keeping track of changes in the Pokémon card market, and he is in e-mail touch with other Pokémon fans in England and Spain. "Pokémon isn't only from the U.S. It's from everywhere," he told me. "All kids, all over the world, are playing Pokémon."

Even more than Pokémon, the computer is at the center of Yasseen's life. Although it is the household computer, sitting on a desk in the family room where it is prominently displayed for guests to see, and is used for e-mail and web browsing by Yasseen's mother and father, the family describes the computer as Yasseen's. He turns it on immediately when he wakes up in the morning, he said, and again as soon as he gets home from school. He confessed that he hardly ever reads *Al Arabi Alsaghir* any more except for the website reviews, and most of the time he already knows better sites than the magazine recommends.

Yasseen's friend Ismail was visiting during my interview. Yasseen and Ismail both attend the Modern Language School (MLS) in Ma'adi Gadida, a private English middle school charging EGP 14,500 (US$3,000) per year, but their family backgrounds are quite different. Yasseen's father owns a small electronics business, and his mother, Soraya, works for the public relations office of a large corporation. They have decided to limit their family to only two children, Yasseen and his two-year-old brother, Adly.

Ismail's father, Amin, works for a pharmaceutical firm. His mother stays home to raise the four children. Although Amin makes a good income and owns some property, the tuition at MLS is a strain on his budget. A school-age daughter goes to a less expensive, less prestigious language school. Amin says he is not bothered by the tuition at MLS, but is disturbed by the many extra expenses, which he had not expected. To fit in with the other children at MLS, Amin says, his son says he needs to have *this* kind of book bag and buy *these* kinds of chips.

Ismail has a subscription to *Majid,* which he reads, he said, from cover to cover.[17] He does not participate in any of the contests or pen pal games, but he spoke enviously of the children in the magazine (both real and in stories and comics) who have computers. He sometimes uses the computers at school to visit sites reviewed in *Majid.* He has asked his father many times for a computer, but his father insists that computers are not toys for children. Ismail also collects Pokémon *tazu,* a practice his father disapproves of. When he started at MLS, Ismail was given fifty piasters a day to buy lunch, but he began to use the money to buy chips instead. "They have no value," his father, Amin, told me when he came to pick Ismail up. "These crisps are no lunch but everyone eats them, so he must too." Ismail's parents upped his allowance to a pound so he could get chips *and* a hot lunch. Then came the Lay's Pokémon campaign, and Ismail began spending his pound to get two packages of chips a day, for the *tazu.*

Yasseen offered to sell some of his extra Pokémon cards to Ismail at a reduced rate, and even offered some of them as a gift, but Amin refused to allow it, insisting that if his son begins collecting these "bits of cardboard," he will end up begging to buy more. If the thought of spending a pound a day for chips is irritating to Amin, the thought of spending twenty pounds for a handful of cards is ridiculous. Amin's words were clearly directed in part at Yasseen's mother, who was making tea in the kitchen but could certainly overhear our conversation. Amin said he knows that Ismail gets some of his ideas about what he must have from *Majid,* but he hesitates to cut off his son's subscription because "he would just get his ideas all from television. At least this way, he is reading."

After Amin and Ismail left, Soraya commented on what she'd heard Amin tell me. She said that she and her husband recognize that the costs of Yasseen's computer, his Pokémon cards, and other commodity purchases are high, but they see it as part of his education. "The web pages, the books and posters are all in English," Soraya said. "They are to help him learn for his future." Play, education, and future work are thus conflated in Soraya's discourse, just as in the magazines. Moreover, Soraya insisted that the family's upward mobility, as expressed in these expensive purchases, is part of her own contribution to the family. She said she knows that some parents at the school think she spoils her sons, but "all these men who complain about computers and cell phones and Pokémon, their wives don't work." She insisted that men who want their children to have better lives need to marry educated women who can contribute to the family's income. But she said many men are afraid people will see them as unable to support their families without their wives' help if their wives work.[18]

These brief accounts of Yasseen and Ismail, Soraya and Amin indicate some of the complex ways in which children's magazines, school, peer groups, and families interact around consumption. For Yasseen, the magazine, the computer, and the expensive, imported goods are all part of how he imagines himself as part of a wider community that extends beyond the Arab world into a world community of affluent children engaged in the same activities. This global identity is encouraged by his parents, who recognize its potential contribution to Yasseen's upward mobility through education and language skills. It is particularly important for Soraya, whose substantial salary pays for the goods required to meet Yasseen's desired identity. Soraya's own Westernized modernity, expressed in her education, dress, work, and easy talk of family planning, both justifies and is justified by Yasseen's transnational imagination.

Ismail's and Amin's imaginations are more troubled. Ismail's desires outstrip his parents' sense of appropriate spending, a model of the liberal economic problem: how to manage unlimited desires with finite resources. Amin's expenditures on school tuition represent his desire for his son's upward mobility, but he is troubled by his son's desires for expensive, brand-name commodities. Yasseen's life is not what Amin would have for his son; Soraya does not represent the kind of woman he would choose to be the mother of his grandchildren. The problem of how to spend enough to let Ismail keep up with his peer group while not giving in to the endless consumption of pointless goods or creating a taste for a lifestyle he may not be able to afford, is a reflection of the larger problem of how to balance modernity with the values Amin grew up with.

AN IDEOLOGY OF DIFFERENCE

The differences between Ismail's and Yasseen's families are not as great as the gulf between the young man from Unity College and his age mate from ASC. Yet they are significant, and growing, as both families seek to create social futures for their children that embrace the contradictions of Egyptian modernity. This is one of the fundamental problems facing middle- and upper-middle-class Egyptian parents: how to ensure that their children are simultaneously modern and Egyptian. That a union of these two identities should be a problem lies in a deeply rooted notion that while Egyptianness is about faith, family, patriotism, and regional ethnic, religious, and political affinities, modernity is tied to the post-Enlightenment values of Western Europe: rationalism, secularism, industrialization, education, democracy, and increasing public and political roles for women. The polarity between local and modern constitutes an ideology of difference, an ideology that "divides spaces, moralities, types of people, activities and linguistic practices into opposed categories" (Gal 2005: 24). This ideology is objectified particularly in goods and expressed in consumer choices: the English school over the Arabic school, the *higab* versus the salon hairstyle, the *galabiyya* versus jeans and a button-down shirt, the sermon versus the television. These distinctions in turn produce hybridities: the sheikh with a cell phone, the televised sermon, the stylish *higab* as high-fashion accessory. But these hybridities do not solve the problem of balancing local and modern identities, they merely rearticulate and complicate it. Hybrid signs become incorporated into practices of differentiation as they raise questions of the authenticity both of Egyptianness and of modernity. The source domains of such hybrids are never themselves pure but, when scrutinized, always turn out also to be hybrids: *galabiyyas* bought in village markets are machine woven on German-manufactured power looms, and the locally manufactured television stands in contradistinction to the expensive foreign import. Commodities multiply, and as they do, so do distinctions.

Modernity in the Middle East, as Armbrust (1996a) points out, is often less about clearing the past to make way for modernity than creating new kinds of connections between past and present—and, I would add, especially where children are concerned, future. Linking regional history and mythography with international popular culture and consumer goods, *Samir, Alaa Eldin, Al Arabi Alsaghir, Bolbol, Majid,* and the like offer children tools for generating hybrid identities that are simultaneously Muslim and modern, Arab and cosmopolitan, child and consumer. They continue an ongoing historical effort since at least the mid-nineteenth century to create media representations of "modern but authentic Egyptians" (Shechter 2006: 10). Reading Arabic children's magazines allows children, and their parents, to imagine social presents and futures as Arab technocrats and consumers in a global world, connected to other consumers both at home in the region and in the wider world. Nor are these identities limited to the imagination. In purchasing Arabic children's magazines for their children, and in supplying the pocket money needed to buy the chips, drinks, gum, and candy advertised in their pages, parents enter into the ritual process through which children use these magazines to construct hybrid identities and to make themselves modern.

What is at issue, then, is not particular commodities perceived as local or modern or hybrid in and of themselves, but the ideologically ordered social fields in which they carry particular meanings and values. The effect of modernity or Egyptianness is carried out through contrasting practices of consumption, work, and play that *become* contrasting through meta-discourses that comment on and interpret these practices. These metadiscourses presuppose that certain values and images are local/Egyptian and others are global/modern, and they select and identify what will count as modern or local (or hybrid) in particular events and actions. Thus are the ideologies and practices of differentiation intertwined. The widening gulf between Yasseen and his friend Ismail is about Yasseen's larger and growing range of choices, empowered by his family's economic choices and his own growing competence in and taste for those goods understood to be particularly modern. Yasseen's declining interest in children's magazines indicates that they no longer offer him resources for developing his identity as a modern Egyptian boy. Awareness of the importance of regional and transnational goods and of global children's phenomena, and the communities they invite Yasseen to imagine himself part of, no longer need to be mediated through Arabic-language print media. As Yasseen becomes the kind of child portrayed in the magazines, he moves on to the consumption of alternative media. His parents' relative affluence and willingness to invest in Yasseen's cosmopolitanism, combined with Yasseen's rising English competence, allows the internet to take the place of Arabic children's magazines. Meanwhile, Ismail remains tied to Arabic children's magazines as one of the resources for his own quite different class development, which is constrained by his parents' different level of affluence and their sense that appropriateness requires that their son's spending more nearly resemble their own.

New private language schools
are continually emerging.

Above. The incorporation of pharaonic elements in this fountain in a walled community testifies to the continuing links between this type of imagery and Egyptian national identities.

Above right.
Cilantro is representative of the transnational coffee shops popping up all over Cairo.

Below right.
A typical *'ahwa* is marked primarily by its openness to the street.

3

POKÉMON PANICS: CLASS PLAY
IN THE PRIVATE SCHOOLS

It is not a coincidence that one of the key signifiers of difference and differentiation between Yasseen and his schoolmate Ismail was Pokémon. At the turn of the twenty-first century, Pokémon was a crucial commodity for children of both the middle and upper classes. Their cosmopolitan identities are constructed in part through the creation of imagined communities of other young people who appear to possess similar attributes and interests, expressed in large part through particular commodities and technologies. For many middle-class children, these interests may remain aspirational for much or all of their lives. For the children of Egypt's upper classes, these aspirational practices are reinforced through institutionalized activities. Consumption, after all, is only one of many ways in which identity is constructed. Consumption occurs within a matrix of other social practices and sites, all of which involve various degrees of social interaction. To mean something, a commodity has to be used and incorporated into everyday life.

The global Pokémon fad reached Egypt by 1999 and was quickly incorporated into local webs of meaning by which goods become part of class production. Yasseen discovered Pokémon through the magazine that became, with the financial support of his parents, his entrée to the internet. As the predominantly English internet replaced Arabic magazines as the medium of his growing cosmopolitanism, expensive imported game cards replaced his burgeoning collection of plastic tokens. Ismail's experience of commodities was quite different. Facing strong paternal disapproval and limited cash flow, Ismail's consumption of Pokémon was limited to the tokens found in bags of Lay's chips. Because Yasseen's cards are imported and thus "authentically" foreign, they invite him to imagine himself part of a cosmopolitan community of Pokémon consumers. Ismail's *tazu*, locally produced and transliterated into Arabic script, offer him a more limited range of connectivity. The distinction between these ranges of imagined communities is not inherent in Pokémon, of course, nor is it a product of different imaginative capacities. The values of these different ranges and forms of connectivity are culturally produced in homes, schools, peer networks, and other social fields where the nature of connectivity can be metadeictally discussed and the symbolic capital of Pokémon collecting and ownership can be converted into the social capital of status and identity.

Pokémon at the turn of the millennium was a powerful resource for the imaginations of Cairene children and their families. From about 1999 to around 2001, Pokémon provided a commoditized virtuality that organized not only children's play but also the social relations in which that play was embedded. Knowledge about Pokémon and access to Pokémon commodities were partially structured by existing social distinctions, and they, in turn, partially reconstructed those social distinctions in face-to-face situations of cooperative and competitive play. In the process, Pokémon was both loved and reviled as parents, educators, and politicians assessed its hold on their children, sought to construct moral frameworks for understanding it, and developed modes of resistance. Anti-Pokémon activities drew heavily on discourses from the Gulf states, where Pokémon was investigated by religious authorities and ultimately banned. Pokémon became an important site for class differentiation not simply because Pokémon play indexed a global community but also because resistance to Pokémon indexed a regional Arab community. This tension generated a field of possibilities for families to use Pokémon discursively to define themselves in relation to others.

SCHOOL SOCIALITIES

While Pokémon enters into many of the domains that make up children's social worlds, I will limit my discussion to their school worlds. Although Pokémon play takes place in many sites, school is perhaps the most central, the most social, and the most common location for Pokémon play and display. As in most places in the world, schools in Egypt are key sites for identity formation while at the same time functioning as locations through which parents imagine and attempt to construct their children's social futures (Cope and Kalantzis 2000). Schools transform children's identities, socially as well as subjectively, transforming them into "educated persons." But "while the educated person is culturally *produced* in definite sites, the educated person also culturally *produces* cultural forms [as] people actively confront the ideological and material conditions presented by schooling" (Levinson and Holland 1996: 14).

Schools are also useful sites for the ethnographic study of children's social worlds since children spend so much of their social time with other children in these institutions. Their behavior there is public and observable, and students are often excited to discover an adult who will listen rather than talk, is interested in those aspects of their lives to which parents and teachers pay the least attention, and does not pass judgment on their activities and language. Schools, moreover, constitute conveniently organized and circumscribed systems in which children's play and social activity intersect with the demands of adult society as to what they should be and become. Schools are sites of acquiescence, negotiation, and resistance among children as they recognize and exploit or do not exploit structural contradictions.

Egypt began importing Western models of education in the early nineteenth century under Muhammad Ali, and with a few exceptions this pattern has been retained (Heyworth-Dunne 1968; Starrett 1998). Although nearly all Egyptian schooling is "Western" compared to the old *kutub* system of memorizing classical texts, some forms of education are seen as more Western and modern than others. Today, schools are evaluated in the light of Egypt's supposed educational crisis and the extent to which people believe a school will provide students with skills—especially fluency in international languages—and disciplines that will suit the social futures their parents imagine for them (Abu-Lughod 1998a). Western modes of education have become a highly desirable commodity, a form of cultural capital that is valued in the job market. Yet parents want their children to take from school only those aspects of Western modernization that are positive, not those that are bad. Exactly which are which is one of the central conundrums of Egyptian life (Abu-Lughod 1998b; Ghannam 2002).

Most public schools are taught in Arabic, with a second language (usually English, French, German, or Italian) introduced in the fifth grade.

Children also take classes in modern standard Arabic (MSA), a form of the language quite different from what they speak outside of school. Because it is taught as a literary language, usually without classes in conversation (Fellman 1973), students usually associate it exclusively with formal and academic purposes. Only a few master the "educated spoken" register that signifies a well-educated Arab (Ennaji 2002: 79–80). Moreover, most people recognize that mastery of MSA will rarely get them jobs, while proficiency in a foreign language is crucial in the job market (Barsoum 1999, 2004; Haeri 1997).[1] It is generally accepted that public school students will face enormous hurdles in entering and succeeding in either the university or the workforce. One answer to this has been the creation of hybrid public-private schools, the so-called experimental schools (*mudaris tagribiya*) which teach certain subjects, particularly math and science, in English but teach others in Arabic. Although operated by the government, parents must pay a small tuition fee to enroll their children in these schools.

The significance of language in school commodification cannot be overstressed. Egypt is complexly multiglossic. Arabic is read and spoken in many different ways in different contexts (Armbrust 1996a; Haeri 1997, 2003). Some proficiency in MSA is required for most public sector work. In the private sector, however, foreign languages, especially English, are far more valuable (Haeri 1997). The efforts of the Egyptian government to attract foreign capital have led to the paradoxical situation that, after Egypt's independence from British colonialism, English has come to play an increasingly important role in the country. Nor is it sufficient to have a mere competence in English. A "good" American or British accent and comfort with idiomatic expression can mean a salary difference of hundreds of pounds per month (Barsoum 2004). Parents pay significant fees to send their children to language and international schools so that they will gain a mastery of this symbolic capital, which will be reconvertible into economic capital as their children enter the labor market. Different kinds of schools, hierarchically organized by the kinds of language learning they provide and the prices they charge, hold out promises of varyingly prosperous social futures.

But language is only the most visible of the many forms of symbolic capital children learn and internalize in and through the school environment. As there are idiomatic forms of language, so there are idiomatic forms of bodily comportment, styles of dress, and tastes in media, food, goods, and leisure activities. As with language, schools are crucial sites for the acquisition of these idioms. Comparing Pokémon play in two private schools can offer important insights into the functions of children's play, and the commodities through which such play is expressed, in class differentiation.

IMSUKUHUM KULHUM!

> Well it's not just a game! It's a whole world. There's
> TV shows, comic books, little figures and card games.
>
> —Ten-year-old Scott, United States (Joyce 1999)

> Pokémon isn't only from the U.S. It's from everywhere.
> All kids, all over the world, are playing Pokémon.
>
> —Ten-year-old Yasseen, Egypt

Pokémon began as a Nintendo Game Boy electronic game in Japan in 1996 and quickly became wildly successful across a vast range of commodified forms. Pokémon traveled rapidly "from East Asia and Australia to the Americas (North, South and Central), Western Europe, Israel, the Middle East, Eastern Europe, and Southeast Asia" (Allison 2003: 381). A number of theories have been offered to explain its phenomenal success. Kline et al. (2003) suggested that it was the game's family friendliness in a market of increasingly violent games. Cook (2001) argued that the game's central theme of a quest for a mastery, which is always ultimately withheld, parallels the structure of unfulfilled desire that is at the heart of consumer capitalism. Buckingham and Sefton-Green (2003) suggested that Pokémon offers children a pedagogy into forms of knowledge significant to them but esoteric to adults. Jordan located in the logic of Pokémon an "ethic of love" (2004: 478) in which relations of mastery and submission are translated into relations of mutual respect and care, an ethic particularly significant for children on the cusp of adolescence and their struggle to understand family roles. Allison (2003) suggested that Pokémon offers a species of "cuteness" that renders high technology, portability, and other aspects of global consumerism reassuring. Pokémon's spread into the wider world may also have been aided by its success in the United States through the so-called megaphone effect, which describes how "cultural products that succeed in a large market such as the United States have added force when they reach a smaller, downstream market" (Lemish and Bloch 2004: 167).[2]

These universal explanations are helpful, and one can find elements of all of these in Egyptian children's discourses. But these explanations should not distract our attention from the important role of localization in Pokémon's success. Cuteness, the psychology of social relations, mastery of knowledge, family friendliness, and so forth all emerge at various times in Cairene discourses about Pokémon, but all are limited to specific contexts. Pokémon was carefully adapted for its North American audiences so as to minimize cultural differences that might interfere with its popularity. Such localization went beyond the mere translation of verbal signs to involve the renaming of Pokémon characters, selective editing, changes to plot narratives, new music, and changes in basic plot themes (such as a reduction in the ambiguity of good and evil) (Katsuno and Maret 2004). Yet at the same time, "Japan has marketed Pokémon as clearly 'Japanese.' National origins are imprinted rather than effaced here, indicating a shift away from what Koichi Iwabuchi has called Japan's policy of 'de-odorizing' the cultural aroma of its products" (Allison 2003: 383). Thus, Pokémon can at once be localized *and* signify "Japanese."

In the Pokémon game, the player becomes a trainer who has to capture one of each species of wild Pokémon to advance to higher levels of mastery. The trainer whips his or her Pokémon into fighting shape, then sends them into one-on-one matches against another trainer's Pokémon. Pokémon who lose a fight do not die, however: they faint. Each Pokémon has a special power of attack, and as they use these successfully over time, they "evolve" into more powerful forms. The Game Boy technology for which Pokémon was designed invites certain forms of sociability, since separate Game Boy machines can be connected by a cable to allow dual play. What's more, in the original version of the game, two machines had to be connected in order for players to capture the rare 151st Pokémon species.

Pokémon also evolved into multiple forms. Roughly categorized by media, we can group these into four primary domains: electronic games, cards, animation, and figurines. *Electronic games* include not only the original Nintendo game and its supplemental editions but also various CD-ROM games and online games. The category *cards* includes game cards, which can be used to play a competitive strategy game in which players seek to capture one another's cards, and also collecting/trading cards in multiple sets and series (with each new release of a game or movie resulting in the release of a new series of cards). *Animation* refers to the Japanese television series, which is available in various dubbed and re-edited versions throughout Europe, North America, and, via satellite, the rest of the world. But it also includes a highly lucrative movie series. Both the television shows and the movies moved quickly from broadcast and theater release to video. Some children collect the videos as avidly as the cards or other goods. *Figurines* include various plastic figures, stuffed animals, and other material forms of the Pokémon.

In addition to these four primary media, a vast secondary domain of production emerged, which feeds off of and comments on the primary domains. This secondary domain includes books on collecting various Pokémon products; illustrated books recounting stories from the animated series; posters enumerating the total number of monsters; "studio" computer programs that allow owners to produce Pokémon stationery, tattoos, greeting cards, stickers, and T-shirts; Halloween costumes; school supplies; apparel; and so on, ad infinitum.

Pokémon has been a transnational phenomenon of astonishing complexity that defies simple labels or explanations. Tim Jordan writes:

> Pokémon is both its material manifestation in a series of games, movies, branded towels, and so on, but it is not only these things. No single product, even the first foundational games, constitutes Pokémon by itself. In addition to the various objects that make up Pokémon, there is a set of logics about what the Pokémon world "is" that ties all the varied products together as Pokémon. (Jordan 2004: 461)

Pokémon involves a web of commodities in which each serves as an indexical sign for all the others, connecting diverse activities and goods across social, political, and economic boundaries.

Pokémon is a perfect example of a *simulacrum,* a set of identical copies for which no original ever existed (Jameson 1984: 66). Children encounter

Pokémon not as a game or a television show or a card game or a motion picture but as a lived totality encompassing many or all of these. Pokémon constitutes what Arjun Appadurai (1996) has called an "imagined world." It serves as an intertextual resource for children's play, for their art, for their discourse. It serves as a reference point for myriad social activities and as a resource for private fantasies. Pokémon players are not only consumers, however; they use the media they acquire to create their own texts, to engage in play, to generate social relations, and to resist institutional authority. Children consume Pokémon, but in turn, Pokémon becomes a resource through which they become producers of social worlds.

The theme of acquisition promoted by Pokémon in all its myriad forms, together with Pokémon's capacity to link children to a global community of other players and collectors, allowed it to rapidly became an important part of the practices of differentiation by which class is produced and reproduced in Cairo.

THE POKÉMON PANICS

Pokémon arrived in the Middle East in 2000 simultaneously in the form of electronic games, collector's cards, an animated television series, stickers, toys, stuffed animals, coloring books, and so forth, and immediately began to colonize children's attention with the same viral capacity it showed throughout the world. It arrived first in the oil-rich states—especially Kuwait, Saudi Arabia, and UAE—where it became the most popular children's fad in decades. Newspaper columnists compared its reach and the loyalty it inspired to Mickey Mouse, Captain Majid,[3] and Tom and Jerry, but the comparisons were always negative. These earlier commodified characters had built up their popularity over many years, and they appeared in only a few forms, primarily comics or animated television shows. Pokémon appeared suddenly and was immediately everywhere, with every child clamoring for cards, games, videos, notebooks, pencils, T-shirts.

My attention to Pokémon's reception in the Gulf came as a result of my Egyptian informants' references to the vociferous debates about the games, cartoons, and related commodities. Discussions of Pokémon in Egypt frequently referenced mediated accounts of the moral debates about

Pokémon in the Gulf states. During my interviewing at the Modern Language School, I received photocopies of six newspaper or magazine articles, all of which were unidentifiable. Although Saad, the father of two children at MLS who supplied four of the articles, insisted that they came from Gulf publications, internal evidence suggests that at least three of them came from Egyptian magazines reporting on the Gulf controversy. A review of an index of Arabic periodicals yielded nine articles. Another six from English periodicals like the *Star* (Amman), *Egyptian Gazette,* and *Middle East Times* derived mostly from Reuters, AFP, and other news services. I will focus primarily on the Arabic texts, both because I can clearly source them and because they are themselves the media through which the public debate was constituted.

These articles initially focused on the genius of Pokémon as a global marketing phenomenon: its capacity to mutate and replicate, infiltrating every part of everyday life. Like many other contemporary phenomena, Pokémon consists of a multimedia, multiple-commodity system in which each component indexes the others. One of the things that has made Pokémon particularly powerful is that the internal narrative in all its forms is about acquisition ("Imsukuhum Kulhum!" says the Arabic slogan, a translation of the English "Gotta Catch 'em All"). Whether as a Nintendo game in which players gather Pokémon, an animated series about children accumulating Pokémon, or as cards, disks, plastic figures, and other objects that can be collected, Pokémon is about the acquisition of an always-increasing number of desirable commodities. Pokémon creates a symbolic reservoir from which symbols can be borrowed and cobbled together into new games and activities. And because new card series, new game cartridges, and other commodities continue to appear, "we see acquisition constantly elicited and refused, the possibility of mastery (catching them all) offered and avoided" (Jordan 2004: 467).

It is just this viral pattern of commodification that was the subject of the most commentary by parents, educators, political leaders, and journalists in the Gulf. Articles with titles like "Globalization Starts with Children," "Pokémon Conquers Children's Minds," "A Pokémon in Every Home," and "Pokémon: Legendary Characters Sneak into Arab Children's Bedrooms" speculated on the power of Pokémon as a representative of globalization and its hold on children's imaginations. A few articles suggested that the Arab world should take note: Pokémon was proof that countries outside the West could create products expressing their cultural identities, and these could enter and even dominate the global economy (Al-Qurani 2000; Nagi 2000). Most, however, agreed with the father quoted in the October 30, 2000, issue of the Qatari magazine *Mulhaq li Watan wa lil Muwatin:* "This is like anything imposed on us by the West. They produce and we consume. They have their own ways to attract our minds, so it is not difficult for them to steal our children's minds and to turn their products into a profitable trade." This notion that Pokémon came to the Arab world from "the West" is not farfetched, in spite of the Japanese origins of the game, the fact that Nintendo is a Japanese corporation, and the claims that Nintendo has sought to emphasize Pokémon's "Japaneseness" (Iwabuchi 2002). With the exception of some stickers and other commodities that require neither sound nor text, very few of the Pokémon commodities in the Gulf are of Japanese origin. Most are imported through licenses with Nintendo North America. Nintendo had hired specialists to assist in adapting the game to suit North American audiences (Katsuno and Maret 2004). With the exception of dubbed versions of the cartoons (which retain the American names of the characters), no similar efforts were made to tailor Pokémon for a Middle Eastern market. As a result, Pokémon products are indexed by English script and other elements of "Western" origin.

Opposition to Pokémon was not simply based on the fact that it is Western, however. A vast quantity of Western commodities are available in Gulf markets, after all, but few stir up controversy at a regional level. As critical metadiscourses emerged, it became clear that the very capacities that generated Pokémon's global success were the subject of moral critique among families and others charged with the upbringing of children. Pokémon's sin is that it draws children's attention in utterly compelling ways. It fills every aspect of their lives, usurping the person-formation roles of family and school. The same article in *Mulhaq li Watan wa lil Muwatin* quoted a teacher and mother of four:

> If Pokémon were limited only to the cartoon serial, the matter would be easy. However, it has turned to games, pictures, and various other forms. As a result of the child's attachment to the serial and to this character, he became eager to get all the Pokémon games, and it even has a site on the internet. . . . The problem is that in the school, children

chat about Pokémon because it doesn't disappear from their vision. His picture is on the school bags, on the pen case, and on the notebooks. His bravery is great in their eyes. Then how does a mother protect her child from it? It is an actual invasion. I don't say that it causes a direct harm but it is not useful to our children, and it gets in the way of useful things.

Here, it is the fundamental nature of Pokémon as simulacrum that is concerning parents and educators. The synergistic capacity of all Pokémon products to index the others is constructed as an "invasion" of children's lives that extends beyond leisure into school and other sites where their future is being shaped.

The problem of Pokémon refusing to stay just a game or television series, stealing children's minds so they do not attend to the social, educational, and religious dimensions of their lives, was only one part of the anti-Pokémon discourses. Another strand expressed the notion that multimedia phenomena like Pokémon teach values and principles which may not be good for children's morals or education. An unsigned article in the sports column of *Al-Rubai'* argued that Pokémon is different from other cartoons (it mentioned *Captain Majid, Bakar,*[4] and *Tom and Jerry*) not only because Pokémon is much more heavily merchandised but because it affects matters of religious faith and practice (*Al-Rubai'* 2000). A Saudi Arabian journalist suggested that Arabs needed to make the best compromises they could in the Huntingtonesque "clash of civilizations" created by globalization when he opined, "If we must choose between the American Miki and Pokémon, who comes from the Confucian culture [*sic*], on the one hand, and [Disney's] Aladdin, who is a distortion of the Arab character, on the other hand, then the mind will say welcome to the Arab character Aladdin, who at least expresses Arab and Islamic heritage and fame" (Al-Qurani 2000: 11). Adopting an essentialist view that imagines "the culture" of a place to be embedded in its products and spread (like a virus) by the global distribution of these products, Al-Qurani sees Disneyfied hybrids as an uneasy compromise to the alternative: the loss of any distinctive "Arab character" like that proposed in the Arabic children's magazines.

Outside the mainstream press, wilder accusations flew, charging Pokémon with Zionism and with promoting immoral ideas and practices. It was charged that Pokémon was owned by Israelis (or American Jews backing Israel) and that the money made was being spent on weapons used to kill Palestinians. Pokémon was said to encode Zionist symbols like the Mogen David.[5] Other charges included the promotion of evolutionary theory and, in the case of card collecting, the promotion of gambling. An anonymous flyer in circulation claimed that the strange names of the monsters encoded blasphemous meanings: "Onix," for example, the name of a black, stone snake Pokémon, was said to "really" mean "Say no to God." To an English speaker, the etymology of the names of the Pokémonsters is usually self-evident. Onix clearly derives his name from the stone of which he is made (onyx). To an Arab monolingual speaker, the meanings of the words are by no means clear. The decision by marketing professionals to transliterate the names of the Pokémon universe but not to Arabicize them at the morphemic level created ambiguities that were exploited by the anti-Pokémon protesters.[6]

The public debate over Pokémon was never a simple mask for a more general attack on globalization but remained fairly concrete and focused. Most of the articles called on the state, and on the religious authorities linked to the state, to protect the community against the dangers Pokémon specifically posed.[7] An unsigned article in the Qatari magazine *Mulhaq li Watan wa lil Muwatin* asked in October 2000 whether government agencies were doing their part to protect consumers. What, the author asked, does the Measures Control Office have to say about the description of children's toys? What are the criteria for deciding how to control children's serials on Qatar TV? What is the opinion of scholars of psychology, education, and medicine regarding Pokémon? And a respected sports columnist in Saudi Arabia's *Al-Rubai'* argued that since Pokémon monsters die and come back to life—a false religious teaching—it should be suppressed by the state and by religious authorities charged with upholding correct religious practice (the columnist seems to have mistaken what is supposed to be the monsters' unconsciousness for death). In addition, he argued, because some Pokémon are worth more than others but one buys the packets without knowing what is inside them, collecting the cards is effectively gambling, which is forbidden by Islam. He asked why the Ministry of Trade and the Committee for Public Morality haven't done something about this.

Nearly all the authors of these articles invoked the responsibility of the state and its institutions to safeguard the family. Occasionally, this argument was explicitly linked to religious teachings. A columnist for *Al Riyad*, Dr. Hafez Medalag, interviewed the prince of Riyad, Salman Ibn Abdel Aziz, who

> emphasized the message of the Prophet (God bless him and grant him salvation) saying: "You all shepherd and you are all responsible for his people." This is a lesson about the relation between the responsible person and their responsibility. We should learn to know our responsibility and prevent the dangers that surround us. The responsibility of the father goes beyond spending money on his children. He has to know where they go, what they play, and how they spend their money. The responsibility of the education sector goes beyond the boundaries of teaching. It should be ready to support students with culture as well as knowledge to develop their abilities to protect themselves and to distinguish between what is useful and harmful to them. This is why the education ministry is called the Ministry of Upbringing and Education. Likewise, the responsibility of the Ministry of Trade is not limited to allowing games to enter the country but it has to make sure of the goals and values behind these games, which children learn from them. The responsibility of the Committee of Public Morality should exceed its laudable efforts in stores and watch markets and sellers of the game and it should investigate the reasons behind the crowd of children in such stores and their interest. The responsibility of the Ministry of Information should exceed entertainment and transmitting information to protecting society from the dangers coming as a result of the intellectual invasion that threatens the youth of the nation in different ages and cultures. (Medalag 2000: 27)

Medalag links parents, community, state, and religious authority into a single economy of responsibility in which all are responsible for all—and each is responsible to God. Children are the only ones who do not carry a social responsibility; it is for them that all these other responsibilities must be mobilized. It is worth noting that Medalag is not a political or religious journalist but an investment columnist. He opened this column with an apology to his readers for the digressions of his Pokémon columns, but explained that he, too, by virtue of his public position as a columnist, must play a responsible role as shepherd.

This Arabian debate over Pokémon constitutes a "moral panic," a concept originated by Stanley Cohen (1972) and subsequently developed by Goode and Ben-Yehuda (1994), Thompson (1998), Critcher (2003), and others. Moral panics have frequently been linked to issues of modernity and childhood (Drotner 1992; Springhall 1998; Cook 2001). A moral panic occurs when a threat to purported "common" values or interests is defined, labeled, and characterized in the media. It is a *panic* because there ensues a spiraling upsurge in public concern, which in turn draws responses and solutions from various authorities. The panic is *moral* because it is organized around the notion that the "threat is to something held sacred by or fundamental to society" (Thompson 1998: 8). The moral dimension of the panic need not be tied to a religious framework. It can invoke a purely secular moral framework centered on "waste," "poor education," or other values that public speakers do not specifically frame through religious references.

Moral panics involving children are often constructed around the notion that child leisure is something pure, which is being corrupted by market incursions (Cook 2001). In the Pokémon case, the corruption of Arab youth was explicitly tied to external forces, whether Japanese, American, Zionist, or the abstract "globalization" itself. These agents are thus not the "folk devils" of Cohen's formulation—agents of disruption arising from within the social order—but foreign devils threatening the social order from without. In pursuit of profits or political ends, these foreign agents focus the power of their astonishing psychological knowledge of how to manufacture desire on to children. Moral panics are clusters of metadeictic discourses that seek to explain global interconnections, to morally evaluate them, and to pursue possible changes that will either break these connections or bring them into conformity with the moral order they have violated. Pokémon, as Yano points out, "becomes a means by which different societies may describe themselves [as] at risk, as vulnerable to threats both externally and internally. Talk of Pokémon points directly to the vulnerabilities of global consumerist citizenship" (Yano 2004: 109).

These metadiscourses about the risks of globalization are complicated by a recognition from many participants in this public debate that their own childhoods were not innocent of similar global comics, games, and goods. They invoke fondly their own engagements with such foreign children's media as *Tom and Jerry, Miki,* or *Captain Majid* and their nostalgic memories of global consumption, but they construct Pokémon as a threat because it is different not only in form but in kind from their consumption. Pokémon is different because of its capacity to multiply endlessly and to colonize multiple commodified domains, from television to movies to school bags to games and more. It refuses to stay leisure, but finds its way into children's school time and their social relations. Because it is inescapable, it is more corrupting than other foreign goods, in at least three ways. First, Pokémon distracts children from truly important things like education. Second, the cost to parents of meeting their children's unending and never fulfilled desires for ever more Pokémon goods places an unacceptable burden on the domestic economy. Finally, the goods may be expressive of negative, even soul-threatening values. Particularly interesting is the strident tone taken by media commentators and interviewees alike in constructing this debate. It stands in contrast to the humorous tone common to moralistic debates about Pokémon in the United States and Canada, where "many find it difficult to take cuddly creatures and cartoon characters seriously, yet seem impelled to do so" (Cook 2001: 93).

The critique of Pokémon in Egypt thus revolved around three closely interconnected discourses. The first represented Pokémon as an example of the power of the Western culture industry to dominate local markets. The second discourse amplified the nature of Pokémon's domination of the market. Pokémon's sin is that it draws children's attention in utterly compelling ways. It fills every aspect of children's lives, usurping the person-formation roles of family and school. The final critique claimed that Pokémon teaches values and principles which are not good for children's morals or education. Taken together, these critiques offered a model of globalization in which the market is desecularized, its moral character emphasized. Marketing psychology has become a kind of magical force that creates desire. These desires are so powerful they colonize children's lives, preventing them from bettering themselves through education, socializing, and religious practice. Meanwhile, the objects of their desire teach them values and attitudes that are, at best, alien to their "natural" Arab and Islamic character and, at worst, outright immoral and blasphemous.

Although moral panics often simply fade away, as public debate about Pokémon did in the United States (Cook 2001), they can also end in laws or regulations designed to protect the community from the threatened social disorder; Critcher (2003) argues that moral panics are essentially modes of social control. This was the case in the Gulf. The prince of Riyadh in November 2000 organized a committee to study Pokémon, the reports of which were forwarded to Mecca. Ultimately, the question of Pokémon was settled for families, communities, states, and markets by a fatwa issued by the grand mufti of Saudi Arabia in March 2001, urging all Muslims to beware of the game and to prevent their children from playing it so as to protect their "religion and manners." Although the primary reason given for the ban was that the game "resembled gambling," Sheikh Abdul Aziz Bin Abdullah Al Sheikh also mentioned that many of the commodities contain Zionist symbolism and that Pokémon promotes evolutionary theories that are incompatible with Islam. Saudi Arabia promptly banned all Pokémon commodities and seized and destroyed those already on the shelves. Dubai followed suit in April, and Jordan and UAE informed distributors that they were considering bans, which led most vendors to stop importing Pokémon products.[8]

POKÉMON IN EGYPT

Pokémon's place in Egypt was very different than in most of the Gulf states. The reach of the primary Pokémon products, Game Boy cartridges and game cards, was low. Egypt's per capita GDP ranges between one-fifth and one-third those of Kuwait, Qatar, UAE, and Saudi Arabia, where the Pokémon phenomenon and controversy were most apparent. Imported Pokémon goods began to appear in Cairo in late 1999, but the Nintendo games and playing cards were extremely expensive by Egyptian standards and largely out of reach of most middle-class families. Indeed, they initially existed primarily in venues where middle-class children would be unlikely to encounter them, and children could mainly be found playing and collecting Pokémon only in the most expensive private schools. Pokémon discourses in Egypt thus reflected these differences.

Pokémon came to the attention of middle- and working-class Egyptians in the fall of 2000, when the animated television program arrived in an Arabic-dubbed version on the national television network. In response to the growth of satellite television, the local government channels had expanded children's programming. Whereas children's television had once been largely a Ramadan season phenomenon, 'Alam Simsim and Pokémon became among the first daily television programs for children, especially rural children, "who can't get Cartoon Network," as one ministry official said.

In December 2000, Lay's Egypt, the local branch of multinational food corporation Frito-Lay, began including *tazu* in its Lay's and Ruffles brand potato chips. The disks, used to play a game also called *tazu*, had pictures of Pokémon creatures on them, with the word "Pokémon" rendered in Arabic script. The American name of each monster was also rendered in Arabic script. There were twenty-four disks in all, and as with the American trading cards, some were easier to get than others. The promotion was immensely successful—far more than previous Lay's *tazu* campaigns featuring the Teenage Mutant Ninja Turtles and Mighty Morphin Power Rangers—and the company extended the campaign for almost a year.

The success of the *tazu* game and the cartoon show produced a small number of local products as well. While the selling of the Arabic-dubbed videos of the cartoons was authorized, many of the other commercial appropriations, such as Rokémon Crisps, a brand of locally manufactured corn chips, were clearly not. Nor was all pirating local. Kiosks near schools for several weeks carried packets of Pokémon treats imported from Turkey, which contained forged Pokémon cards, sticks of gum, lollipops, and stickers. To feed the desire for Pokémon, local stationery stores began carrying inexpensive imports, such as stickers from Japan. Upscale stores increased their stock of expensive, imported games and trading cards. While still out of reach of most Egyptians, many upper-middle-class children learned about these goods and pestered their parents for them. When they got them, they took them to school to show their schoolmates.

POKÉMON IN THE MODERN LANGUAGE SCHOOL

The MLS, attended by Yasseen and Ismail, is a private, co-educational school which follows the national curriculum but offers primary instruction in English. It is composed of three buildings housing the elementary school, junior high school, and senior high school, all surrounded by a wall. There is a large swath of garden fronting the school, so that the view from the gate as one enters is of grass and trees. The remainder of the compound is asphalt, including a large parking lot and two athletic courts for football, basketball, tennis, and other games. The wall around the school abuts another wall, which encloses an older private language school owned by the same family that built MLS. This school charges substantially lower fees, offers instruction in Arabic, and follows the national curriculum, advertising itself to parents as a premier opportunity to prepare their children for the national exam.

At MLS, students are offered two tracks, one designed to prepare them for an international baccalaureate, the other for the Egyptian national exam. Unlike the public schools, which offer Islamic religious instruction in Arabic, MLS offers no explicit Muslim or Christian instruction. Private language schools like MLS are crucial instruments through which middle-class Egyptian parents attempt to ensure that their children are simultaneously modern and Egyptian. Administrators are keenly aware of their responsibility to guide children—and perhaps their parents—in the struggle Egyptians face "to appropriate what they perceive as positive aspects of modernity and avoid what is considered negative" (Ghannam 2002: 133).

I was introduced to the Modern Language School by Saad, who had a son and a daughter enrolled there. One of my graduate students had told me that some schools were burning Pokémon, and when I pressed him for details he introduced me to Saad as a man who "could tell me everything about it." Saad was a thoughtful man with an intense manner, an unexpected sense of humor, and a deadpan delivery that kept catching me unaware. He was skeptical but intrigued by the anti-Pokémon rhetoric, but seemed equally skeptical of my interest in the controversy. Saad introduced me to Mrs. Maryam, the principal, who welcomed me warmly. Over several weeks in the spring of 2001, I interviewed my way down the school hierarchy from Mrs. Maryam through the administrators to the teachers to the students. My reception was due more to my status as an AUC professor than because they welcomed my study of Pokémon as an example of globalization and localization processes. There was considerable confusion among staff, faculty, and students as to what exactly I was doing there. Some teachers were convinced I was studying Pokémon as an example of the problems facing teachers in the classroom, while others grabbed onto the notion of "globalization" and waxed eloquently about the pros and cons of foreign influences in Egypt. One teacher introduced me to her class as a professor from AUC who had come to observe them in such a way as to make it seem that I might be recruiting students for the university. In all, I paid nine visits to the school, interviewed three administrators and five teachers, and observed classes and recess play. Over the summer, I visited the homes of six families with one or more students enrolled at the school—including Yasseen's and Ismail's—to get a deeper perspective on Cairene attitudes toward school, education, play, and social futures.

The faculty and students at the school are nearly all Egyptians of the middle classes, but a considerable income gulf exists between more and less affluent parents of the students. MLS's fees are about one-half those of ASC, but still quite expensive by Egyptian standards. This income gulf was expressed through Pokémon as a distinction between those who collected and played the card games and Game Boys, and those who collected and played *tazu,* the colorful plastic disks given away inside bags of Lay's potato chips.[9] While students who collected and played Pokémon cards also collected and played *tazu,* the price of the cards led to a class distinction in that only those with greater spending power could collect the cards. With imported Pokémon cards running at a price of twenty pounds or more per packet, card collectors clearly had parents either with higher incomes or with very different ideas about how to spend their limited money on their children, or both. Indeed, the chief predictor for card collecting among the six families I interviewed was (as Soraya predicted) whether or not the mother was employed. Two-income families not only had more money to spend but tended to display different attitudes toward Pokémon. The distinction between the cards in English and the *tazu* in Arabic served as a reminder of why the students were at MLS at all: to learn English and to learn *in* English, the current language of social mobility, modernity, and economic advancement. This goal is not consistently reached. One afternoon, the principal of the junior high school was explaining that at MLS "all the children speak English all the time. In the classrooms and even out on the playground at recess, everywhere within the walls of the school," even as the excited voices of children playing football, shouting in Arabic, drifted in through his window.

School authorities at MLS worried about Pokémon's influence on students, calling it an "obsession" and saying something had to be done about it. The school lacks extensive playground areas and, as a result, Pokémon *tazu* games, which often gathered large crowds of spectators, clogged hallways and stairwells. Mrs. Maryam, the MLS principal, told me that Pokémon "was getting completely out of hand." Children were playing with and trading *tazu* in hallways not only at scheduled recesses but between classes, and some were even skipping extracurricular activities in order to play *tazu*. Seeing Pokémon as an attack on the scholastic order, the MLS banned all display of Pokémon objects and activities. Teachers confiscated books, notebooks, stickers, and other paraphernalia, even resorting to body searches in gym classes.[10]

Official MLS discourses about Pokémon, some of which were shared with parents at a general meeting, reflected many of the same concerns as those expressed in the Gulf newspapers. Pokémon's ubiquity meant that even when children were not actually playing, the Pokémon icons on their notebooks and pencils, backpacks and lunchboxes, pointed them away from the world of education and back to the world of play. For MLS staff, one of the purposes of education is to teach children to differentiate between what is good from Western modernity and what is not. Pokémon distracts from this important goal. Mrs. Maryam and two other administrators discussing Pokémon with me began our conversations with a focus on specific ways Pokémon threatens school discipline but inevitably moved into a discussion of a more general breakdown of the moral order in the face of globalization. This became particularly clear when Mrs. Maryam spoke about the failure of parents to stop children from playing Pokémon at home. "We cannot stop this craze without the parents," she said. "If the children do not play at school and then go home to play, it is as if we've done nothing." But why, I asked, if the problem is school disruption, should the ban extend into the home? "You must understand," she answered. "The Egyptian parent is weak where their children are concerned. If their children ask them for something, they must give it to them. It is part of our Egyptian character. Parents must learn to be stricter about giving children only those things that are good for them." This notion that Pokémon represents a far greater challenge than a breakdown of school discipline was not peculiar to school administrators but was part of a larger public discourse through which displays of Pokémon play and paraphernalia came to be read.

Although media reports from the Gulf fed into it, the moral panic over Pokémon in Egypt was quite different from that in the richer Gulf states. For one thing, it was far more limited in scope. The mainstream Egyptian press, such as *Al-Ahram,* and the English-language upper-class magazines almost failed to notice Pokémon, and when they did, it was usually to comment critically on the panic among the middle classes. The defense of the morality and purity of Egyptian children was thus left to the popular magazines, which reported all that happened in the Gulf states. There were many additional local flourishes. Some were modest, such as the claim that children were buying packets of chips for the *tazu,* then throwing them away.[11] Most were not. In rapid succession, it was put forward that Pokémon was Jewish, then satanic, then poisonous. Pokémon's Jewishness was mainly supported by two claims. The first is that one of the symbols on the cards, a stylized asterisk, has six points and therefore is "really" a Star of David, which is understood as a symbol of international Zionism. This claim may have been picked up from Gulf sources where the cards were more widely distributed. In Egypt, most people know Pokémon from *tazu* and the TV show, which do not feature these symbols. The other claim, suggested by at least one journalist, is that the Pokémon Stario, a starfish with a jewel on his back, could also be characterized as a Star of David. The fact that Stario, like all starfish, actually has only five points, was ignored in these stories and, as with similar claims in Gulf newspapers, no illustrations of Stario were printed in the two articles I read making such claims.

Satanism and Judaism were often linked in such accounts, not directly but indexically, by co-association. In some cases, items like an anonymous Saudi flyer asserting blasphemous meanings for the names of Pokémonsters circulated widely, brought, faxed, or mailed, at least in the case of the copy I received, by Egyptians living and working in the Gulf. One parent informed me that the names on the flyer were the "Jewish" meanings of the words, although there was nothing in the text of the flyer making such a claim. Calls for the authorities to step in and shepherd the community went unheard. Neither Al-Azhar University, the primary religious authority in Egypt, nor the Mubarak regime took the slightest public notice of Pokémon. Families found it necessary to resolve their moral dilemmas on their own, in response to community and public discourses.

Yasseen does not read the popular press. He nonetheless encountered these controversies via his older cousins. Coming from a family with less disposable income than Yasseen, the boys used to collect *tazu* but destroyed them after their father read them stories about Pokémon from the newspapers. For several months, they harassed Yasseen about his collection. "They told me Pikachu was Jewish. They said if I buy Pokémon I am putting money into the pockets of the Israelis that they will use to buy guns to kill Arabs." Yasseen's mother said Yasseen became increasingly depressed, torn between his passion for his collection and his fears that his cousins' stories might be true. "Finally I called my brother and I told him, don't let your sons talk to my son any more. They're messing with his mind," Soraya told me.

DR. REEM'S POKÉMON PARTY

In the spring of 2001, the entire fifth-grade class at MLS was invited to the home of their classmate Yussuf for a "Pokémon party." About half attended. For nearly an hour, the children showed their various Pokémon paraphernalia. One girl showed her collection of some 200 Pokémon *tazu*. One boy showed his collection of expensive imported game cartridges— yellow, red, and blue.

When they were finished, Yussuf's mother, Dr. Reem, gathered them in a circle and read aloud two magazine articles. The first described the fatwa against Pokémon issued by the grand mufti of Mecca because it taught children behaviors incompatible with Islam. The second article asserted that Pokémon was part of a Zionist conspiracy. Pokémon, the author claimed, was ultimately owned by Israel. Its colorful characters and fascinating story lines were designed by professional psychologists to seduce Arab youths into buying Pokémon products. But every pound spent on Pokémon was ultimately used to buy guns to kill Palestinians. The children, I am told, listened with growing shock, dismay, and horror. When she had finished reading aloud the articles,[12] Dr. Reem led them outside, where a bonfire had been prepared. Under the urging of Dr. Reem and one or two other parents, the children consigned their Pokémon materials to the flames. After the immolation, food and drinks were brought out, and the children celebrated.

I was not at the party. It was described to me by two parents, one who was present and one who heard about it from another parent. I was subsequently able to briefly interview Dr. Reem, in the company of two of her co-workers, near the free women's clinic she operates in association with a large mosque. Dr. Reem said that her concerns about Pokémon started when she realized how much of her son's pocket money was being spent on chips and Pokémon stickers. Searching his room, she found entire notebooks filled with his drawings of Pokémon characters. She took the notebooks to the clinic, where one of her co-workers showed her a magazine article detailing the dangers of Pokémon. That night, Dr. Reem confronted her son with the magazine and ordered him to destroy his collection. She said her son agreed to stop buying Lay's chips and stickers, but explained that everyone at the school collected Pokémon. Fellow students often asked him to draw Pokémon characters for them. Dr. Reem told me that she knew how difficult it is for a child, or even an adult, to resist something everyone else is doing, especially when most people see it as harmless. One of the purposes of the party was to relieve her son of the burden of social nonconformity by teaching his schoolmates the dangers that Pokémon posed to their moral well-being. The party served as a powerful ritual that enacted both political and moral resistance to globalization, emphasizing that the purchase of foreign goods takes money out of people's hands and injects it into global flows in which its ultimate destinations and uses are not under the control of the consumer.

Dr. Reem is highly respected in the school community as a devout Muslim who wears the *higab* and prays publicly in the mosque on Fridays. In addition to her work at the clinic, she serves as a *da'wah,* or female religious teacher. Other parents at the school claim that she gave up a highly successful medical practice to devote herself to the poor. As an educated, professional woman who chose to give up her income to devote herself to Islamic moral activities, she is a direct contrast to Soraya, an educated, professional woman who chooses to work and bring income into her family. Yet Soraya's choices are also framed as morally acceptable because she emphasizes that her income is spent on bettering her children's futures. Both women stand in contrast to "traditional" middle-class women like Ismail's mother, who stays at home, and the putative "Western" woman of movies and soap operas, who selfishly spends her earnings on herself.

In spite of her religious activities, there is nothing specifically "religious" or "Islamic" about Dr. Reem's anti-Pokémon activities. To Dr. Reem, the moral issues surrounding Pokémon go beyond the psychological or educational effects on children that exercise Mrs. Maryam. Rather, they are fundamentally economic. In Dr. Reem's view, spending money can be a quintessentially moral act that links us to others, including those who would use our money to do evil and those who are harmed by it. Dr. Reem asked me several questions about Pokémon, particularly its ownership, and I answered them as clearly as I could. In many cases, my answers contradicted the information she had gleaned from the articles she had read. But Dr. Reem said the ambiguity of the knowledge only sharpened her argument. She told me that, even if the commodities available in Cairo are not Zionist products but are produced by Nintendo in Japan (as in the case of her son's stickers) or by Nintendo North America (from which Lay's purchased its rights), the fact remained that some of the money that Egyptian children spent would end up as U.S. taxes, and some of this would be given to Israel. To spend money when she knew that it would, or even that it might, end up working evil in the world was not acceptable.

CLASS, EDUCATION, AND COMMODITIES

While middle-class families with aspirations send their children to the language schools, upper-class families usually send their children to the international schools. While there is a range of these, the top tier schools cater primarily to expatriates, allowing Egyptian students to learn their cosmopolitanism directly from Western peers. There are more than 10,000 expatriates in Egypt and nearly all multinational corporations and embassies pay to send their employees' children to one of the major international schools. The schools thus become centers of expatriate community activity. The American School in Cairo (ASC), in the southern suburb of Ma'adi, is currently the largest, most prestigious, and most expensive of these institutions, with fees of between $10,000 and $12,000 per year. In 2000, the student body was composed of 725 Americans, 284 other foreigners,[13] and 184 Egyptians.[14] The school is accredited by an American accreditation system, uses American curricula, conducts all courses and extracurricular activities entirely in English, and is operated by U.S.-certified teaching staff and administrators, some of whom are Egyptian nationals.

For Americans, the primary purpose of the school is to provide an American education such that their children's acquisition of educational capital is not impaired by their parents' relocation to Egypt. For Egyptians, a primary purpose of the school is to provide students with a "quality" education far removed from the Egyptian system. These purposes combine to create a system in which middle-class Americans set social standards for Egyptians of the highest elite class, including owners of major American and European franchises and Egyptian partners in multinational corporations. At ASC, cultural and economic capital meet in a social hierarchy organized by access to commodities. One of the most crucial social questions among expatriates in Ma'adi is whether or not a student is "commissary"— that is, comes from a family with access to the military base's commissary with its American goods at American prices. Commissary privileges extend to all U.S. embassy families, military families, and some USAID staff. The importance ascribed to having access to American goods among the children at ASC is very high; particular brands that are readily available in Cairo from local factories of multinational companies, like Nestle's, Coca-Cola, and Frito-Lay, are discounted in favor of American versions of the same products. The meaning of commissary goods at ASC is tied to their mode of distribution. Because they are available only at the U.S. "territory" of a military base, and they are mostly transported by the military, they are not "imported" in the usual sense, and they powerfully index their American origins. A secondary option indulged in by many petroleum families is to pool money to pay for a "shipment"—a container of American products shipped from the United States which might include not only brands unavailable in Egypt, but American versions of brands sold at every kiosk in Cairo. Egyptians, as well as Americans whose incomes do not permit indulgence in containers, must bring back what they can in sporadic trips overseas, or rely on the occasional and heavily overpriced (and often stale) imports that find their way into the local stores.

The three tiers—"real" American, imported, and local—are linguistically marked. Egyptian local versions of multinational brands like Coca-Cola are labeled in both English and Arabic script. Imported goods are marked by a small white import sticker printed in Arabic characters. Arabic in this system indexes a lack of authenticity. English script indicates American goods, which in turn index and emphasize a consumer's Americanness. This is a class system but not one based solely on income. Jim, an oil executive, reported to me with amusement that his eight-year-old son had complained that his father was "just" in oil, instead of being a Marine sergeant like his best friend's father, who had commissary privileges. In this system, the children of military families, despite their relatively low salaries, are put on an equal status with their more highly paid embassy cohorts and in a superior position to higher-salaried oil workers, academics, USAID project staff, and wealthy Egyptians.

Commissary families tend to be generous with their American goods. Kids bring snacks to their friends and may even pass money from friends to their parents with requests that they pick up some of a particular product. A student-written school play intended to dramatize everyday life included a scene of an Egyptian friend visiting an American friend after school to do homework, saying, "I'm sure glad you're commissary," as he munched on Cheez Doodles. As in any community, patterns of exchange express social relations. Those who give construct and reproduce their own position in the social field through their presentations.

This system is familiar to us as Bourdieu's "symbolic violence," in which one group in a social field establishes certain symbols and tastes, of which they have a monopoly, as constituting more valuable capital than that possessed by others (Bourdieu and Passeron 1977; Bourdieu 1990). Within the school system, the symbolic value of commissary goods and imports greatly disadvantages Egyptian students, since their access to these commodities is usually quite limited. Bourdieu's notion of symbolic violence is meant to emphasize the extent to which the students are complicit in their own delegitimation. He argues that a system like this is not imposed from above but rather is maintained dynamically as people experience the institutions and structures that comprise it and come to internalize the system as part of their taken-for-granted understandings of school.[15] At the same time, in submitting to this subaltern status, wealthy

Egyptian students receive benefits: they accumulate the kinds of cultural capital that will let them move freely among other cosmopolitans in Egypt and around the world, particularly an attention to, and a taste for, particular brands and trademarks.

Pokémon is beautifully adapted to this system. As a trademarked term for a panoply of symbols disseminated internationally in a variety of media, toys, games, apparel, websites, and more, Pokémon perfectly fits definitions of globalization: it involves the simultaneous circulation of people, capital, images, media, ideas, and technologies along routes ordered by a capitalist world system. Pokémon's success at traversing and colonizing the scapes of the global derives from its essential fluidity, its ability to infiltrate local imaginaries and be transformed to fit local socialities. Whether as a Nintendo game in which players accumulate Pokémon; as an animated series about a child accumulating Pokémon; or as cards, disks, plastic figures, and other objects that can be collected, Pokémon is about the acquisition of desirable commodities. Pokémon entered ASC in the form of commodities carried in by foreign students as they arrived in Cairo, whether newly arrived or returning from the summer vacations that allow them to stay abreast of what's cool and what's not back home. Students brought Pokémon cards from Europe in various languages, but these were quickly discounted in favor of English versions (my daughters once received a whole packet of Italian Pokémon cards in trade for a single, not-very-rare English card).

It is common wisdom that globalization occurs through a form of trickle down. Global commodities arrive through the cosmopolitan upper class, then trickle down to the middle classes. In fact, cosmopolitan Egyptians in the international schools constitute themselves as the lower class emulating the upper class. Meanwhile, middle-class Egyptians like Yasseen encounter Pokémon through local manifestations mediated by locally owned and run franchises of multinational conglomerates, entrepreneurs, and the government's Ministry of Information. But there is evidence for a trickle-up theory. While the primary target of Pokémon, kids aged nine through twelve, rejected the *tazu,* their younger brothers and sisters in kindergarten did not. Too young to be able to recognize the difference between Arabic and English, but able to recognize the visual icons, five- and six-year-old kids at ASC began collecting the plastic disks.

This temporarily stood the commodity class system on its head. Suddenly, it was those children who lived closer to the Egyptian economy and bought their chips for twelve cents at the kiosk or at local shops who had access to desirable commodities, while the children whose parents bought "real" Lay's chips at the commissary for fifty cents found their chip bags empty. For about six months, Egyptian chips were valuable and American chips denigrated in ASC's three kindergarten classrooms.

ALINE'S IDENTITY

One of the ASC students I knew best was ten-year-old Aline, who lived just around the corner from my family. Aline was quick to recognize the importance of Pokémon to establishing her cosmopolitan identity, and that a crucial component of this involved differentiating herself from "Egyptians." For Aline, the daughter of an Egyptian businessman and a French mother, her Egyptian identity has always been troublesome. "Egyptians," for many ASC students and their parents, are servants, taxi drivers, shop tenders, and street cleaners, people who speak poor English and often seem to be out to cheat you. Many Egyptian students at ASC spend a good deal of time attempting to manage this identity, emphasizing alternative citizenships, Western modes of dress, and American or European ways of speaking.

For Aline, this meant emphasizing her Frenchness. Aline managed her identity in a number of ways, including ritual displays, language practices, and taste in commodities. Scholarly work in the ethnography of education has emphasized the ways in which the architecture of schools and school rooms, the design and alignment of desks and other furniture, and the technology of teaching are designed for surveillance and constitute what Foucault termed "pedagogical machines" (1979: 176). Bodily disciplines extend beyond class regimentation to team sports, marching bands, school plays, and other performances and ceremonies that train the body in "the microgymnastics of power" (Margolis 2007: 11). The material bodies of teachers, administrators, aides, staff, and security guards also serve as visual models whose dress, comportment, and speech can be emulated in acts of identity or rejected in acts of differentiation. Foucault's machine metaphor is unfortunate in this regard because it tends to occlude the agency that the "products" of the apparatus have in their own production. The school provides the structure, but it is Aline who appropriates and uses this structure in pursuit of her own (albeit institutionally shaped) goals.

One of the major "rituals of identity" (Nash 1989: 83) at ASC is "international day," a celebration of the multiethnic, multinational character of the school which is open to families and their guests. The day begins with a parade around the track ring, in which students dress in "national costume"—Aline's was supplied by her French maternal grandmother—following the flags of "their" countries. Booths selling crafts or foods associated with different countries are open for the rest of the day. The tendency of schools to categorize international identities in monocultural or binary ways has been described and critiqued for constructing "closed and limited subject positions for students based on difference and sameness" (Koehne 2005: 104). Less frequently addressed are the opportunities such categorizations offer to students like Aline, who recognize that articulating public selves in terms of multiple subject positions may lower their status. The physical ritual limits identity possibilities. One may have dual citizenships and multiple ethnic identities but physically one cannot simultaneously march with the French and the Egyptian group. Because international day constructs identities in terms of mutually exclusive, bounded groups labeled by nation, it gives Aline an opportunity to simultaneously enact and display her French character and erase her Egyptianness.

Arabic is another signifier that can be strategically deployed to downplay Egyptian or Arab identity. The language politics of Arabic, with its multiglossic character, has been the subject of considerable attention over the years (Ferguson 1971[1959]; Badawi 1992; Armbrust 1996a; Haeri 2003). Arabic has a complex set of dialects and registers such that how one speaks a particular variety of Arabic in a particular context positions one in a variety of social fields. Less attention has been given to the politics of English and French use in Egypt.[16] Language choice can be a significant element in establishing social identity. Aline's family primarily spoke French and Arabic in the home, switching to English if there were guests more comfortable in that language. The family employed six servants, all but one of whom—a Filipina—were Arabic monolinguals. At ASC, however, Aline not only spoke English like most of the rest of the students but pretended that she did not speak Arabic and that she understood only a very little.

Aline, of course, was not commissary. Access to the commodities valued at ASC came through her father who, having gone through the same process with three older children, was alive to the nuances of his daughter's social needs and ensured that each business trip included a bag of snack foods, candies, and popular toys not readily available in Cairo. Aline first became aware of Pokémon through seeing other children collecting, trading, and exchanging the cards. Fearing to betray ignorance or naïveté, Aline did not ask questions: "I listened to what everybody was saying until I knew what to ask my father for." Her father bought her dozens of packets of American game cards on his travels, as well as a binder to keep them in. They were carefully placed in plastic sheets and frequently brought to school and displayed. Aline's possession of the cards was not initially matched by a knowledge of the Pokémon mythos and the values of the cards. She once admitted to me that she did not understand the card game at all or the values of the cards. She was frequently taken advantage of in play and exchanges until two American girls started helping her by explaining what the numbers meant in play and which cards were worth trading.

Aline was not the only one being cheated in exchanges or games. Complaints from parents and teachers that Pokémon was getting "out of hand" led to a rule against Pokémon trading on campus. An administrator told me, "We e-mailed to several schools in the U.S. and asked them what they were doing about Pokémon; then we took similar steps."

By this time, however, Aline had obtained a panoply of Pokémon merchandise which she could continue to display: notebooks, stickers, shirts, a backpack. In addition, her father had purchased for her a Nintendo Game Boy and one of the original Pokémon game cartridges. For the first time, Aline began to speak to me about Pokémon with pleasure, rather than in terms of strategies for fitting in. She enjoyed the game in a way she had never enjoyed the cards. Videos followed, and she eventually collected "all" the videos, mostly in English although a few in French. When the battery case on her original Game Boy cracked, her parents purchased a second one, and she gave the first to an American girl whose parents had refused to buy her one, considering the game a waste of time. The two girls began to play the game together, and Aline had her father buy a cable that could connect the two Game Boys.

The growth of Aline's personal pleasure in Pokémon, however, coincided with the decline of Pokémon display at ASC. Pokémon backpacks, notebooks, clothing, and other paraphernalia increasingly came to be seen as babyish and out of fashion. Fifth- and sixth-grade girls began to eschew Pokémon at the beginning of the fall 2000 semester (even as Pokémon was just beginning to significantly enter into the consciousness of students at MLS), and by the end of December boys, too, had stopped displaying their Pokémon artifacts. Twelve-year-old Stephen told me in December 2000 that "there's a couple [of] boys in my class I think still play Pokémon but they don't talk about it at school." He told me that many fifth-graders still played Pokémon, but "they don't play it as much as they did last year. It was like a huge fad and everybody was into it and now it's, like, over."

Egyptian identity, says Walter Armbrust, "rests on an ideology of transformation from 'traditionalism' to 'modernity'" (Armbrust 1996a: 25). Class identity, as we have seen, rests on an ideology of differentiation according to which the upper classes distinguish themselves from the middle and lower classes by emphasizing their connectivity with larger global structures through consumption. But class identity is not the whole of Egyptian identity, and global neoliberal capitalism is not the whole of connectivity. The middle and lower classes not only forge connections with wider global communities through consumption but also draw on mediated connections with regional communities like the Gulf states. Consuming Pokémon by itself does not make anyone "global" or "cosmopolitan." But Pokémon can play a part in helping people position themselves and others within such categories. Whether and how one consumed Pokémon, what metacultural discourses authenticated their decisions, and to which audiences families displayed their consumption, however, *was* an important part of Egyptian identity for children and their families at the turn of the millennium.

4

TALK LIKE AN EGYPTIAN: NEGOTIATING IDENTITY AT THE AMERICAN UNIVERSITY IN CAIRO

In 1998, producer Muhammad 'Adl released what became one of the most commercially successful films in the history of Egyptian cinema: *Sa'idi fil Gama'a al-Amrikiyya* (*A Southern Egyptian at the American University*). The title alone was enough to bring chuckles to many Egyptians, linking a person from a place representing the depths of Egyptian backwardness to a place that represents the pinnacle of its Westernized modernity. Sa'idis—inhabitants of the rural south—are subjects of jokes throughout the rest of the country. They are usually portrayed as honest but dumb, good-natured but naïve to the point of stupidity, and chivalrous but quick to avenge a slight (the *tar*, or "blood feud," is one of the most ubiquitous stereotypes in popular representations of Sa'idis). Poor, backward, speaking heavily accented Arabic, grubbing in the dirt for a living, lacking basic technologies—such stereotypes of Sa'idis are often used in jokes, novels, movies, and television melodramas as examples of all the things modernity is supposed to be an escape from. By contrast, the American University in Cairo (AUC) represents to many Egyptians all the best and worst aspects of modernity. It is the pinnacle of academic excellence but also of elitism. It represents wealth and social mobility but also Westernization and loss of authenticity. As Egypt's major private university, it is an embodiment of Egypt's aspirations for a place in a global market economy—yet it is hopelessly out of reach of more than 90 percent of the population. The movie's success stemmed from its capacity to juxtapose these stereotypes for laughs.

Muhammad Heneidi plays Khalaf, the academically brilliant but naïve son of a provincial farmer from the governorate of Sohag. Passing the *thanawiyya 'amma* with the highest score, he receives a scholarship to the American University, where he chooses to major in political science. His initial appearances at the university are a classic Sa'idi joke: he trades in his *galabiyya* for a suit, but it is a suit of red-orange, a bumpkin's notion of fashion. Most of the first half of the film is a series of such jokes as Khalaf, who doesn't dance, flirt with women, drink alcohol, or speak English outside of class, encounters one culture shock after another. Eventually, some AUC students take pity on him and introduce him to the delights of cosmopolitan consumption. Beginning with a shopping spree to the sprightly music of *Kazhwaluh* (*Dress Him Casually*), which became a big pop hit, he learns to wear imported jeans and polo shirts, talk (and flirt) casually with women, and enjoy the commodified pleasures of the upper class. Khalaf's full acceptance by his fellow students, however, comes not from his adoption of their commodified lifestyle but happens when he stumbles across a student protest marking the fiftieth anniversary of the creation of the state of Israel. The AUC administration is shown seeking to stop the protest, calling in the police. When one of the student organizers is arrested, he throws the Israeli flag to Khalaf, who sets it ablaze, then dances around it in a movie version of a rural folk dance. The incident reawakens Khalaf to the fact that his family sent him to AUC to become someone who could make the world a better place. He buckles down seriously to his studies and graduates at the top of his class.[1] He gives the graduation speech, saying, "When I first came here, I was overwhelmed by America. But after three years, I would like to say that even though we graduate from an American University, it does not make us Americans."

The film became controversial in a number of ways. Internationally, it got play in some American news stories as a supposed example of anti-Semitic trends in Middle Eastern media because of the flag burning.[2] Locally, it got play because of a lawsuit filed against its producer for using AUC's name and logo without permission. Although the university cited trademark regulations, popular rumor insisted that the lawsuit was filed because of the flag-burning scene. These rumors persisted even after the producers apologized and the university withdrew the suit and invited star Muhammad Heneidi to visit the campus.

The flag-burning scene, however, cannot be understood without linking it to the scene where the AUC students assist Khalaf to dress like them. These are the two scenes most Egyptians evoke when talking about the film. Khalaf is portrayed as wanting to be like the AUC students; his parents did not send him to AUC to stay provincial, after all. At the same time, the film underscores his struggle to grasp the pleasures of consumerism without compromising the Egyptian values that make him who he is. The flag-burning incident serves to solve his identity issues in part by establishing a common ground between him and the other students. Even the police called in to stop the protest sympathize with the protesters: all share a common Arab identity, a "community of sentiment" (Appadurai 1996: 41) expressed by their strong support for the Palestinian people. But the scene does far more work than this. The scene indexes actual protests against Israel and the burning of its flag on AUC's campus in 1996, after the Israeli shelling at Qana.[3] Yet there is a significant difference. In the real event, AUC supported and defended the student protests as protected free speech. In the reel event, the "American" university is portrayed as forbidding the event, even calling in police to stop it. The difference is crucial. For most Egyptians, any protest against Israel is a protest against the United States, and AUC here stands indexically for the United States. The movie AUC's decision to stop the protests represents one of the many hypocrisies that most Egyptians say bother them about the United States, in this case, preaching democracy but seeking to censor political speech when it is aimed at itself or its allies. The climax of the film occurs as the limits of the promises of Westernization are revealed: one cannot be simultaneously Western (Americanized) and Arab in *this* context. Faced with such a choice, Khalaf chooses to join the community of protest and, in doing so, establishes the limits of his Westernization, confirming the moral bedrock under his increasingly cosmopolitan veneer.

Khalaf's struggle is everybody's struggle. In my first year in Egypt, I must have discussed this film with dozens of people: students, colleagues, shopkeepers, tourist touts, taxi drivers, strangers riding the metro with me. Telling people who took me for a tourist that I was a professor at the American University who had come to live in Egypt served as a natural segue into discussion of the film. I never met anyone who had failed to find the film funny (although more than a few protested its "vulgarity"), and I never found anyone who did not sympathize with Khalaf.[4] No one is as naïve as Khalaf, which is why everyone can laugh at him. Even the lowliest laborer has seen enough TV to know better than to wear an red-orange suit. But Khalaf's ambition, his desire to seize his opportunities and to better his life through education—these are easily understandable, as are his struggles to figure out what he can take from globalization and what he must reject.

Sa'idi fil Gama'a al-Amrikiyya was a star vehicle for Muhammad Heneidi, a comedian who has built a career making films about ambitious but naïve characters who discover that their solid traditional values don't work as expected in the careers to which they aspire, or the places to which they travel, and who must find successful compromises. These films, such as *Hamam fil Amsterdam* (*Hamam in Amsterdam*) and *Ga'ana al-Bayan at-Tali* (*We Have Just Received the Following Report*), often have similar resolutions, as the hero finds a seminal event in which the hypocrisies of globalization force him into a clear choice that defines the limits of his cosmopolitan identity and establishes him as authentically Egyptian underneath his Western facade. The difference between Khalaf and his audiences is that *his* story has a structure and a defining moment. For most of those who attend the real American University in Cairo, the articulation of identities is an ongoing and never entirely resolved process. As students make the transition from their private schools to Egypt's most elite academic institution, they struggle to find the core of their Egyptianness and the limits of their cosmopolitanism.

INDEXING IDENTITIES

To articulate an identity is to use indexical signs to map oneself to a community. Although these often occur in narrative accounts, as people offer stories of experiences that they believe shaped their identities, real lives lack the clarity of reel lives like those of Khalaf. Embracing modernity and globalization by finding the limits of Westernization is an ongoing process in which identities are daily articulated through narrative, dress, consumption, social intercourse, and all the other practices of everyday life. The symbols and values provided by the media and consumer culture are part of the semiotic reservoir people draw on as they engage in this process, but they are never complete.

As we've seen, the construction of identity is already a problem for children like Aline, Ismail, and Yasseen, even at age ten. At first glance, their struggle seems to be a straightforward matter of managing conformity to the classroom and peer cultures. But as we have seen, identities shift with changing circumstances, and individuals are never in complete control of their identities. As children mature, managing such identities as "French," "American," and "Egyptian" becomes increasingly problematic, as they become more and more affected by overlapping identity categories like "male," "female," "modern," and "authentic." As they moved into junior high and high school and began to prepare for college, both new ASC students like Yasseen and longtime students like Aline became increasingly concerned with their Egyptianness.

In part, this is due to changing demographics. Many upper-middle-class families like Yasseen's cannot afford twelve years of tuition at ASC, but are willing to pay for four years of high school there after eight years at a less expensive private school like MLS.[5] At the same time, many expatriate businesspeople stationed in Cairo while their children are younger find themselves promoted to more prestigious positions in Europe, Asia, or North America as their children are reaching adolescence. These factors alter the ratio of foreign and Egyptian students in the higher grades, giving the latter a greater voice in what constitutes social and cultural capital in the school. In most high school classes, Egyptians make up about half the students, while Americans have become the largest minority among Canadians, South Koreans, Swedish, Indians, Israelis, and others. The new Egyptian students like Yasseen often come from private English middle schools with more nationalistic, and sometimes more Islamic, curricula. In addition, many of the children I spoke with said that, as they reached adolescence, their parents spent more time talking to them about identity-related issues: who they were, what they wanted to be, and what kinds of behaviors were or were not acceptable. As a result of these factors, Egyptianness increasingly ceases to be something to be ignored or erased and becomes rather something to be explored and articulated in more complex ways.[6]

Anthropological accounts since Mauss (1985[1935]) have demonstrated that Western notions of person, with their clear distinctions between private selves and social persons, are not universals (M. Rosaldo 1984; R. Rosaldo 1980). Anthropologists have described "collective, relational" concepts of persons among many of their host communities (Battaglia 1995: 7) and have argued that "inner" selves are often "inchoate" (Fernandez 1986: 8) until enacted through social performance. Even in societies that conceive of persons as distinct units, identities can be shown to be both co-constructed (Goodwin 1990; Goodwin and Goodwin 1992; Ochs 1992, 1993; Ochs and Capps 2001) and continually emergent in performance (Moerman 1993; Livia and Hall 1997; Sidnell 2003). *Who am I?* (and, perhaps more correctly, *who am I to you?*) is a question always in flux, never fixed, yet necessarily reified from moment to moment in social actions.

Perhaps the most crucial point is that, while identities are shaped by social processes, identities "do not precede the semiotic practices that call them into being in specific interactions" (Bucholtz and Hall 2005: 588). Identity production does not simply map selves to fixed categories; the categories of personhood to which students lay claim (including "global" and "local") are themselves always in flux and capable of being rearticulated.

In the following discussion, I will draw heavily on the work of Mary Bucholtz and Kira Hall (2005), who summarize current theorizing on the social production of identities in five key points. First, identity is *emergent* in speech and social action. Second, identities emerge in concrete moments of interaction in which people *position* themselves with regard to one another. Third, the key semiotic process in identity formation is *indexicality,* the active creation of links between persons (selves and others) and social meanings. Fourth, people always construct selves in *relation* to others whom they imagine as like and unlike themselves according to some criteria. Finally, because they are co-constructed in interactions with others, identities are always *partial* and incomplete; they are never constructed once and for all.

Students like Aline, Yasseen, and their families invest heavily in acquiring the social capital to become members of the global cosmopolitan class. They construct these identities indexically, by linking themselves to particular categories of person: Western, French, European, Egyptian, Arab. This is accomplished through discrete indexes—languages, accents, fashions, tastes—that indicate the places from which these categories of person are derived, and yet they are available not only in those distant locales but, through the space-condensing power of globalization, in Cairo in commodified forms for those who can afford them. But these identities are always emergent, never completed. Every act is a performance and its outcome is determined relationally, by the positions they have in the social field comprised by themselves and their audiences. Aline may perform Frenchness, but her identity is co-constructed by those for whom she performs. This process takes place through a metadeictic discourse, a discourse that articulates the modality of the indexing signs Aline produces. This is a discourse of *authenticity,* an effort to establish who someone "really is." Authenticity in this use is an ideological structure used to pass judgment on the indexical claims produced by social actors performing particular identities. Part of the process of becoming cosmopolitan is learning to manage metadeictic discourses.

NEGOTIATING AUTHENTICITY

How far one can go in adopting cosmopolitan styles and still claim to be Egyptian or Arab is thus a matter of considerable debate and discussion. Irony is ubiquitous as students strive for the essential core of an identity category, only to realize that the particular persons they wish to apply it to, including perhaps themselves, don't quite fit their characterization. Thus, many young women at ASC and AUC will joke about having *u'dit il-khawaga* (foreigner complex) because they lighten their hair, wear makeup, follow international fashion trends, and try to get their parents to buy them tinted contacts. The claim is usually made with a laugh, assertive and defensive at the same time, indicating their underlying discomfort with these choices, a fear of being criticized, and resentment that it is not always possible to adopt styles of foreign origin without being cast by others as someone who is losing her "true" character as Egyptian. Students often explain that they adopt Western styles and attitudes because of a failure of Egyptian culture to provide a coherent "system" of belief and action that can help them make sense of their everyday experiences. Growing up with the uncertainties of the dismantling of the Nasserist economic structure and the growing availability of new goods and new lifeways, students complain that it is no longer clear what it means to be Egyptian. They struggle to discursively establish the limits of their cosmopolitanness so that they can claim their essential Egyptian character.[7]

These issues were well illustrated in a conversation I had with a small group of tenth- and eleventh-graders at ASC. My entrée into the group was Eiman. I had met her through her brother, a fifth-grade Pokémon and Game Boy expert. Unlike her younger brother, who had started at ASC when he was in the first grade, Eiman had attended a less expensive private school until high school. We had spoken briefly about *u'dit il-khawaga* when she picked up her brother at my flat after a gathering of younger students talking about Pokémon. When I ran into her at ASC, I asked if she'd be willing to talk further. She introduced me to her friends as someone writing a book about Pokémon. When I explained that I was actually writing about globalization and how it affected people's lives in Cairo, the students began to speak rapidly and vociferously.

"The kids at this school are a bunch of American wannabes," complained Mona, Eiman's friend. Also a tenth-grader, she was relatively new to ASC, having lived three years in the United States and four in Canada. "They show off with their English and pretend it's the only thing they know. Not all of them but a lot are like that. What I really hate is that they try to act like Americans but they say they hate Americans and that Egyptians are better because they have *adab* [manners] and *akhla'* [good character]." On the indexical plane, the articulation of identity often turns around token distinctions. Categories of person are discursively constructed, often by contrasting two *types* of persons in opposition to one another, such as wannabes and their implicit opposite, real Americans or Europeans. These types are then mapped to specific *tokens,* actual persons whose behavior can be described as exemplars of the type. However, as Chock (1987) notes, exploring how particular real-life examples fit the categories often forces speakers to reconsider and rearticulate their categorical types. Thus, most students who complain about Egypt or who comment ironically on their own Westernization point at others who, they say, have gone *too* far, whose adoption of foreign mannerisms and display of goods smack of artifice. These students, they say, are *mitfarnagin* (trying to act foreign). Critical terms like *mitfarnagin* and *u'dit il-khawaga* have their own opposite: persons who have struck the right balance between authentic Egyptianness and Westernized modernity.

Mona's complaint draws our attention to something that emerged in most of my interviews and conversations with Egyptian ASC students: the attribution of whether or not a particular student is *mitfarnagin* depends on whether they feel his or her behavior indexes *interior* elements of Egyptian character. The students almost inevitably express such categories of essential Egyptianness in Arabic. These include *akhla'* and *adab* for all persons and, for young men, *shaham* (gallantry), and for young women, *mu'adab* (decency). Fifteen-year-old Hassan, who earlier in the conversation had emphasized that his ASC education made it easier for him to get along with people of many different backgrounds, disagreed with Mona. *Some* students were hypocritical, he acknowledged, but others, like himself, just "don't believe in their [Americans' or Westerners'] way of doing some things. I think the Egyptian man is *shaham* [gallant]. Like, if he sees a fight in the street, he won't think twice but will jump in to stop it but American men don't do this."

These categories are important because they are invoked to establish who, under their Western veneer, is truly Egyptian. *Adab* is often translated as "manners," "comportment," or "etiquette," but it means far more than those words. *Adab* also means culture, in the sense of a high culture opposed to the vulgar and uncultured.[8] These two meanings are both invoked by the students' use: *adab* consists of disciplining the body to a cultural code of proper behavior. It calls for the moderation of emotion "in accord with an authoritative model of the virtues" (Hirschkind 2006a: 47).[9] Similarly, the idiomatic *akhla'* has multiple meanings. The classical Arabic word it is derived from, *akhlaq*, is usually translated as "moral virtues" or "ethics." *Akhlaq* stands for the "traits of man's moral character" (Siddiqi 1960: 58) or the "system of norms" (Alam and Subrahmanyam 2004) and the ethics the person is practicing. Yet, as the plural for the word *khulq* (disposition), *akhlaq* also implies moral habits that emerge through the repeated practice of these moral virtues, which thus have an enduring character.

Egyptian consultants with whom I shared the students' interviews warned me that, as a non-native speaker of Arabic, I was missing the fact that *akhla'* and *adab* were being used in this conversation to jointly infer a set of relational values toward family and the opposite sex. Among teens, values associated with *adab* and *akhla'* include a respectful demeanor toward one's elders, recognition of parental authority, chastity, and avoidance of behaviors that would embarrass one's family, such as smoking, dating, or staying out too late. "*Al walad da akhla'a* [a child with morals] is a line used to describe youths who make decisions with their family," wrote Dalia, an AUC sociology graduate student and mother of two. "Most Egyptian adolescents are raised in a protective family where absolute autonomy is not seen as a positive." Mustafa, a teacher at a private school, pointed out that, while many of the ASC students may violate these norms in their actual behaviors, they have nonetheless internalized them: "They are still shocked if someone calls the teacher by his first name. If they engage in premarital sex, there is still a sense of shame, they think of it as adultery. A pregnancy out of marriage is still a disaster." Mustafa, like many other Egyptians, believes that American and European students view premarital sex, teen pregnancy, and disrespect for adults as "normal," without shame, and it is their possession of this contrary internal moral sense, rather than their actual behavior, that distinguishes Westernized Egyptian youths from their authentic Western peers.

Shaham, an "Arabic term that has no exact equivalent in English, [means] gallantry mixed with nobility, audacity, responsibility, generosity, vigor and manliness" (El-Messiri 1978: 49). According to Wassef (1999), *shaham* or *shahama* refers to "fairness and gallantry" but is also linked to a man's sureness of his own sexual prowess. It refers to a self-possession bordering on audacity, which reveals a noble character. Idiomatically, *shaham* refers to a man who "will insist on walking you home or to your car at night," said Eiman, when I asked the students to explain the term. "And he walks in front of you, not because he thinks he's better but to help you from the crowd." Like *adab* and *akhla', shaham* is not only an individual characteristic but is linked to social order. An editorial about the decline of civility in Cairo written a few years after my conversations at ASC claimed:

> [S]ociability and *shahama* (valor or decency), a source of Egyptian pride, once guaranteed the city's safety. If someone was shortchanged, had their pocket picked, was involved in a car accident or otherwise slighted or injured, a crowd would form and the victim consoled or bundled off to hospital. The perpetrator would be caught and chastised, and scented tissues or cigarettes distributed all around. Not anymore. (Golia 2004: 7)

Yet the line between protection and control is a fine one; a boy may also exhibit his *shaham* in the ways he polices gender relations. Mona complained that her boyfriend used his *shaham* as an excuse when he didn't approve of some of her American habits and wanted to change her behaviors:

Everybody here is obsessed with having a boyfriend or girl-friend.[10] Your parents tell you it's not allowed, like *mu'adab* [decent] girls don't do this. But you have to have one or people think you aren't cool. Only, like, there's all these rules. Like, an Egyptian girl isn't supposed to have an American boyfriend but it's okay if [an Egyptian boy] has an American girlfriend. And one time I was sitting on the floor in the theater doing stretches and my [Egyptian] boyfriend came up and told me I was losing respect and I had to sit on a chair.

Mu'adab—literally "one who has *adab*"—is used almost exclusively by these teens to refer to the characteristics of modesty and good behavior that girls need to display to show that they come from decent families.

The traits of *akhla'* and *adab, shaham* and *mu'adab,* combined with the advantages of wealth and privilege, constitute the characteristics of *wilad an-nas,* "children of the people." Deriving historically from a term used to describe the high-status children of the Mamluk aristocracy, *wilad an-nas* continues to refer to a child of privilege, someone from "an elevated social background" (Barsoum 2004). *Wilad an-nas* is usually contrasted with *wilad al-baladi* (son of the country), a complex symbol meaning someone whose character is rooted in a particular place. The rural *ibn al-balad* is represented by the Sa'idi, or *fallah,* while the stereotypical urban *ibn al-balad* is someone who lives in a traditional neighborhood (*hara*), wears a *galabiyya,* and works at a trade. Such an *ibn al-balad* may represent "the salt of the earth" or a "diamond in the rough" (Armbrust 1996a: 25) but may also indicate someone crude, ill mannered, and ignorant.[11] Armbrust (1996a) and Shechter (2006) point out that *ibn al-balad* can also be contrasted with *ibn az-zawat* (son of the aristocracy), a term implying wealth but also frivolity, greed, sloth, and effeminacy (in men) or immodesty (in women), and with *bitu' l-infitah* (those of the open door), referring to the new rich who made their wealth in the post-Nasserist economic liberaliza-tion. Often shortened to *infitahi,* these new rich are the "inauthentic imita-tion foreigners" (Armbrust 1996a: 27) who have the economic privilege but lack the manners and dispositions that should accompany it.[12]

Wilad an-nas, I would argue, has to some extent come to be used for those who are seen as having attained an appropriate balance—the best of what is Western with the best of what is local and authentic. Students use terms like *akhla'* and *adab, shaham* and *mu'adab* to describe those characteristics of Egyptianness displayed by someone who has properly integrated the best of both worlds. Terms like *ibn al-balad, ibn az-zawat,* nouveaux riches,[13] *infitahi,* and *mitfarnagin* are used pejoratively to refer to those who have failed to find balance. But these are shifting targets; behaviors that indicate a person who has found a proper balance for one audience may well indicate someone who is an American wannabe or nouveau riche to other audiences. One of the functions of private schools like MLS and ASC is to construct students who can credibly claim to be *wilad an-nas.* These private foreign-language schools, although different in their costs and capacities, are designed to operate as systems for inculcating in Egyptian students the attributes of *wilad an-nas.*

What we see here is a process through which identities are doubly articulated. Students construct identities by mapping themselves and others into such categories as *u'dit il-khawaga,* wannabe, and *mitfarnagin.* But these are not coherent, bounded categories. They must themselves be articulated by describing some of the characteristics whose inferred presence or absence defines them: *akhla', adab, shaham, mu'adab.* In actual discursive performances, pronouns, categories of person, and characteristics of selves are all indexical signs whose reference "shifts" according to the context of the performance. Thus, Mona can claim that she and her cohort ("we") are all *mitfarnagin* and wannabes because of their common pursuit of Western, commodified educations, goods, and lifestyles. Hassan rejects this identity by claiming that it is not material goods (*al-mada*) that define their identities but rather moral character. He removes himself from Mona's "we" to establish an "I" that he immediately maps to another "we" labeled "the Egyptian man." He then identifies the essential characteristic of this category as possession of *shaham.* Mona's response is to redefine *shaham* as an index of an inauthentic identity by claiming that (some) men use it hypocritically to establish a double standard in which they can enjoy Western-style dating even while refusing Egyptian girls the status of *mu'adab* if they do the same.

Authenticity is thus not a given but is negotiated as people judge their own and others' internal characters according to their external actions. Yet while this tension over authenticity is linked to distinctions between inner selves and outer behaviors, people also recognize that identities, whether inner or outer, are not entirely under one's personal control. A young woman may claim *u'dit il-khawaga* because it suggests an internal state, an inferiority complex in the face of foreign goods and manners. It is a condition one suffers from, whereas to be *ibn az-zawat, infitahi,* or *mitfarnagin* is to be a phony, to claim a status and identity that does not match what is inside. The distinction turns on the authenticity of one's experience. One of the most interesting questions in identity co-construction is thus where people place the agency for social action. One of the things that emerged from my conversations and interviews is the tendency to redistribute agency from the self as an acting individual to a general social "other" who constrains the narrator's actions. These others may be individuals (like Mona's boyfriend) or a general sense of the public scrutiny. Students construct themselves in part as persons who "are not unified, autonomous individuals exercising free will, but rather subjects whose agency is created through situations and statuses conferred on them" (Scott 1992: 34).

But to where is this agency displaced? In language reminiscent of some of the moral panics over Pokémon, Eiman and her friends speak of Egypt as a collapsing cultural system faced with the strong Western society. "I think that American society has been able to overcome Egyptian society because Egyptians *makabarin dimaghum* [just don't care]." Another girl in the group, Bilqis, referred to Egyptian society as "*mutakhalafin* [retarded]." Hassan said, "We live in a shitty society [*mugtama' zibala*] where everyone is concerned with themselves." His friend Ashraf added, "I think the reason we want to be like America is because we live *fi mugtama' hamagy* [in a chaotic society]." Asked for an example, several of the students described their experiences going as a group to the Sting concert in April 2001 at the Sound and Light Theater outside the pyramids. Egyptian pop star Hakim, who was scheduled to open for Sting, was more than a half-hour late, and when he didn't show, his instruments were removed and Sting's band took the stage.[14] Furious, Hakim strode on to the stage and made an impromptu speech about Egyptians being insulted in their own country. He urged the audience to leave, and Eiman said with a laugh, "Like I paid 120 pounds to hear Hakim." The students expressed their admiration for Sting's professionalism against Hakim's unprofessional behavior. "[Sting is] world famous but he was on time, very respectful of the audience," said Ashraf. "These guys [Arab musicians] are always late. They have no respect."[15] But their criticisms about Hakim's behavior were nothing compared to their contempt for how the concert was organized. Crowds were packed into areas far too small for their numbers, there were no instructions for parking, the buses that were supposed to take concertgoers from the parking lots to the concert area were too few and unmarked, and security forces turned away some ticket holders for no apparent reason. "Total chaos," said Hassan. "[There was] no order, no system."[16]

Phyllis Chock (1987) has argued that when people attempt to articulate identities with any complexity or detail, the difficulty of pinning down the characteristics of those identities often leads them into an ironic recognition that these identities are constructions that do not fully encompass all the complexities of real life. In her work, informants often dealt with such ruptures with irony, or by starting over the process of defining their identities. In my interviews, students labeled themselves and others as more or less authentically Egyptian by describing behaviors and then interpreting them as involving inner characteristics definitive of Egyptianness. In the process, however, and especially when reflecting on their own actions, they displaced some of the agency for these actions from the actor's own choices to the failures of the larger society in which they were embedded. When students told stories like the one about the Sting concert, they blamed the ironic ruptures in their narratives of identity on an agency outside their control, e.g., on the chaotic society. Because people in general do not behave with *shaham* any more, it is difficult for them as individuals to behave with *shaham*. Because society pressures the students to be Western and modern *and* Egyptian and moral, they see the behaviors that might connote modern, educated, *mu'adab, akhla'*, and *adab* as unclear, shifting, and perhaps impossible to keep in balance. Globalization, usually glossed as Westernization or even Americanization, is constructed as an external force before whose onslaught the Egyptian moral system crumbles. Indeed, given the systemic nature of *akhlaq* and the claims made about *shaham* as concepts that once ordered social behavior, their discourse suggests a sophisticated model in which the internal disorder of Egyptian teens is a mirror of the external disorder of Egyptian society. Like personal identities, social order is doubly articulated. The goal of finding the right balance—a balance that includes establishing the credentials necessary to make a living—is carried with them to the university.

WHAT'S AMERICAN ABOUT *GAMA'A AL-AMRIKIYYA?*

Even as they were beginning to locate the limits of their Westernization and explore the authenticity of their Egyptianness, Eiman and her friends were beginning to think seriously about college. Although most hoped to go abroad, all of them were at least considering the American University in Cairo, the university attended by the fictional Khalaf and where I taught for five years. For generations, class, modernity, and cosmopolitanism have been intertwined at the American University in Cairo. Founded in 1919 as a Presbyterian mission school focusing on secondary education, AUC evolved into an elite, private, secular liberal arts university with a strongly cosmopolitan character and a reputation for being able to place its graduates in high-paying jobs with multinational corporations.[17] Many Egyptians with upwardly mobile aspirations continue to turn to AUC to help them acquire the social and symbolic capital of cosmopolitanism.

The adoption of Western models of education in Egypt can be traced back to the reign of Muhammad Ali (r. 1805–1849). The chaos created by the French invasion disrupted the traditional *madrasa* system, opening opportunities for the monarch to import a secular European model of education and to send Egyptians to schools abroad in Paris, Livorno, Milan, and Florence (Boktor 1936; Heyworth-Dunne 1968). By bringing in "the influence of Western thought and technology . . . he set the stage for the emergence of a new 'managerial' class of Egyptians, imbued with a new national consciousness which expressed itself in a desire to improve society and to secure for themselves a greater share in its control and development" (El-Hamamsy 1982: 286). He also firmly established foreign languages and styles as the premier social capital for the professional classes in spite of their recent liberation from foreign (Ottoman) dominance. These changes barely survived the next two monarchs, who shut down several schools in an effort to diminish foreign influences, then enjoyed an efflorescence under Ismail Pasha (r. 1863–1879), who famously said, "My country is no longer in Africa; we are now part of Europe. It is therefore natural for us to abandon our former ways and to adopt a new system adapted to our social conditions," and established a series of government-run language schools for the teaching of French, German, and English. While many of Ismail Pasha's reforms were reversed under the British occupation, the foreigners established English and French "mission schools." These schools were primarily aimed at educating the children of European expatriates, and while the children of wealthy Egyptians could attend, the "people these schools produced were naturally somewhat alienated from [Egyptian] cultural traditions and sometimes showed little pride in [Egypt's] values" (El-Hamamsy 1982: 291). This emphasis on "cultural traditions" is a common complaint and reflects the fact that most Egyptians treat modernity as style rather than structure. Mitchell points out that the reforms of Muhammad Ali, Ismail Pasha, and their successors introduced significant structural transformations of education, in which a pedagogy focused on "the practice of the particular profession or craft to be learned" was replaced by a pedagogy organized by timetables, syllabi, and abstract letter grades, which "had the effect of re-presenting—or exhibiting—an autonomous 'realm of order' or structure" of modernity (Mitchell 1988: 85; see also Starrett 1998). Although there have been many debates in Egypt over whether the specific content of textbooks or other educational materials reflects an "Egyptian" character, there has been little criticism aimed at reforming the modernist structure of the institutions to reflect an "Egyptian" structure.

The modern state of Egypt, based on Western institutions initiated by Muhammad Ali and Ismail Pasha, with its requirement for a class of civil servants produced a literary establishment and body of secular public intellectuals "historically dominated by the political field" and consequently "dependent on it for status and power" (Mehrez 2008: 9). At the same time, modernity was always an elite project, and the state has had to balance its commitments to modernity through education with concessions to the conservative religious establishment, which lays claim to moral and cultural authenticity. In this system, the elites espouse Enlightenment values, all the while seeking to incorporate elements of regional and local authenticity, while the religious establishment lays claim to traditional cultural and moral authenticity and uses it to pass judgment on the practices and products of the intelligentsia. The state has attempted to both sustain and control these rival establishments to shore up its own power and to successfully administer "the masses." Universities have been one of the central arenas in which these tensions have played out.

Established as both a preparatory school and a university,[18] AUC was part of this process whereby expatriates maintained their children's Enlightenment cultural values and upper-class, mostly Christian Egyptians learned these values as part of their training as Egypt's professional class. But the university, along with the rest of Egypt, was dramatically changed by the Nasserist revolution that began in 1952. While the new regime sought to expand education, it also sought to expel the foreign "advisors" whose sons and daughters were an important part of AUC's clientele. Land tenure reforms left many of the elites who had been a primary local source of AUC's students in greatly diminished financial condition, and the very existence of an elite, private university ran counter to Nasser's promotion of free education for the masses. At the same time, it was clearly unwise to close down the only internationally accredited school in the country at the very moment Egypt was seeking to create fledgling institutions along modernist lines. Deals were struck by which the faculty was opened to Muslim professors, and Egyptian and U.S. faculty were hired in roughly equal numbers.[19] Subsequently, the 1962 Egyptian-American Cultural Cooperation Agreement established AUC as a "private cultural institute" whose declared purpose is to "contribute to the intellectual growth, discipline, and character of the future leaders of Egypt and the region" while simultaneously "advancing the ideals of American liberal arts and professional education and lifelong learning" (American University in Cairo 2000: 15–17). During the Nasserist heyday, AUC had little stature; it was largely seen as a way for those who could pay to get an education when their low scores prohibited admission to the national universities. This changed with the *infitah*; by the 1980s, "[a] recent graduate of the American University in Cairo . . . working for a foreign institution usually receives a starting salary that is at least ten times the size of his counterpart's who has graduated from a national university and is working for a national institution in Egypt. Little wonder that the AUC . . . is now the ultimate dream for many young Egyptians" (Ibrahim 1982: 52–53).

At the time of my study, AUC had an undergraduate student body of about 3,500, with roughly equal numbers of men and women. Highly competitive, admission required both high scores on national exams and an ability to pay fees roughly three times the mean GDP (equivalent, in fact, to the cost of ASC). The university's operating budget was about $80 million of which half came from tuition and fees. There was very little financial aid available for undergraduates, although free tuition for the children of staff and a handful of scholarships did open the doors to a small number of high-achieving students with lower incomes. The majority of undergraduate students had attended private language schools like MLS or private international schools like ASC.

Egyptians tend to have an instrumentalist view of education as a route to social mobility, which has been shaped in large part by postcolonial history. Under Nasser and until a moratorium was placed on the practice in 1986, the government promised to hire anyone who graduated from a national university (Nicol 1991: 6). A private university education—which until 1996 exclusively meant AUC[20]—is primarily seen as a good to be consumed or a service to be purchased (El-Messiri et al. 1992; Russell 1994: 207). A key aspect of an AUC education is its promotion of liberal arts and critical thinking, which are instrumentally touted as essential to Egypt's future in the globalizing world. "What we are trying to engender in our students is the willingness and ability to question," said former AUC president Donald McDonald in a 1995 interview in *Egypt's Insight.* Ahmed, a student who spent two frustrating years at Cairo University's School of Medicine before switching to AUC,[21] made a distinction between the national schools, "where you learn *fi akhud ala afaya* [from a smack on the neck]," and schools like AUC, "where they teach you that your ideas matter." The former, he told me, produce "thoughtless people" who are helpless to do anything to change their situations, while the latter produce people who know they can change the world. It is AUC's ability to lay claim to education of this special kind and quality that justifies its existence as a place where the Khalafs of the world could conceivably rise above their origins.

Yet, "the ideology of a liberal arts or American-style education by which the institution markets itself is not the reason students enroll there" (Russell 1994: 207). The description "liberal arts education" and AUC's articulation of it are transformed into a language of credentials by other institutions feeding the growth of Egypt's globalized economy. In 1999, for example, Microsoft hired for jobs in its Seattle offices eleven Egyptians, nine of whom were AUC grads, a fact noted both in the press and by AUC's publicists and apologists. Many human resources professionals argue that only AUC offers Egyptians the skills that high-end employers are looking for. It isn't enough to be able to speak English and have computer skills, said Nadia, director of a human resources consulting firm that serves foreign clients doing business in Egypt: "Companies want people who have team spirit, leadership ability, initiative, [a] serious work ethic, and good communication skills, not just language but [the] ability to communicate effectively."

Nadia graduated from AUC, then took a degree in human resources management at a U.S. university.[22] Her company was initially bankrolled by an uncle but is now thriving on its own, she said. "When a company wants to hire a skilled manager, they have to interview a hundred people. I save them that step." She does most of her recruiting at AUC because "AUC offers this multiskilled workforce. . . . There are good people . . . at Cairo and Alexandria [universities] but they are one in a hundred."

Nadia speaks the language of human resources she learned at AUC and in the United States, but her list of the characteristics that make a good employee also sounds very much like common definitions of *wilad an-nas*. In interviews with employment agents who claimed that the best jobs went to women who were *bint an-nas* (feminine singular of *wilad an-nas*), Barsoum extracted some of the characteristics that define this category: they have the "right manners" and the "right attitude." They can both give and accept orders. Because they are children of privilege, they do not look with wonder or envy at the wealth displayed by their employers. They have good posture and grace of movement. They speak English correctly, with little or no accent. They know how to dress appropriately for different kinds of occasions (Barsoum 2004: 52–55).

> [*Wilad an-nas* is] capital in disguise. It involves moral qualities as well
> as intangible issues of grace and style. It is a perfect example of what
> Bourdieu calls symbolic capital. It is a capital monopolized by those
> who come from privileged classes. It is also a capital readily changeable
> for economic capital, since having *bint nas* criterion [*sic*] opens doors
> to prize jobs in a country with job scarcity. *Bint nas* is also a means
> of symbolic violence since it serves as a mechanism for exclusion. By
> valorizing the qualities of those who come from the cultivated classes,
> poorer graduates are excluded from the realm of prize jobs. (Ibid.: 54)

In this view, schools like ASC and, later, AUC are not so much institutions providing opportunities for acquiring valuable skills and achieving social mobility as they are "ideological mechanisms by which the educational system tends to transform social privileges into natural privileges *and not privileges of birth*" (Bourdieu and Saint-Martin 1974: 346).

The argument that AUC is less an institution by which people pursue and attain social mobility and more a site in which upper-middle-class and upper-class children and their families launder their privileges of birth by acquiring cosmopolitan credentials is made by Russell (1994), drawing on similar arguments about university educations in Britain and France. On the basis of a survey of 279 students (about 8.5 percent of the undergraduate body), Russell argues that AUC valorizes cultural capital that students already possess because of the set of life chances into which they were born. Family wealth, high levels of education attained by parents and grandparents, secondary schooling at institutions like MLS and ASC, and English-language competence are crucial to success at AUC, and they are already largely possessed by the families whose children enter the school. Although many families—like Yasseen's—make considerable sacrifices to send their students to AUC, they are unable to send their children to the school unless they have accumulated economic capital well beyond that of most Egyptians. Private secondary schools with foreign curricula, like ASC and MLS, prepare students "for the assignments given at a Western university: term papers, essay examinations, oral presentations, science lab work and the like" but, perhaps more important, prepare students for "how to *act* in the cosmopolitan manner that an institution such as AUC valorizes" (Russell 1994: 203–204). AUC validates the cultural capital students possess by virtue of their privileges of birth, transforming it into the credentials necessary to enter into the kinds of work that will allow the students to continue living at the level of affluence of their families of origin.

There is more to cultural capital than simply having it or not. Russell's study captures some of the internal complications of prestige hierarchies at AUC as well. The most prestigious majors—engineering and laboratory sciences—require the least knowledge of English, while lower-prestige majors, like comparative literature or history, have the highest requirements. Gender distinctions are significant, with women reporting far lower expectations not only of anticipated career goals but even idealized goals.

Particularly interesting for my project is the subtle distinctions created between students who buy new or used books, wear particular styles of dress, or participate in school activities. Student activities entirely funded by the participants, such as Model UN meetings in Europe, weekend jaunts to Alexandria and Sharm El-Sheikh resorts, four-day scuba-diving excursions, and even trips to Disney World, act as filters through which economically homogeneous groups within the student body can befriend (and exclude) one another, and create social networks that will extend beyond school as important aspects of graduates' social capital.

AUC contributes to the reproduction of existing class structures not only by providing "a restricted setting for recruitment into the high prestige occupations necessary for the elite to maintain their positions at the top" (Russell 1994: 213), but by reinforcing and refining the sets of styles by which cultural capital is to be displayed. AUC graduates have been characterized as the "Westernized wing of the Egyptian bourgeoisie" (Hinnebusch 1982: 535). Certainly, students who come to AUC have different backgrounds than those at the national universities. In a 1987 survey, they were nearly twice as likely to say they were well-off, to have lived abroad, and to have parents who had lived abroad than were students at the national universities. And, as we might expect from the comparison of Yasseen's family with Ismail's above, AUC family size averages 2.7 children against 4.0 among national university students (Sell 1990: 62).

Egypt has always been cosmopolitan, politically as well as socially. From around 350 BCE until the 1952 revolution, Egypt's ruling class was composed of foreigners—foreign both in terms of heritage and languages spoken among them, but also in the perception of the indigenous population. These foreign ruling classes, in turn, encouraged other foreign groups (Armenians, Greeks, Iranians, Jews, Lebanese, Syrians, Turks) to reside in Cairo and act as intermediaries between the rulers and the indigenous population. "Are the perceptions of the Westernized bourgeoisie, as suggested by AUC students, sufficiently different from the mainstream of Egyptian sentiment, in a sense replicating previous eras when ruling classes neither spoke Arabic nor shared the majority customs?" asks sociologist Ralph R. Sell (1990: 67). "The answer is a qualified no" if we go by "affinity surveys" that compare how AUC students rank various foreign countries with how their colleagues at the national universities and non-degree students taking technical courses rank foreign countries. Such instruments, though simplistic, suggest that there are popular moral economies out there that link elites and their middle-class counterparts in spite of claims made on both sides for the complete alienation of the upper classes from the wider world of "real" Egyptians.

Yet the idea that upper-class cosmopolitanism *could* be an alienating factor—rendering one *mitfarnagin* or a wannabe—remains a central element of cosmopolitan identity construction. "The idea that AUC is an isolated island worries me," said former AUC president Donald McDonald in a 1999 interview with *Egypt's Insight*. A polemic against AUC by a self-styled Egyptian Islamist argued that AUC's presence is part of an ongoing historical conflict between Arabs and Egyptians and the West (Sidahmed 1985: 10). Aside from being a haven for CIA operatives, Sidahmed claimed, AUC promotes values that are likely to produce increased political, economic, and cultural dependence on the West in general and the United States in particular.[23]

Young Egyptians, both in high school and college, often demonstrate mixed feelings about the Westernized identities they have worked so hard to construct. ASC's Egyptian students are caught between the Western, American-inflected cosmopolitanism their expensive educations are supposed to provide them, and the desire to find value in their Egyptianness. In interviews, conversations, and observations of student behavior, two general strategies for finding this balance emerge: familial nationalism and Islamic renewal. Neither of these strategies turns out to be simple, straightforward, or completely successful.

COSMOPOLITANISM AND THE NATIONAL FAMILY

"I hate Egypt," Aline told me casually one day when she was about fourteen. Many students like Aline, who continued to almost exclusively employ European or American signifiers (speech, dress, manners), usually expected to go abroad for college and to settle and work abroad for the rest of their lives. Some of these students had mixed parentage and, like Aline, they invested heavily in the foreign parent's identity. Aline's older brothers had settled in Belgium and Switzerland, her sister was in Britain;

she hoped to settle in the United States, England, or France. By her freshman year in high school, she was already traveling abroad independently during school breaks, visiting family but also school friends in Europe and the United States. A substantial trust fund ensured that she could attend any university that accepted her and that she could live comfortably in any career she chose.

When cosmopolitan young adults like Aline travel, however, the social distancing supposed by claims to "hate Egypt" is not always easy to sustain. Their identity is not a choice that is entirely theirs to make. Identities are co-constructed and the negotiations through which identities are managed are not always pleasant. Successful as Aline became at managing cosmopolitan identities, she recognized both from her travels and her experiences at ASC that her Arabic last name and toffee-colored complexion marked her as "not really" French, British, or American. She told me of a playground incident when she was in ninth grade when a boy called her an "American wannabe"—particularly insulting as Aline had been emphasizing the Frenchness she derived from her mother. When she got older, she said, she realized that the boy himself had similar issues: he had a British father and an American mother but had spent fewer than two years in either country. He sought to position himself as "American"—a higher-prestige nationality at ASC—in spite of his UK passport.

Khaled related a similar incident that occurred in Germany. The son of Osman, a successful businessman whose projects included part ownership of two Red Sea resorts and a German-Egyptian export business, Khaled had always expected to attend a German university and settle in Germany or Austria, like his brothers. Khaled had studied at the German school in Cairo and transferred to ASC in his freshman year. In spite of his European tastes in dress and idiomatic command of German, he was called a racist epithet while visiting his brother in Germany, and when he returned to Egypt he changed his plans and enrolled at AUC. For both Khaled and Aline, a crucial problem is managing a cosmopolitanism that anchors itself through links to a global community that dubs their place of origin inferior and, especially since the terrorist attacks on the United States, Great Britain, and Spain, potentially dangerous and frightening.

Many young cosmopolitan Egyptians manage the ironies of their relationship with Egypt through social networks with Egyptian travelers.

This has been hugely facilitated in the twenty-first century by the availability of e-mail, instant messaging, cell phones, and social networking technologies. The Facebook group "I Will Bitchslap the Next Foreigner Who Asks Me if I Go to School on a Camel," for example, was founded in 2007 as a site for Egyptians to share stories about the ignorant, rude, or just plain stupid misconceptions they encounter in their travels. It quickly evolved beyond this. In the photo section, for example, members began mocking ignorant foreigners by posting photos of camels with captions like "This is what I drive to school" and pyramids captioned "Here's my school." Other photos offered images of high-tech buildings, resorts, and internet cafés as contradictions to the stereotypes they have encountered. These quickly gave way to nostalgia photos featuring common sights that expatriate Egyptians say they miss about Egypt, and critiques of Egypt from an insider perspective, such as poorly translated signs transposing p and b, or men on bicycles transporting huge weights on their heads. In the latter case, someone inevitably posts the comment "only in Egypt."

This mix of nostalgia, insider critiques, and humor aimed at "dumb foreigners" offers a powerful means of managing cosmopolitan identities by indexically linking oneself to a national home toward which one is at once highly critical and also affectionate. Vanessa Fong refers to "filial nationalism" as a description of the way teens in China attempt to resolve a similar contradiction between an inescapable national identity and an "identification with a global community that [has] deemed China inferior" (Fong 2004: 631). The dream of pursuing the good life abroad is ubiquitous, as are complaints about the "chaotic" nature of Egypt's infrastructure and social organization. The desire to go abroad permanently is seen as selfish, even as a betrayal of society. "We would like to stay in Egypt if things would get better," complained Hawass, an AUC computer science graduate who obtained a job with a German firm and was preparing to relocate to Bonn. "[But] if we all go abroad, who will make the country better?" Yet the decision to stay in Egypt is often characterized as quixotic and even stupid. "I only know one guy who turned down a job abroad, and everybody was, like, 'Hey, are you stupid? What's up with that?' But I think it was really a family thing, like his mother just didn't want him to go abroad," said Aida, an AUC junior majoring in anthropology.

Hawass's complaint echoes those of the ASC students: Egyptian society has become so chaotic that it has become impossible to pursue a balanced lifestyle. Yet he recognizes that the abandonment of Egypt by its most educated elites can only continue to leave Egypt chaotic. Aida's story reflects the same contradiction but introduces a rational reason to stay: family. This is important because, as Fong's work in China suggests, these accounts of family can serve not only as modifying discourses for explaining motives to turn down global opportunities but can in turn become metaphors for relations with the nation.

Family played a big part in Aida's life. Aida had grown up in California until she was twelve, and her wish was to study sports medicine at UCLA. Both brothers had gone back to the United States for their educations, but her parents had refused to send Aida for fear she would "get into trouble." Since she smoked, dated boys, and went clubbing in Cairo, she said, she couldn't figure out what they thought she'd do there that she didn't do in Egypt. Aida complained frequently about her parents' treatment of her, but bristled if anyone else criticized them. One day, when a discussion in my office somehow turned from assignments to her parents, I suggested how I might deal with my own daughters' educations, which she took as an oblique criticism of her parents. "They're my parents, you know?" she retorted. "They're trying, you know. They're wrong, but they're just trying to do what's best for me." Fong argues that this idiom of family—an intimate community whose members can criticize it but will defend it against outsiders—serves as a model for many cosmopolitan youths trying to make sense of their relations to the homeland they want to leave.

Contemporary students may find expression for this filial nationalism in popular culture products that hark back to older expressions of secular nationalism. *Nasser 56*, a film by Muhammed Fadel, eclipsed *Sa'idi fil Gama'a al-Amrikiyya* to become the most popular film in Egyptian history. Filmed in black and white to resemble a newsreel or a film from the era it depicts, *Nasser 56* shows an Egypt united under a popular, secular, but moral leader unafraid to make difficult decisions. Eiman's friend Hassan, one of the ASC students who told me Egypt has no "system," specifically pointed to *Nasser 56*. He told me that his father had taken him to the movie and they'd gone out for dinner afterward to talk about it. "Everyone was willing to make sacrifices," he said. "Not like today." *Nasser 56* was a powerful film that galvanized discussions of the Nasser era, but they were not the careful, nuanced discussions of shifting nationalist ideologies identified by historians: pharaonicism, Easternism, Islamic nationalism, integral nationalism, and Arab nationalism (Jankowski 1986; Jankowski and Gershoni 1995). Rather, conversations I had with students and Arab colleagues about the film centered on a nostalgic nationalism, an imagined state of affairs. Nostalgic for a media image of a unified society with a paternal leader and citizens willing to work together for the common good, Hassan's personal plans to attend Boston University and pursue a business career abroad stand in ironic contrast. It is an irony of which he is keenly aware, as he blames the broken Egyptian system for his inability to stay and be the kind of Egyptian portrayed in the film.

Pharaonic images may also play an important role in filial nationalism. Even while they mock foreigners who ask them questions that confuse ancient Egyptian lifestyles with their contemporary lives, students' websites and instant messaging icons frequently feature scarabs, pyramids, and hieroglyphics, as do professional websites offering an "Egyptian" web portal to the internet (Peterson and Panovic 2004). The use of such imagery is not new, but reflects a discourse of secular nationalism that dates back at least to the turn of the twentieth century, associated with important political and intellectual leaders such as Mustafa Kamil, Ahmad Lutfi al-Sayyid, Salama Musa, Saad Zaghloul, and Taha Hussein (Gordon 1971: 126–127; El-Shakry 2007: 55–86). Such pharaonic imagery can be used to assert the existence of a unified collective Egyptian character rooted in thousands of years of civilization. Unlike the comparable symbols reminiscent of Arab nationalism that fill the pages of Arabic children's magazines, pharaonic nationalism emphasizes Egyptian uniqueness. It functions "as an exclusionary discourse, situating Egypt within a heritage highly prized by the West and disembedding it from its African and Arabian contexts" (El-Shakry 2007: 83).

The Nahdet Misr movement emphasized a common Egyptian character in battling the foreign domination of the British (especially in a 1919 uprising) and during the 1922–1923 final break with the Ottoman Empire. Howard Carter's discovery of the tomb of Tutankhamun coincided with these events, laminating pharaonism and Egyptian nationalism in the popular imagination. Some pieces of national architecture, including the

tomb of nationalist leader Saad Zaghloul and the new High Court building, and the incorporation of pharaonic elements in malls and walled
communities testify to the continuing links between pharaonic imagery
and Egyptian national identity. At the same time, these are contested links,
particularly when appropriated by the state. Nasser, whose contemporary
image has had a huge boost among teens because of the film, downplayed
the country's pharaonic heritage in order to emphasize links with neigh-
boring Arab states. Sadat attempted to restore the significance of pharaonic imagery so pointedly that his assassin called him a "pharaoh." More
recently, cosmopolitan Egyptians at home and around the world—Dubai,
London, Oslo, Sidney, San Francisco—celebrated the Egyptian New Year
on September 11, 2006, with celebrations that included televised coverage
of a dance at Giza said to be recovered from an ancient papyrus. The celebrations were masterminded by Egyptian Salon, an NGO with ties to the
secular nationalist Egyptian Liberal Party, and advertised through scores
of "Year 6249" websites (Darwish 2007). Yet if pharaonicism distinguishes
Egyptian national identity from Arab and African identities, it remains
open to global appropriations. Many of the websites promoting Year 6249
were established not by cosmopolitan Egyptians but by just the kinds of
people Aline and Khaled disparage as inauthentic and "ignorant": new
age "Egyptofreaks," belly dancing schools, and pan-Africanists. Because
modernity is conceptualized as largely *external* to Egypt, and because the
external world has already colonized pharaonic and orientalist imagery,
authenticity remains elusive. An alternative for many students is to find
the limits of their Westernized cosmopolitanism not in Egypt but in some
"modern" form of Islam.

MORAL MODERNITY

As I entered my graduate course in social thought one afternoon in 2000,
I found two students in the midst of a heated argument. Sherif had apparently told members of the class that he had been driving all the way to the
Al-Hosary mosque in Sixth of October City to hear the sermons of the
well-known preacher Amr Khaled. Nora had dismissed Amr Khaled as
"an accountant who preaches," and an argument over the authenticity of

the wildly successful Islamic preacher had begun.[24] What was fascinating to me about the debate was that it once again came down largely to a matter of style. Amr Khaled, his supporters claimed, "speaks to *us*," that is, to Westernized, upper-class Egyptian Muslims, and "is easy to understand." Nora and her fellow critics argued that he was an inauthentic sheikh precisely because he wore jeans, was clean-shaven, and "carries a cell phone." To Sherif, Amr Khaled is powerful because he speaks to well-to-do youth in their own idioms. To Nora, he is a fraud because the very idea of a "hip" (*rawish*) sheikh is absurd and inauthentic. No mention was made by either side of the fact that Khaled's "doctrinal views hardly differ from those of the orthodox Azherite sheikhs who dismiss him" (Bayat 2002: 23) and who both Nora and Sherif hold up as counters to him because of their conservative styles of dress and paternalistic, authoritarian modes of speech.

With Amr Khaled, the medium is very much the message. Clean-shaven, dressed in a suit and tie, or in jeans and a polo shirt, instead of the customary *kiffiya* and robe, Khaled is the leading proponent of a growing trend in popular Islam expressed by sheikhs in mosques, on television, and through youth organizations that presents faith and ethics in compelling and contemporary ways to young middle-class consumers. He did not originate this movement—he was preceded by 'Umar Abdel-Kafi, Khalid al-Guindy, Mustafa Mahmud (Conermann 1996; Salvatore 2000; Wise 2003), and others—but he is without question its most successful proponent. He began preaching in mosques and private clubs in the early 1990s, and by the early years of the new millennium his cassette tapes were bestsellers to rival those of pop musicians, his website counted more than a thousand hits per day (a significant number given that only 4 percent of the people in the Arab world have access to the internet), and his television shows were being broadcast via satellite to millions of Muslims worldwide.

The most common way to explain Islamic revival is as a reactionary force: people who are poor and unemployed, who are excluded from political participation, or who are frustrated at their exclusion from Western modernity turn *away* from the desire for greater wealth, the promise of democracy, and the unreachable world of modern goods to something else, something that makes them feel better about themselves and that exposes material satisfaction as illusory. But how can we then explain the increasing attraction of an active Islamic renewal to Egyptians like Sherif, who are wealthy and educated with good job prospects; who have opportunities to enter the corridors of power through kinship relations, social networks, and cultural capital; and who express their cosmopolitan class identities through consumption of transnational goods?

The attraction of this kind of Islamic renewal to this affluent population can better be explained by an emerging literature that describes resurgent Islam as a kind of action that many people see as a relevant and powerful tool for *bettering* their situation rather than turning from it (Wiktorowicz 2003; Sparre and Petersen 2007). In this understanding, mass literacy spread by national educational reforms took Islam out of the hands of the small class of scholars, preachers, and jurors (Eickelman and Anderson 1997; Eickelman 2002) and made it possible for individual Muslims to "put Islam to work" (Starrett 1998), especially in new (often commodified) public spaces not yet dominated by the older religious authorities, such as television (Abu-Lughod 2005), cassette recordings (Hirschkind 2001, 2006a, 2006b), and the internet (Anderson 2003a, 2003b). For AUC students like Sherif, the Islamist modernity represented by Amr Khaled offers an opportunity to achieve that elusive balance between modernity and authenticity because "according to Amr Khaled, Islam is not only about praying five times a day and wearing the *higab* the correct way, and *da'wa* is not just a call to live by those rules. Islam is about changing and improving yourself and your community, and *da'wa* is a call to actively engage in this change" (Sparre and Petersen 2007: 14). The Islam articulated by such preachers offers a way to link a personal authenticity rooted in a commitment to shared Islamic values and practices to social renewal. In the face of complaints by young people that the nation is chaotic, crazy, and disordered, activist Islam promises to create a society that is shaped by moral practices and self-sacrifices for the common good.

Central to Amr Khaled's message is an effort to link moral commitment with social (and political) behavior (Rock 2010). In the first year of his television show *Sunna al-Hayah* (*Lifemakers*), he called for and publicized the collection of secondhand clothing and its distribution to poor areas (Sparre and Petersen 2007). Borrowing the buzzwords of Western modernity, Khaled ties "capacity building" and "sustainable development" to the traditional social values of Islam, especially the requirement for Muslims to care for one another. Khaled, in other words, portrays an Islam that sounds authentic, because its theology is conservative, yet it looks and sounds like the contemporary, globalizing world with which AUC students are familiar. This form of Islamist activism thus offers students like Hassan and Sherif a promise of the kind of society worth making sacrifices for. The movement he represents is an important part of the ongoing "objectification" and "functionalization" of Islam, which have transformed Islam in the minds of many Muslims from "an unexamined and unexaminable way of life" to "a coherent system of practices and beliefs" (Starrett 1998: 9) that can be put "to work for various types of social and political projects" (10). Above all, like contemporary fundamentalist and evangelical preachers and teachers in the United States (Wise 2003; Bielo 2007), he validates a personal piety that is consistent with upper-middle-class wealth, power, and prestige. Like proponents of pharaonic nationalism, Amr Khaled and his ilk offer a stylish authenticity that cosmopolitan Muslims can adopt as part of their efforts to manage the limits of their globalization and to locate authenticities in which their identities can be rooted. The most visible public sign of this authenticity is the veiling of cosmopolitan women.

TRANSNATIONAL VEILS

At one of the main entrances to Cairo University stands a statue that represents the Nahdet Misr movement. The statue features a woman in a *galabiyya* looking to the dawn, peeling off her *higab* with one hand while the other hand rests on a sphinx. The statue captures a particular moment in Egypt's ideology of modernity—rooted in the pharaonic past, looking to the future, and abandoning the shackles of tradition. The ideology represented by the statue remains a potent force in contemporary Egypt, but it is no longer exclusive, or even dominant. This was driven home to me when I visited the elegant, high-tech offices of the Nahdet Misr corporation, the largest publisher of educational materials in Egypt. Founded in 1938, Nahdet Misr's logo is a drawing of the famous statue, and the corporation certainly serves as a model for women's employment: not only is the director of the publications division a woman, but so are many of the editors, including the editor of *Miki* (*Mickey Mouse*), the bestselling children's magazine in the Arab world. Yet, in a company whose logo is a woman unveiling, nearly every female employee wears the *higab*. The re-veiling of women in Egypt has long been a sign of their entry into the public spaces of work, education, and politics rather than a symbol of domesticity and containment.

One of the things for which Amr Khaled is famous is facilitating and publicizing the re-veiling of actresses (van Nieuwkerk 2007). As the veil grows in popularity, the movie and television industries remain an important and influential holdout, a bastion of women displaying their bodies in the Western style. Teaching that college and the workplace are potentially dangerous places, Khaled and other sheikhs call on men and women to discipline themselves accordingly. Chief among these disciplines is veiling, a bodily discipline that not only conceals women from the male gaze but, as these sheikhs define it, helps them to embody that submission to God which is the core of Islam.

Nireen was a young woman of twenty-one, dressed in a long skirt and modest blouse, when I interviewed her in the winter of 2001. A graduating senior in psychology, she had taken two classes with me and asked me to write a letter of recommendation to a U.S. graduate program. When her self-account became increasingly personal, I asked if I could record and interview her. Nireen told me she had been "in self-destruct mode" in her teens, taking drugs and cutting and burning herself. Her parents sent her to a psychiatrist, who put her on antidepressants that turned her "into a zombie." In her sophomore year, she was hospitalized for a drug overdose and began praying for the first time in years. When she returned home, she said, she stopped taking her medications and seeing her psychiatrist and turned to the Qur'an. About six months later, she caused a car accident because she'd been drinking, so she swore off alcohol. Giving up alcohol meant giving up most of her friends and evening social activities. With more time on her hands in the evenings, she began listening to Amr Khaled tapes and thinking about ways she could improve her life. She was unveiled at the time of our interview, but thinking seriously about taking the *higab*, and she asked my opinion about how people in the United States would see her if veiled, especially after 9/11. "I never believed in the veil," she said. "Now, I'm not sure. . . . If it's meant to happen, if God allows it to happen and gives us enough time, then it becomes part of your life." She had no immediate plans to veil, but the *higab* would come, she told me, "in God's own time."

Amira wore tight jeans or short skirts when she first appeared in my class during the fall semester of her sophomore year at AUC. Suddenly, in the last week of class, she came wearing the *higab* and a skirt that fell to mid-calf. She told me that she had always been convinced that being unveiled was irreligious but chose to put it off until she was married. "I wanted to look good," she said. "I was very sensitive about my appearance" especially at engagement and wedding parties. Yet her conscience was bothering her. "I kept saying to myself, 'if you are convinced of something, why don't you do it?' But all my friends were the same. We all thought the veil was a good idea, but we all wanted to wait." Then, one of those friends called her to tell her she'd taken the veil. Amira rushed over to her flat, and the girls talked it over. Her friend played her a tape by Amr Khaled that impressed her because "it sought to answer all the questions girls have. He pointed out all the common excuses teenagers make to escape from their duties. . . . I started crying because of all the bad things I used to do."[25] She was particularly impressed, she said, with one motto he offered: "If you do something that upsets your mother, you make sure you don't do it again. So why don't we do the same with God?" Amira went with her friend to one of Khaled's lectures and was deeply moved by his argument that Islam was submission to the love of God, not to arbitrary rules and laws one obeys from fear. Finally, she said, she was impressed by his argument that veiling is not an unfair imposition on women. "Boys have a job not to stare at ladies, so it is divided among the two," she said. "And if they stare, that is their sin, just as if I don't cover up, that is mine. It's as if I had a brother who didn't show my mother the same love and respect I do. I wouldn't stop showing respect because of his bad example."[26]

Amira's narrative of taking the *higab* follows a particular structure. She already believed that veiling was a rule for women, but while accepting the rule she found it easy to evade it. Amr Khaled gave her a different metaphor for submission; instead of following rules, she was showing love. He offered filial devotion as a model for that love, and directly addressed the issues of peer pressure and gender inequality that served as obstacles to her acceptance of veiling. More than this, Amira, like most women I talked to about veiling, saw donning the veil not as a singular act but as the beginning of a new self-discipline that made her, day by day, a better person. She no longer touches boys, and she carries a Qur'an in her bag with her school books and reads bits of it each day. Above all, she said, her thinking has changed:

> Before I wore the veil, I had this close friend, this guy I used to talk to every day on the phone for hours. And one day he called me up, maybe a year ago now, and says he won't be able to talk to me any more because it's irreligious. I was very mad at him and told him what he was doing was not logical and crazy. But now, I agree with his decision. I respect him for making it.

The students who said their lives were transformed by Amr Khaled emphasized the extent to which they laid claim to agency. Amira's and Nireen's stories are consistent with Saba Mahmood's description of veiling as an act of self-making (Mahmood 2005; Bautista 2008). Donning the veil is no easy thing, but it is a powerful means of practicing the requirements of virtue oneself. Another interesting thing that emerged from my interviews with these students was the way that they indexically positioned Khaled as a conduit to a wider "Islamic transnational space" (Bowen 2002) that is global but non-Western.[27] Amira and the others spoke repeatedly of the international reach of his ministry: his travels, the transnational broadcasting of his television shows, and his internet presence. Transnational references played an even larger role in follow-up interviews I conducted with Amira and Nireen on my return to Egypt in 2005, after Amr Khaled had left Egypt, claiming he was being pressured by "certain authorities."[28] His camps for Muslim teens in England, his sold-out performances in Jordan, and the shift of his broadcasts to wider-reaching satellite channels were all pointed to as evidence of his importance. Yet when Nireen said, "He speaks to all of us," she did not really seem to mean all Muslims but rather those well-off, educated Muslims caught between the "contradictory orientations" (Bayat 2002) of being Muslim and being global.[29] Students like Amira, Nireen, and Sherif use Khaled in part to establish the limits of their Westernization by locating a parallel modernity (Larkin 1997), also global in its reach, that allows them to feel both rooted in a tradition while free to maintain their privileges.

THE LIMITS OF AUTHENTICITY?

In order to be "sensitive to the social mores of this country," as former AUC president John D. Gerhart put it, the American University in Cairo has made numerous accommodations over the years to such rising expressions of Muslim piety, including developing a special class schedule for the month of Ramadan, allowing a student-built mosque to exist on school grounds, and responding to political and legal pressure to ban "offensive" books.[30] But the university found the limits of its own accommodations when some students attempted to adopt the *niqab*, concealing themselves behind black facecloths.

When an undergraduate student named Heba El-Shabrawy adopted the *niqab* in the fall of 2000, her action produced enormous consternation. The majority of the faculty clearly opposed allowing students to wear the *niqab*. A large number of vocal students supported the student's right to "free expression," and the irony was not lost on administrators that many of these student leaders had also supported the government's right to ban certain books "offensive to Islam" at AUC. A small number of other women, perhaps three to five, were emboldened by El-Shabrawy's decision and similarly adopted the *niqab*. By the end of the fall semester, the university had warned El-Shabrawy that, unless she removed the veil, she would not be allowed to enroll in spring classes.

Women in the *niqab* were not entirely unknown on the AUC campus. Many women taking degrees through the university's School of Continuing Education programs wore the *niqab*. While most of these took classes in satellite programs off campus, some occasionally came to campus to visit faculty members or administrators. The university was unprepared, however, for the possibility that regular AUC students might adopt the full *niqab* and wear it to classes. A 1994 Egyptian regulation bans the *niqab* from being worn on college campuses, and the university argued that it was bound by its charter to uphold the law even though the government does not enforce it at the national universities. AUC explained to its students and faculty in a 2001 memo banning the *niqab* from campus that it did not have a written policy dealing with this matter previously because the issue had never arisen in the eighty years of the school's existence.

A minority of faculty shrugged the whole business off, arguing that women at AUC were unlikely to ever cover their faces in large numbers. While most of the faculty seemed opposed to students taking the *niqab* on campus, they split over the reasons for their opposition. Many American faculty, especially those in the freshman writing program, perhaps the most homogeneously non-Egyptian faculty cluster, expressed fear of women in the *niqab*. Faculty said they found the face veil "alienating" and even "frightening." One said she felt that her personal security was threatened in the classroom because "you don't know who might be behind that veil." Many Egyptian faculty members, in contrast, said they were disturbed and angered by the trend they believed the *niqab* represented, a "step backward," as one Egyptian woman faculty member put it. In classic Egyptian ideologies of modernity since at least the late nineteenth century, "the woman's veil was the symbol of her relegation to the private sphere and of the appropriateness of her invisibility and nonparticipation in public life" (Hoffman-Ladd 1987: 23). These narratives of modernity remain strongly convincing for many Egyptians, albeit sometimes in transformed ways (Armbrust 1996a). Other faculty referred to the *niqab* as "excessive" and "not Egyptian," both references to the practice's roots in new transnational forms of Islam.

AUC's official policy banning the face veil but not the head scarf reflected these concerns.[31] The official reason given in a memo e-mailed to faculty was security: "This policy was enacted because all members of the AUC Community have a basic right to know with whom they are dealing, whether in class, the library, labs, the bathroom or anywhere else. This is a matter of personal security and safety, not a religious issue. . . . We use photo IDs for a reason—to enable us to identify people by matching the person's face to the picture." To the argument that AUC need only hire some female security guards to help check IDs at the gates, the university responded, "[F]aculty are not security personnel and should not be put in the position of having to call security in order to verify the identity of students who come to class or office hours covering their face." But the university also tied the visibility of the face to the mission of a liberal arts institution, arguing, "A liberal arts education requires dialog and intellectual interaction with colleagues and with other members of the University community. Face veiling inhibits this interaction. Students who choose to cover the face should seek another type of education." The university thus constructed a model of dialogue privileging face-to-face interaction as central to the university's mission in Egypt. According to this model, wearing the *niqab* is both alien and alienating, and so contradicts the liberal rationality that is AUC's stock-in-trade and that makes its graduates attractive in the global labor market.

Such a model is consistent with transnational debates on veiling around the world, in which veiled Muslims are repeatedly singled out for failing to respect the fundamental distinction between the public, secular realm and the private, religious realm, and hence veiling is represented "as both foreign and irrational" (Klaus and Kassel 2005: 335). The establishment of the boundaries of this public-private distinction has been part of political struggles in European and North American nations for decades. What AUC's dilemma demonstrates is that this distinction is complex and nuanced, a continuum or field rather than a dichotomy. The limits of liberal tolerance are drawn not at public expression of Muslim identity through the wearing of the *higab,* but at what the administration describes as an excessive expression of religion that complicates an understanding of liberal discourse as a "great conversation." Some faculty applauded the rule. One professor who wore the *higab* insisted that the *niqab* was rightly banned because it is "not Egyptian." Others expressed disgust at the rule. A few noted the ironies inherent in the unveiled approach to liberal education. In a public forum inviting faculty comments on the policy, one professor (who did not cover her head) asked, "Why is liberal education always so reluctant to support these women's rights to veil as a matter of freedom of expression? The university is telling her, in essence, your dress shows you aren't liberal, so stop trying to get a liberal education. . . . These kinds of rules always seemed to be aimed at restricting women's access to education." Another professor asked, "So why are we sinking money in web-based coursework if we can't teach students whose faces are hidden from us? On the web, all the faces are veiled."

This professor's point that there is more than one way to conceal one's face also occurred to the handful of AUC students who desired, but were denied, the opportunity to wear the *niqab.*[32] Most of them continued to wear the plain, black, long-sleeved dress and head covering as before but without the cloth veil. Instead, as they moved around campus, they covered their faces below the eyes with open books or sheets of notebook paper. This use of the paraphernalia of education to pursue a personal agenda that the university insisted undermined education left many students and faculty nonplussed. Some faculty wrote into their syllabi rules against concealing one's face with books or papers, but the three or four students engaged in the practice simply avoided those classes. A growing support, not so much for the pious act as for the students' persistent willingness to buck the system, allowed the young women to seek out a handful of sympathetic professors, mostly women. They would sit in the front rows of the classes and lower their "veils" before the female professor, then take them up again at the end of class. "The boys in the class always respect our choice and sit in the back so as not to offend against us," one of the young women told me. Nor did the practice disappear when these girls graduated. Although women covering their faces never exceeded a handful, the administration felt it necessary in February 2004 to issue a memo reiterating its opposition to face covering in any form on university property or at university events and urging faculty to report the name and ID number of any girl covering her face by *niqab*, piece of paper, book, or any other means.

While most studies of veiling either uphold it as a sign of women's dignity or condemn it as a sign of women's repression, veils can have multiple meanings, serve different functions, and be used in myriad ways depending on contexts (Shiraz 2001). Elizabeth Fernea pointed out as early as the 1980s that women in Cairo were adopting the *higab* in order to escape the constraints of the domestic sphere, enter into public spaces (including mosques and schools), and enter occupations previously dominated by men without having to abandon local values of modesty and femininity for Western versions of femininity (Fernea 2002). It is important to emphasize, however, that the veil is not only a marker of *mu'adab* and *al-haya* (reserve, restraint) but is, for many women, an action that helps them to create a more pious self. While the veil manages public personhood by signifying a more modest public woman, for many women it also serves as a form of "bodily comportment considered germane to the cultivation of the ideal virtuous self" (Mahmood 2001a: 202). Finally, in adopting the *higab* or *niqab*, Egyptian women connect themselves to the millions of previously unveiled Muslim women globally who have begun to take the veil as a sign of their common identities as Muslim women and as acts of pious self-discipline. In addition to its purely local functions, veiling can be seen as creating a gendered but "global public space of reference and debate" (Bowen 2002: 879) and hence, for a handful of women at AUC, as an attempt to manage the balance between the modernity represented by the American University and new forms of religious authenticity coming to Egypt from elsewhere in the Islamic world.

THE AUTHENTICITY OF AUTHENTICITY

The problem faced by the fictional character Khalaf in *Sa'idi fil Gama'a al-Amrikiyya* is a problem confronted by countless Egyptians: pursuing the balance between a social mobility characterized by cosmopolitanism and the limits of one's globalization—and thus the core of one's rootedness in a place or people. Modernity and authenticity are continually contested, and their proper balance must be perpetually negotiated. New practices of speech, dress, consumption, education, and uses of technology emerge as significant indexes of both cosmopolitanism and authenticity. Interior character, Egyptian nationalism, and transnational Islam all offer repertoires of symbolic actions that can be drawn on in particular situations to root a person's authenticity. But authenticity—like cosmopolitanism and modernity—"is a field of contestation rather than an essence" (Salamandra 2004: 4). Admonishing a girlfriend, posting a funny photo about Egypt to a website, or covering one's face with a sheet of notebook paper are performative activities that generate links between persons and social meanings. At the same time, they link one to other persons who draw on the same or similar repertoires for their own performances. Yet, ultimately, all these authenticities are continually subject to various public interpretations. Identities are constructed not merely through the enactment of cultural categories but through performances that can be reinterpreted by an audience drawing on metadeictic discourses that interpret and reinterpret actions. The biggest challenge for Egyptian cosmopolitans seeking to find the limits of their Westernization is that the authenticity of one's authenticity is always in doubt.

Advertising of global and local products
is ubiquitous in the Cairene cityscape.

Above. International chains serve cosmopolitan consumers
and upwardly mobile members of the middle class.

Below. In Egypt, every fast-food company delivers orders to customers.

5

COFFEE SHOPS AND GENDER
IN TRANSLOCAL SPACES

"These towers are for the very rich," Maged told me, pointing to the thirty-two-floor First Residence complex adjoining the First Mall shopping complex in Giza. "The flats cost $3 million, just for one. Inside, there are elevators for automobiles, so they can rise up to their flats. And on the rooftop, there are helicopters. If there is trouble, they can fly out of the country."

I'd asked Maged to drive me to see the towers and the First Mall complex after my curiosity was aroused by a research paper written by one of my undergraduate students at the American University in Cairo. Yasmin, whose father was one of the investors in the complex, had spent weeks visiting Cairo's luxurious First Mall, interviewing staff and customers, and had concluded that the complex is a site of spectacle on three different levels. At one level, the buildings themselves are spectacles, demonstrations to Egyptians and foreigners alike that Egypt is a part of the global flow of commodities and has shopping malls as luxurious as anything boasted by London, New York, or Paris. Second, the shops are sites for displays of goods, a vast array of luxurious clothes, shoes, and other commodities from around the world. Finally, the First Mall is a place in which wealthy elites display themselves to one another in all their finery (on one occasion, when Yasmin asked a friend to go to the First Mall with her, she was refused because the friend "didn't want to get dressed up"). These levels, moreover, interrelate: for businesspeople, the status of the First Mall as spectacle makes having a branch of their retail store there a prestige marker, even when it is not the most lucrative branch. To visit the mall, to see and be seen, is also to expose yourself to objects of desire, and, of course, the objects on display are just the sorts of clothes and accessories in which one might wish to display oneself in a place like the First Mall. The First Mall is thus a self-contained world of consumption in which one exchanges economic for social capital. The residential towers attached to it—allowing one to literally live at the mall—just add to this sense of overwhelming splendor.

But the construction of class through consumption is not only about the accumulation of goods and the display of taste. It is also about the exclusion of those who cannot, and should not, be shopping here. My interest in the First Mall developed in part from the fact that the place is not only beyond Maged's experience but likely to remain so, since even in his best clothes he would be unable to pass the scrutiny of the security guards at the entrance.[1] Hence his tall tales about the First Mall. False though they may be in their specifics, Maged's stories concretize a reality of his world: members of the economic, social, and political elite—like those who take my classes at AUC and those who live and shop at the First Mall—live in places from which the poor and middle classes are excluded, except those who work in them as clerks and security guards.[2] Even though their Mercedes and SUVs contribute to the noise and pollution of Cairo, in Maged's tales these cars are literally lifted up and out of it.[3] From their vantage points above, the rich who own these cars can look down on teeming Cairo, and if the masses get out of hand, they can escape by flying even higher and crossing borders that, troublesome though they may be for most Egyptians, are open to the cosmopolitan elite.

Men of Maged's class frequently articulate experiences of *abjection,* "the combination of an acute awareness of a 'first class' world, together with an increasing social and economic disconnection from it" (Ferguson 2002: 559). Men like Maged manage this awareness in part by embedding their interpretations of elite Egyptians in moral universes. Working-class people often narrate tales that construct those who inhabit spaces like the First Mall as moral opposites. Maged assumes that no one comes by so much wealth honestly, and that such people are the sources of the corruption of Egyptian society. The children of the rich are often indecent, idle, frivolous, and selfish. He agrees with the ASC students that Cairene society is "shitty" (*zibala*) and "chaotic" (*hamagy*) but would put much of the blame on them and their parents. When Maged spoke to me about Egypt's downward spiral, I shared with him some of the things my students had said about this over the years. He was incredulous. How could those who have so much complain about the society? In a wide-ranging conversation containing allusions to several movies, including the Egyptian classic

Banat al-Yom (*The Girls of Today*) and *Titanic,* he emphasized that the Egyptian upper classes were corrupt, the women immodest and the men effeminate. Most of Egypt's population, like Maged, know the cosmopolitan elites who control most of the country's wealth only through fleeting glimpses, mediated representations, tall tales, and the fabulous exteriors of establishments from which they are excluded.

For upper-class Egyptians and those professional upper-middle-class Egyptians with upwardly mobile ambitions, the exclusion of the middle and lower classes creates social spaces in which they can construct cosmopolitan identities apart from the disapproving moral gaze of the wider public. At the heart of the First Mall is an elegant and expensive coffee shop, La Gourmandise.[4] It is from here, dressed in their most expensive clothes, sipping espresso made from beans imported from Latin America while nibbling on locally baked "French" pastries, that the members of Cairo's cosmopolitan class who frequent the mall observe their shopping peers. Places like this café are sites where consumption not only takes place, but is displayed as a form of social capital. European and American coffee shops are interesting sites because by sipping lattés and espressos people are not only purchasing goods and services but purchasing an exclusive site in which to consume them. Coffee shops, certain restaurants, shopping malls, and resorts are venues whose prices and atmosphere (and sometimes security measures) almost ensure that the public who views one's performances of identity will be of similar background, giving cosmopolitan Cairenes some control over their displays of identity. Moreover, such contexts of consumption offer particularly gendered ways of displaying cultural capital, since mixed-gender socializing is one of the hallmarks of a cosmopolitan lifestyle. Finally, modern coffee shops are especially interesting because of their contrasts with *'ahawi baladi,* the traditional, male-dominated sidewalk coffee houses (singular: *'ahwa*) in which Egyptian men have for centuries constructed their social identities.

Coffee houses of different kinds are sites of gender performance, places where particular kinds of masculinity and femininity are constructed. As my conversation with Maged illustrates, elite appropriations of global modernity are popularly associated with immodesty for women, and sometimes with effeminacy for men. Modern coffee shops on the Starbucks model offer spaces where professional women can socialize both with one another and with men in an environment that is "safe" from the public gaze and the loss of status and *mu'adab* that comes from mixing with the lower classes. The opening of these spaces to women, and mixed-sex socializing, however, make them uncomfortable sites for performances of masculinity among many upper-class men, especially young professional men who have the means to marry but have not yet done so. For some of these men, the *'ahwa*, where men have traditionally gathered to socialize for centuries, becomes a counter-site where they can engage in performances asserting their masculinity against the public scrutiny of men like Maged.

The new "coffee shops"—always referred to by the English term—signify in at least three different ways: *indexically* through their contiguity with a global commodity chain (the bidirectional links that connect producers and consumers worldwide; Gereffi and Korzeniewicz 1994; Bestor 2001; Samper 2003); *iconically* by their resemblance to similar places in Cairo and throughout the world; and *contrastively* by their similarities to and differences from the traditional *'ahawi*, those bastions of masculine public space. To enter a coffee shop in Cairo is to enter a translocal space, at once of Cairo and not of Cairo. In so doing, one constructs a cosmopolitan identity, both to self and others, by being able to afford entry into such a space and by being comfortable in it—that is, knowing one's place in the world. But I particularly want to contrast the coffee shop and the *'ahwa* to explore intersections between the social exclusion of the *bi'a* (vulgar) and *sha'bi* (popular) classes and the gendered construction of cosmopolitan identity in Egyptian translocal spaces. While the exclusion of the middle and working classes provides a safe site for young professional women to engage in leisure activity outside the home, the club, and the workplace, the very presence of so many women, combined with the traditional association of wealth with effeminacy, leads some cosmopolitan men to enter into the popular space of the *'ahwa* to reassert their masculinity.

Class and gender are thus mutually constructed. Mixed-gender socializing is an important part of the cosmopolitan style that serves as social capital for Cairene elites, yet it poses a particular problem for women, for whom participation in leisure activities with men risks a loss of their reputation as decent (*mu'adab*). The wealth of the professional classes allows them access to commodified spaces like exclusive malls and coffee shops where class and gender identities can be performed before selected audiences of peers. Yet the entrance of women into these spaces feminizes them, creating for some men the difficulty that their cosmopolitan style contributes to a loss of masculinity, which can be managed by mingling with the very classes excluded from the malls and coffee shops.

MANLY COSMOPOLITANS

You can tell Ahmed is a regular because when we enter, the *'ahwagi* (head-waiter) hurries to greet him with a flowery: "Hello, master of men and women." Ahmed responds, "Greetings, boss," as we enter the small building. We are immediately hailed by his friends, most of whom I recognize from my previous visit, and we walk over to take a seat with them. Ahmed calls out to the *'ahwagi, "Hat shisha salum wa an-nabi"* (Give me a *shisha* with plain tobacco please),[5] to which the *'ahwagi* responds, *"Minawwar ya pasha"* (You light up the place, O pasha). Ahmed returns, *"Bi-nurak"* ([It's lit up] by *your* light). The young men have cups of tea, and Ahmed orders one as well. I am the only one who orders coffee.

One of the young men, Khaled, turns to Ahmed as we sit down. "So I hear you sucked your teacher's dick for that 'A.'" Ahmed shakes his head. "Ha ha, you're really funny. Don't say this in front of the doctor." "I didn't give you an 'A,'" I say. "They must mean some other doctor." Samir says, "Yeah, I heard the same story, only I heard you let him fuck you." Karim says, "Guys, let him alone. This is Ahmed's only way to succeed in life." "Fuck you all!" Ahmed shouts. The whole group bursts into laughter, Ahmed included.

When the *shisha* comes, the boys are appalled that I don't have a personal *mabsam*, the rubber mouthpiece that covers the tip of the pipe. "You can't use the ones from here," Ahmed warns me. Out come the *mabasim* (plural of *mabsam*), in little cellophane packages, and everyone vies to convince me that his color is the best. Once I've selected a mouthpiece—an auspicious green from Karim—the conversation turns to movies we have seen. I settle back to listen. They speak primarily of U.S. films, only once mentioning an Egyptian movie. They take it for granted that everyone will have seen the same Egyptian comedies—in fact, several of the friends will have gone together. Foreign films are different; a guy might see one at an upscale theater with a date, or watch a banned film on video or DVD. Every time anyone shares an opinion of a film or piece of music, one or two of the others immediately begin deriding it. Then, Samir opens his bag and shows us his new Metallica tape (*Garage Inc.*), which turns the conversation to music.

My charcoal goes out and I raise my hand to order more. The boys laugh at me and mock my polite order for more charcoal, making me sound prim and fussy. Samir shows me how it is supposed to be done: "*Hat wal'am!*" (Get me some fire!), he shouts to the waiter, pointing at his own *shisha*. "Or you can say *sahu!*" (Wake it up!), says Ahmed.

Ahmed and Karim start a game of backgammon. The players insult each other throughout the game ("I'm fucking you up the ass, now"), while the others watch and mock every roll of the dice, every movement of the tokens ("What are you doing? You must be mentally retarded"). When Karim wins, he screams and laughs in Ahmed's face. The others join in with a barrage of insults. But when the next game begins, I notice that nearly all the insults are aimed at Karim, as if by winning he made himself a target.

At last Khaled says he needs to get to a class, "unless the doctor here will write me an excuse." I shake my head. "I can't write you an excuse for fear of rumors about how you got it," I tell him. Everyone laughs and begins to gather up their bags. The headwaiter appears, saying "*Khalih ya bey . . . khalih w'allah*" (Keep your money . . . in God's name, keep it). The students respond, "*Allah yikhallik*" (May God preserve you), but they ignore his request, as he expects them to. Everyone pays for their own *shisha* and drinks, and the combined tip is well over two pounds.[6]

'Ahawi, traditional or *baladi* coffee houses, are visible every few blocks throughout Cairo. Rodenbeck (1999) points out: "Only one Cairo institution is more common than the mosque: the *qahwa* or coffee house. Statistics are less accurate now than when Napoleon's army counted 1,350 coffee houses in the City of a Thousand Minarets, but the ratio of 200 citizens per café has not declined much. By this reckoning, the cafés of modern Cairo must number well over 30,000" (263). A typical *'ahwa,* if there is such a thing, is marked primarily by its openness. Although a few "modernized" *'ahawi* in high-rent districts like Mohandiseen are entirely enclosed shops, complete with air conditioning, the vast majority are open on one or more sides. A street *'ahwa* is typically open on one side if it is in the middle of the block,

on two sides if it is on a corner. Some newer 'ahawi in malls and food courts are open on three or even all four sides. The openness of the 'ahwa extends beyond the shops onto the sidewalks, with tables and chairs sometimes extending even into the street. Tables are usually small, just large enough to hold a chess or backgammon board. The 'ahawi basically sell two things: drinks—coffee and tea—and shisha. Against one wall—or occasionally in an adjoining kitchen—every 'ahwa has a space where powdered coffee, laced with habahan (cardamom), is boiled in a kanaka and poured into tiny cups, which are served with a water chaser. Tea is even more popular than coffee, and many different varieties are available.[7] Shay bi-na'na' (mint tea) is the most popular, waiters tell me, followed by regular tea, then shay mezza (tea with milk). I once heard someone order shay tayyara (airplane tea), which the waiter explained meant that it was made with a tea bag.

On a shelf or against a wall are the water pipes. Shisha is one of the primary reasons for going to an 'ahwa. Men sit in circles, drawing smoke from tasseled pipes, then puffing out the smoke. Tobacco comes in many flavors. Salum (plain tobacco) and tuffah (apple flavored) are the most popular, but mango, cherry, orange, banana, and molasses flavored tobaccos are also available at most 'ahawi. There is a lore to smoking shisha—it is said to be less harmful than cigarettes because the water filters out the harmful effects of nicotine, for example—and a language and set of practices for smoking it. The habitual shisha smoker does not simply order shisha but calls out some hyperbolic phrase, which is answered in kind by the waiter.

Every 'ahwa I have ever entered has had a television. In the daytime, it is often tuned to old movies; in the evening to news and sports. In most 'ahawi, the volume is low to encourage conversation, although it is cranked up for major sports events so that it can be heard even by people in the streets. 'Ahawi are usually at their most crowded during these televised sports events. Besides television, it is common for an 'ahwa to have chess and backgammon sets, decks of cards, and dominoes.

'Ahawi are examples of institutions comprising the public sphere, places "where private individuals come together as public" (Habermas 1989: 27). But such public spaces are not the transparently social sites Habermas seems to imply in much of his writing. Rather, while creating the public, they do so in ways that reproduce such social phenomena as gender and class differentiation. Certainly, this is true of the Egyptian 'ahwa, which is one of the most significant forms of Egyptian public space, a site where social networks are formed and reinforced.

Farid, who works as a waiter at an upscale 'ahwa downtown, off Tahrir Square, spends his evenings after his children go to bed at the 'ahwa on the first floor of his apartment building in the Abu Khalifa neighborhood in Ghamra. Farid earns about 20 pounds per day, and spends about two and a half pounds each day hanging out at the 'ahwa, buying his round of tea or coffee for his brother-in-law and their friends, and smoking one or two pipes of shisha. The expenditure of more than 10 percent of his daily income is not only worthwhile, but seems to be as much a necessity as food and clothing, for it is here he ceases to be Farid the waiter and becomes Farid the man. It is here he is called by his nickname, Maru'a (Generous).[8] It is here that he is able to see himself reflected in the eyes of the men who love him. Most men have an 'ahwa in their neighborhood that serves such a function, operating as what Oldenburg (1989) calls "the great good place," a "third place" between home and workplace where social solidarity is built.

Young men of the cosmopolitan class are frequently less rooted in neighborly sociality, but may, like Ahmed and his friends, still rely on the 'ahwa as a site for building and displaying social cohesion. The insults with which the young men greet one another are phrases which would lead to violence in other settings; here, "Mother fucker, I haven't seen you for a long time," or "You're like your father, a faggot," function as indexes of friendship, since only a real friend is allowed to say such things without inviting violent reprisal. For the most part, these conversations are in English, which Ahmed told me keeps the meanings of the words from shocking the older men and those of the lower classes, who are often presumed to be disapproving of such language. This explanation is a bit disingenuous. In novels, films, and cartoons, 'ahawi are notorious for coarse language, and the young men's verbal behavior, if a bit over the top, is not out of place. Swearing in English is, of course, as much about displaying facility in a prestigious code as it is about protecting the sensibilities of the virtuous poor, whom Ahmed is constructing as the "other."

If Ahmed and his friends see someone they know—or even someone whose dress and bearing suggest he is of their class—they will invite him to join them. If he puts them off, preferring to drink or smoke alone, they will make jokes about his manhood. In one incident I observed, a student put on a faux Austrian accent and accused the solitary smoker of being a "girly man," an intertextual quotation from a *Saturday Night Live* sketch, which only members of the cosmopolitan class would be expected to recognize. The mocking idioms of incest, homosexuality, and effeminacy that recur in the byplay between these young men draw attention to the fact that, for cosmopolitan young men, mixing with the other classes at the *'ahawi* is at least in part about cementing their masculinity. Because they don't actively labor and are associated with Western lifestyles, elite men are said to be *foffy* or *khalawati* (effeminate, homosexual), and are often represented as such in popular media.[9] Many terms for labeling upper-class men, such as *ibn azzawat* or *infitahi,* have traditionally been associated with frivolity, sloth, and effeminacy, and many films and other forms of popular culture contrast men who are modern but effete with men who have found a balance between their modernity and their masculinity (rooted in such Egyptian values as *shaham*).[10] The use of accusations of homosexuality and femininity in performances designed to construct masculine identities is well established in literatures on manhood (e.g., Adams 1993). The playful attacks these men make on one another's masculinity is intended to cement that masculinity by demonstrating that they are "man enough" to take it, and give it back. Significantly, these performances are carried out before a mixed-class male public, the very audience most likely to regard young cosmopolitan men in stereotypical ways.

Masculinity, as de Beauvoir points out (1972: xvi), is generally taken as the norm of social behavior, such that when one speaks of "ordinary" social action, one is speaking of the normal activities of men; only when one speaks of women is it necessary to differentiate. This has problematically influenced anthropology: "Anthropology has always involved men talking to men about men, yet until fairly recently very few within the discipline had truly examined men *as men*" (Gutmann 1997: 385). Yet masculinity, as a social identity, is as much a performance as femininity, and particular kinds of social performances can construct particular kinds of hybrid gendered identities, such as the "effeminate man" and the "masculine woman," but also the especially "masculine man" and "feminine woman" (see, e.g., Butler 1990).

Yet, while all gender is constructed in performance, specific displays of masculinity tend to occur most obviously when one's manliness is somehow in question. *Khalik gada!* (Be a man!) is a common phrase thrown at boys by Egyptian teachers. Demands that girls exhibit decency and boys manliness function at one level as a simple means of classroom control. Both phrases demand that students discipline themselves, and they can be applied by teachers seeking to address all manner of unruly behavior. However, this practice works by invoking characteristics of masculinity which are supposed to be expressed in behavior. Manliness in this context includes *shaham,* but also the ability to work hard, to shoulder burdens, and to face adversity without complaint. True masculinity is often said to only show itself in *wat al-shida* (times of adversity), so upper-class men, who presumably face less adversity in life because of their fine homes, clothes, educations, and lifestyles, have fewer opportunities to exhibit their true masculine character. Normative masculinity in Egypt involves a man's capacity to marry, to have a wife who behaves appropriately, to have children (especially sons), to support his family, and to mobilize a network of male kinsmen and friends (*wasta*) for such tasks as finding employment, meeting financial obligations, or cutting through bureaucratic red tape. In Cairo, it is often men who have not yet married, or whose wives or daughters are deemed to behave immodestly, or who have no sons, or whose wives work to help support the family, or who have few male friends who are especially prone to asserting their masculinity through particular displays.

Exhibiting manliness at the 'ahwa requires the ability to subject oneself to the continual abuse the men hurl at one another, but also to engage in the continual displays that show one is 'ishta (literally "cream" but used idiomatically to mean "cool," "sweet," or "with it").[11] Some of the young men vie with one another to offer the most outlandish compliments to the waiter as they order their drinks and *shisha.* It is particularly 'ishta for a young man to have his own *mabsam,* or rubber *shisha* mouthpiece. These come in various colors, and young men will argue about who has the best. Other conversations focus primarily on new clothes and shoes, new music, what movies one has seen. The volume of the conversations tends to rise as young men show off their new CDs or shoes, but drops when they move on to girls and gossip about people they know in common.

"From the beginning," writes Serdar Öztürk, coffee houses in the Middle East were "male public spaces that enabled transgression of power configurations. They bridged social differences by bringing together men of all social levels and lifestyles, offering ordinary people an opportunity to experience a way of life, outside the bazaar and the mosque, in a place where boundaries had not been defined by one's duties to the family and God" (Öztürk 2008: 435). Yet precisely because *'ahawi* are sites in which social classes may mingle, class displays are inevitable. It is not unusual to see men in *galabiyyas,* men in business suits of varying quality, and men in jeans and button-down shirts all sitting in the same *'ahwa.* Young men of the upper classes, like Ahmed and Karim, often make much of this rubbing together of the classes. Accessibility to the *'ahwa* is very broad because of the accessible prices, a mere twenty-five piasters on the low end, rising to a pound at the high end, and most *'ahawi* will allow a man to sit for the better part of the day nursing a single glass of tea. No one is in any doubt about who is who. Upper-class young men in jeans and polo shirts will speak respectfully, even deferentially, to older men in out-of-fashion suits or *galabiyyas* if addressed, but for the most part, people cluster with people of like dress and speech. The displays described above—code-switching between Arabic and English, displaying imported CDs, style of dress—all serve to index class. The *mabsam* not only distinguishes the upper-class young men from one another but serves to prevent them from mixing bodily fluids with the presumably lower-class people who sucked on the pipe before them.[12]

Class distinctions are evident not only in displays of commodities signifying affluence, but in social interactions between the young men and the staff at the *'ahwa.* Waiters who will chat all day with a man nursing a single cup of tea and accept its twenty-five-piaster price from an older man in a *galabiyya* will expect hefty tips from the students, totaling as much as half the price of the drinks and *shisha.* They get it, too, because these tips ensure cosmopolitan students the continued good humor and exaggerated courtesy they enjoy. On the flip side, students who feel they are being ignored by a waiter will quickly become loud and abusive, sometimes even menacing him physically. "You have to show male dominance," Ahmed said. "If you are rude to him, he'll see that he can't push you around that easily. Then the guy will treat you well and never forget your face." Although by no means universal, the notion that members of the upper classes must shout at and even physically menace members of the lower classes is frequently in evidence in Cairo. Many upper-class men and women explain that they need to treat their servants and employees thus in order to make them listen or perform their work effectively. That Ahmed should characterize the aggressive treatment of an 'ahwagi as "male dominance" emphasizes the degree to which class and masculinity are being co-constructed.

The classes have not always mingled in modern Cairo. For decades, 'ahawi were categorized as lower-class establishments, at which no upwardly mobile man, his class marked by his Westernized modernity, would ever be caught. Shechter describes how after World War I the upwardly mobile, educated classes used cigarette smoking to distinguish themselves from the shisha-smoking habitués of the 'ahwa, who represented a backward-looking world view (Shechter 2006: 122–126). At least since the early 1990s, 'ahawi have made a tremendous comeback among young men of the middle and upper classes. The contemporary hipness of shisha can be seen not only in the rising number of upscale shisha parlors in such venues as five-star hotels and luxury shopping malls, but in bumper stickers reading "I Only Smoke Shisha on Days Ending in Y" (a slogan that is meaningless if one doesn't understand English). Most upper-class men stop visiting 'ahawi as they get older and more settled in careers and family. But for young men in the liminal stage between child supervised by mother and married adult man, 'ahawi had become firmly established sites for the public display of masculine sociality by the late 1990s, when contemporary Euroamerican espresso coffee shops began to emerge.

WOMEN AMONG MEN

At no time does the masculine nature of the 'ahwa as public space become more obvious than when it is entered by women. In the twenty-first century, there have been efforts to open up some 'ahawi to women, especially in and around those public places where men and women already mingle, such as college campuses and shopping malls, and in many areas of Cairo it is no longer uncommon to see women in an 'ahwa smoking shisha. These efforts have occurred in at least three ways. First, there have been attempts by entrepreneurs to establish family-oriented 'ahawi. Second, among the educated classes, an increasing number of young women will go to the 'ahwa with men they are dating. Finally, there have been efforts by some women, including many wearing the *higab* or *niqab,* to enter into the once exclusively masculine social space of the *'ahwa.* The incorporation of *'ahawi* into shopping malls and other "modern" spaces offers interesting hybridities, as designers seek either to integrate them into the contemporary spaces (like the art gallery in the *'ahwa* of the Yamama Center) or to create kitschy representations of Bedouin life, like the tent *'ahawi* in the Marriott and Sheraton hotels.

At the Al Akkad Mall in Heliopolis, the *'ahwa* is located on an open platform just outside the main entrance of the mall. The striking feature of this *'ahwa* is its giant back-projection screen, and the deliberate orientation of tables and chairs toward the screen. One of the jokes among those who frequent the mall is that this *'ahwa* is where women park their husbands, brothers, or sons while they go shopping. But the design also invites men to bring their families, especially for movies or televised sports events. The *'ahwa* seats about fifty people, and during football games when Egypt is playing, as many as 15 percent will be women, nearly all wives and daughters accompanying their husbands or fathers. The *'ahwa* demands an EGP 10 cover charge during football games, ensuring that its customers will be comfortably affluent. While the male audience openly comments on the games, and men freely speak to those around them, women speak only to one another or to their husbands or fathers, and many sat quietly through the entire game, eyes only on the screen. Hedayat, a young AUC graduate student in sociology who watched the July 1, 2001, match between Namibia and Egypt with her family there, commented that being surrounded by men made it difficult for her to even show reactions to the game. She told me she was fascinated by the freedom with which men spoke to strangers, broke class barriers by listening to and arguing with waiters, and created an atmosphere of sociality similar to yet quite different from those that women create in their own spaces, such as the *hammam* (public bath or spa) and the salon.

Hedayat and other women enter the space of masculine sociality, but for most of them their comportment remains that expected of women in the public presence of men. Drawing on norms of *hasham* (shame), they govern themselves by behaviors that they understand will be seen as appropriately modest in the situations in which they find themselves (Abu-Lughod 1986: 108). When introduced into the masculine space of the *'ahwa*, they often remain quiet where men are loud, private where men are social, reserved where men are unruly, contained where men cross borders. What behaviors constitute appropriate modesty vary from situation to situation, but insofar as they are known and understood, they are deeply embodied (Bourdieu 1977: 87–95). Indeed, when I asked Hedayat what would have happened if some man had spoken to her about one of the plays or the score, her body answered for her, reddening before she could even speak. Yet Hedayat is comfortable and loquacious, even assertive in her interactions with young men in her graduate courses at the university. The classroom, the hair salon, and the coffee shop are sites where she feels appropriate being assertive, speaking eloquently, and gesturing expressively. For men, the *'ahwa* may open up a space of bodily freedom in which loud public displays are not only possible but offer ways of expressing masculine sociality. For many of the women sharing that space with them, the *'ahwa* presents an example of Foucault's "structural" organization of space that disciplines and regulates bodies (1979).

That what constitutes appropriate modest behavior changes from situation to situation (Ossman 2002: 77–78) makes it possible to imagine transforming the rules of appropriateness. Perhaps the most successful example of this is the mosque movement. By assuming the veil and disciplining their bodies to display modesty, pious women were able to reclaim space in the mosques, a space that had been for generations monopolized by men (MacLeod 1991; Mahmood 2005; Hafez 2003). Perhaps it is a similar impulse that motivates Karim's aunt and her friends to smoke *shisha*. In the food court of the Ma'adi Grand Mall, Karim told me, his auntie smokes *shisha* at the *'ahwa* with several other women. The family disapproves, he said, but she's a widow and no one can make her stop. The disapproving part of the family, Karim emphasized, was his parents, his uncles, and their wives, not Karim and his generation of siblings and cousins. Karim thought it was *'ishta*. "These days, almost everyone smokes *shisha*," he said. "You find it in the five-star hotels. But women, it's still disapproved of to smoke *shisha* or sit in the *'ahwa*."

Since I lived nearby, I visited the Grand Mall at least a couple of times each month, and I always checked the food courts for the women of whom Karim spoke. To some extent, it is the *shisha* that especially marks an *'ahwa* as a male domain. There are tables throughout the food court at the Grand

Mall, and women, especially young women, sit at many of them, eating French fries, licking ice cream cones, sipping sodas or coffees. There are tables where women sit with their families, and even tables with young lovers—newly married or even dating couples. Drinking tea or coffee is not, by itself, a remarkable violation of propriety. It is only when one does it in the 'ahwa, a self-contained part of the food court roped off from the rest, and when *shisha* is involved that it becomes a subject of moral discourse by families worried about their reputations.[13]

I spotted them one day, five women drinking tea and smoking *shisha*. They were dressed in sober, dark colors. All wore the *higab,* and all had translucent black scarves that they occasionally pulled across their faces, making it difficult to get a good look at them.[14] I had intended to approach and ask if I could interview them, but when I actually saw them I found that I had sufficiently acculturated to Cairene norms that some kind of male habitus kicked in and I couldn't do it. They were grouped together, laughing and talking, and seemed to invite no wider intercourse. The thought of approaching them with some lame line about knowing one of their nephews (and suppose Karim's aunt wasn't there that day?) or writing a book about 'ahawi suddenly seemed impossible, and I contented myself with interviewing the headwaiter.

"I cannot keep them out," he told me defensively, misinterpreting the intent of my question. "But they are enclosed." He gestured, and I saw what he meant. His section of the food court was marked off by ropes running through plastic posts. An extra set of posts bisected the corner where the women sat smoking *shisha,* creating a segregated "woman's quarter."

In both of these cases, entrance into the masculine public sphere of the 'ahwa involved attention to comportment. At the Al Akkad Mall, Hedayat fulfilled rules of appropriateness by being accompanied by a husband or father, and by hyper-attention to her bodily comportment. At the Grand Mall, the women covered themselves from the male gaze as a prerequisite for entry into masculine space and behavior, and even then a liminal space was improvised for them by the men in charge of the space. In both cases, women were able to be *in* masculine space without being entirely *of* it.

A much more dramatic form of hybridity involves smoking *shisha* and visiting the 'ahwa as part of dating practices. Dating and the concept of being "boyfriend and girlfriend" are powerful markers of cosmopolitanism. At AUC, couples who are "going together" take classes together, hold hands, exchange kisses (mostly on the cheeks, at least in public), and play footsie under tables. Outside the campus grounds, however, there are few places they can be together in these ways. One exception, for a small number of couples, is the *'ahawi* near campus.

Although perhaps several hundred young women at AUC date, with varying degrees of family knowledge and approval, only a handful of girls smoke *shisha,* and most of these seem to have been raised partly in Europe or the United States. Knowing that both Ahmed and Karim had such girl-friends, I asked them what young men talk about with their girlfriends at the *'ahwa.* They reported that men censor their speech when women are present—"We don't talk the same amount of filth," said Karim—but they also reported trying to teach their girlfriends the rules of *shisha* discourse, including how to "talk dirty." "At first, you go easy on her," said Ahmed, "until she picks up the habit of talking trash and insulting you." "In the future, if she ever goes to [smoke] *shisha* with some other guy, he'll be shocked that she knows how to talk like this," Karim added.[15] The men's claims reflect beliefs about the gendered nature of spaces and of the verbal and bodily practices appropriate to them. Karim's final words cut to the heart of the transgressive nature of this activity: the effect of such practices on women's reputations.

Though increasingly common, dating remains a transgressive activity, and more so for women than men. For women especially, smoking is also a transgressive activity.[16] Although many women smoke (usually cigarettes but increasingly *shisha*), they are aware of the social stigma it brings and frequently strategize their smoking according to particular spatial zones of comfort and privacy: only at home with friends, only in the car, only at certain restaurants, only on campus. Loud, aggressive, and "dirty" speech is also transgressive for women, and whether and where to use it are like-wise strategized. The young women who exhibit themselves at the *'ahwa* are thus simultaneously violating multiple norms for honorable and ap-propriate feminine behavior. This does not always sit well with their peers. "You have to admire them because they are showing that they don't give a damn," said Salma. "But all they are really doing is, everyone sees them and says, 'See? All the AUC girls are whores.'" Their public display of them-selves with men, smoking *shisha* and swearing, is a powerful technique for constructing transgressive gendered and class identities in performance, establishing their cosmopolitanism by signifying that local rules do not apply to them. Yet precisely because it is public, this display allows for the reinscription of gender ideologies by subjecting the women's performances to public critique. Salma's critique as an "AUC girl" expresses her fear that she will be tarred by her affiliation with the school that produces women who go to the 'ahwa.

'AHAWI AS TRANSLOCAL SPACE

Places like 'ahawi are socially constructed sites and they are polysemic sites, offering multiple meanings to a variety of visitors. People create such sites by investing them with meanings and then using these spaces in meaningful ways. These spaces thus mean and produce meaning at several levels. First, there is an understanding that specific sites inscribe places in ways that give them meaning. Market logics that keep 'ahawi from springing up so close to one another as to overcompete means that the density of 'ahawi becomes a good general indicator of population density. As a result, 'ahawi signify social space: Egyptians will say that every neighborhood has its 'ahwa because the presence of an 'ahwa is part of what defines a place as a neighborhood. Similarly, entrepreneurs who create coffee shops choose their locations carefully to ensure a ready clientele; once established, the coffee shop inscribes the local space as a cosmopolitan site.

Spaces often have significant semiotic dimensions at both the symbolic and social levels—and these levels are overlapping and mutually constitutive (Bourdieu 1979). In occupying these spaces, we "embody" the cultural systems they represent by disciplining (Foucault 1979) our physical persons to accommodate both the spaces and the meanings inscribed in them. By simultaneously training our minds, bodies, and emotions, we reproduce these meanings for ourselves and others in deeply embodied sets of habits (Bourdieu 1977). Learning to display oneself as masculine at an 'ahwa is thus not merely a performance; it helps the bodies of these young men become habituated to these forms of masculine comportment.

To say that some spaces in Egypt are gendered is thus a commonplace. But the gendering of space is an ongoing process, and "[t]he assertion of a traditional division of labor, with the women in the home and the men out in the business world . . . was always class based" (Abu-Lughod 2005: 142). Middle-class women may be assigned the home and the salon (Ossman 2002), but for working-class women the alleys and neighborhoods are equally women's spaces (Hoodfar 1997). The links between space and gender ideologies are complex and cannot be easily reduced to a simple dichotomy that makes masculinity public and femininity private and domestic. Gender ideologies are tied to space through particular kinds of linguistic performances and bodily practices that are appropriate to a particular place. 'Ahawi are not simply "masculine spaces"—they are appropriate places for men to display their masculinity through their verbal and bodily comportment. For many Egyptians, the entrance of women into the 'ahwa is scandalous in itself; for many others, it is *how* women occupy the space and comport themselves within it that makes their performances more or less transgressive. But the most crucial transgressive element may well be gender mixing (see, e.g., de Koning 2006). Public displays that exclude men, as at the Grand Mall, and public entries into mixed-sex spaces accompanied by a father or other close male relative, as at the Al Akkad Mall, allow for different kinds of public scrutiny, while going to an open 'ahwa with an unrelated man on a date elicits very different scrutiny even from young women who would be comfortable in the other two situations (see also Armbrust 2003, 2006). Such links between gender ideologies, spaces, and practices become transformed when new kinds of spaces emerge and new kinds of comportment can be negotiated. The emergence of Western-style coffee shops as an alternative to the 'ahwa created such new spaces in which the rules of appropriateness effective in their locales of origin no longer applied; these coffee shops are sufficiently unlike the 'ahwa to offer opportunities for new modes of gendered behavior.

These new coffee shops constitute what Low and Lawrence-Zúñiga (2003: 25) have called "translocal" spaces, sites where local and state-based notions of territoriality are dissolved. Translocal places are created through a semiotics of space that brings together one or more types of place in distinct sites. However such sites inscribe space, it cannot be quite the same way that local sites do. Whatever cosmologies and social worlds they construct, they cannot be entirely "traditional" or "local," that is, reflective of Egyptian culture (whatever that may be to different publics). And the ways people embody these spaces, and discipline themselves to these spaces, must inevitably differ from the embodiment and discipline associated with more deeply embedded local spaces.

Traditional 'ahawi were once both translocal and transgressive spaces. Brought from Yemen by Sufis in the late fifteenth and early sixteenth centuries to aid in all-night prayer (*dhikr*), sites to brew and drink coffee and to gather spread readily throughout the peninsula, North Africa, and ultimately the Muslim world. The flavor of coffee degenerates rapidly if it is allowed to cool or if kept hot for too long, so a stable kitchen is preferable to a wandering vendor with a pot. One cannot quickly quaff a scalding liquid, so benches and perhaps tables where one can sit and sip the drink are useful. Because there was no tradition of public restaurants in the sixteenth-century Middle East—decent people took their meals in their homes—the spaces that coffee houses most resembled were taverns. Taverns (*hanat*), usually run by non-Muslims ostensibly for non-Muslims, were widely understood to be places of vice and sin, and coffee houses initially partook of this reputation. Debates over the virtue of coffee and coffee houses raged throughout the sixteenth century (Hattox 1985). Such debates have recently been revived, and one can find sermons on cassette tapes that warn Muslims against coffee as a violation of the Prophet's injunction against wine (understood metonymically by these preachers to include *all* intoxicants and stimulants) or that reveal the moral risks to young men exposed to the uninstructive conversations of the 'ahwa.

Sites like Beano's and Cilantro are not the first hybrid European-style coffee houses in Egypt. During the colonial era, when "Europe, and particularly France, was the measure of all things elegant" (de Koning 2006: 227), cafés emerged to cater to the colonial's desire for a taste of home and the upper-middle-class Egyptian's taste for European-style places of leisure. A few—Groppi's, A l'Americain, and Café Riche—became Cairo institutions. Café Riche, for example, founded in 1914 by a German businessman, and subsequently renamed and operated by French expatriate Henry Recine, served for decades as a central site of intellectual and political activity (Bieber-Roberts and Pierandrei 2002). As social capital transformed in response to changes in global trends and tastes, upper-class consumers abandoned the prior sites for new commodified forms of leisure, and these old venues either closed, reinvented themselves, or became sites for consumption by the middle classes they had so long excluded. Thus, Groppi's, for generations a landmark watering hole for colonial and early postcolonial elites, is now a popular spot for dates between bearded students and their veiled wives or fiancées.Like the *'ahwa* in the sixteenth century and the colonial era cafés, the idea of coffee shops came from elsewhere and is being localized. Coffee shops designed along European or American models first emerged in the mid-1990s in imitation of the U.S. specialty coffee craze epitomized by the explosive international success of Starbucks. For expatriates, tourists, and cosmopolitan Cairenes, such coffee shops are immediately recognizable, offering tastes, smells, and appearances that closely resemble similar coffee shops worldwide. These coffee shops did not emerge to compete with the *'ahawi,* though: *'ahawi* are everywhere throughout Cairo, but coffee shops are clustered in the upscale districts of the city; *'ahawi* are relatively inexpensive, but coffee shops are very expensive; and *'ahawi* have deeply institutionalized functions and meanings, while coffee shops offer a new kind of space whose meanings and functions are open for negotiation.

Such spaces cannot simply be understood as "foreign," as part of some global standardization of space ("the global village" or "the flattened earth"), the way some literature on globalization would have us do. Theories that view growing human interconnectedness as processes of global homogenization, such as Ritzer's (1993) McDonaldization thesis, are rooted in an assumption that, for example, a McDonald's is a McDonald's is a McDonald's. To adopt such a thesis requires an assumption that the ideologies and cosmologies associated with a space are inherent in the structure of the site, rather than in the people who come to the site. A more empirically defensible approach is to recognize sites as culturally coded spaces organized to mean particular things for specific people and to function in specific ways in particular contexts. The local businesspeople who (re)create these sites locally have reasons to believe their sites will meet some desire or need among the congeries of publics in the new locality. Their novelty and their foreignness are themselves important signifiers, transforming the nature of the space. However much a McDonald's or a coffee shop in Cairo may resemble one in New York, London, or Jiddah, what it signifies locally will necessarily depend not only on that resemblance but also on its resemblance to, and differences from, various kinds of local spaces.

The key to teasing apart the many layers of the polysemy of transnational space is to focus on indexical signification. The market logic that places coffee shops in Cairo's most expensive neighborhoods—Heliopolis, Ma'adi, Mohandiseen, Zamalek—creates associations of *co-locality,* in which the coffee shops are understood by the company they keep. The iconic resemblance of coffee shops to one another, and to models in Europe and the United States, points back to these models and generates a sense of *translocality,* a resemblance to places that are other than here.[17] The tastes displayed contrast with local *'ahawi,* generating a sense of newness and difference that opens up possibilities for different kinds of social functionality. Cairo's new coffee shops are simultaneously at least three spaces: a global space that derives its meaning from its indexical connections to the global coffee commodity chain, a translocal space that signifies by its iconicity with similar sites around the world, and a local space that signifies by its contrasts with other local spaces, particularly the *'ahwa.*

IT'S ALMOST LIKE YOU'RE NOT IN EGYPT

RAGHDA: It's Westernized, it's liberal. Out there, if people see you have a boyfriend, it's not accepted. But here, we can be comfortable to come in with our boyfriends, or smoke cigarettes, you know, and it will not be out of place.

Having used *'ahawi* in a class lecture as examples of sites where male sociality is constructed and social networks built or reinforced, I found myself being taken by Gazbeya, Omneya, and Raghda to the Beano's coffee shop in El Marsafy Square to get an understanding of "where *we* [women] go for coffee and socializing." I'd been to such coffee shops many times before, but I'd come as a foreigner, seeing and using them much as I would a coffee shop back in the United States. This time, I had local guides who wanted to show me these sites as *Egyptian* coffee shops and to contrast them with the male sociality of the *'ahwa.* As we entered Beano's, the first thing they pointed out to me was the quiet. If part of the significance of the coffee shop is its difference from the *'ahwa,* one of the most dramatic differences is the way the coffee shop is cut off from the street by walls and sheets of glass. The heat and dust are further kept at bay by air conditioning. The window functions as a barrier between inside and out, between the dust, heat, and public gaze of the external world and the clean, cool, "homey" (Raghda's word) atmosphere of the shop. "You can hide away from the crowds," said Hedayat in an interview, contrasting her experience of the *'ahawi* at the Al Akkad Mall with another modern coffee shop, Cilantro. But it is not only walls and windows that make coffee shops like Beano's and Cilantro less public and more private and home-like. The coffee shops tend to be located in quieter, more affluent neighborhoods, and the young women emphasize how clean and quiet the shop is. Yet it is by no means hushed; groups of girls, mixed-gender groups, and couples occupy six of seven tables, chatting amiably, laughing, and drinking their coffees. There are twenty customers besides us, none of whom appears to be over thirty. They are grouped into two sets of two girls, a boyfriend-girlfriend couple, a male-male pair, and two mixed groups of men and women. There are seven men, three of whom are foreigners—two from the United States and one from Serbia. There is no *shisha* in evidence nor is it on the menu; the waiter looks at me doubtfully when I ask and tells me he could send someone down the street to get a pipe. Only a tiny number of coffee shops serve *shisha*,[18] and one almost never sees men or women hunched over a game of dominoes or backgammon. Instead, newspapers and magazines are available. Beano's, Cilantro, and similar coffee shops are places where people can come alone to read or study, meet a friend to chat, or arrive with their *shilla* (group of friends) for an outing.

"It's almost like you're not in Egypt any more," Omneya says. The foods arrayed in the glass display cases are certainly not local or regional foods; they include croissants, crepes, endive and Roquefort sandwiches, bottles of Perrier. There is a menu on the wall behind the display case listing coffee drinks and prices. Traditional Arab coffee with cardamom, boiled in a *kanaka,* is not available here; the beans are imported already roasted from American coffee suppliers, and the emphasis is on flavored coffees and espresso-based beverages like cappuccinos and lattés. What Ellis has called "the lactification of the coffee house" (2004: 258) is a crucial defining characteristic for distinguishing the new coffee shops from both the *'ahawi* and the older European-style coffee shops, like Groppi's and Café Riche. The menu at Beano's is in English, and I looked around the shop in vain for a word of Arabic. The reading materials in the rack by the door include the

English-language *Al-Ahram Weekly,* the *International Herald Tribune,* and a number of the glossy, ad-heavy magazines that cater to the Egyptian upper class: *Man, Cleo, Enigma, Pharaoh.* Although they draw their inspiration from such international chains as Starbucks, these new Cairene coffee shops are not clones. Many serve light meals, and the emphasis is rarely on take-away but rather on creating sit-down opportunities for social interaction.

The menu features the Beano's logo: two aromatic brown coffee beans against an orange circle. The logo is repeated on the napkins, something Gazbeya draws my attention to as a sign of "elegance." The logo does not strike me as particularly elegant in an aesthetic sense, but this is not really what she means. Logos are indexical signs. They connect advertisements and the paraphernalia of the shop—cups, napkins, menus—with the shop itself in a semiotic web. If the shop has multiple locations, as Beano's does, the logo helps fold them into this web, providing reassurance that, when one visits any location, one will find essentially the same food, beverages, and atmosphere of "quality." Finally, logos signify luxury because they signify expense. Thanks to low labor costs, putting a logo on a napkin runs a business owner about one-third less than the same process in the United States, but it is substantially more expensive in the context of Egypt's GDP. No *'ahwa* charging twenty-five or fifty piasters—or even a pound—for a glass of coffee could afford such paraphernalia. Beano's can, because the cheapest item in the shop is five pounds. Beano's offers not just a shop but a *brand.*

The creation of these new espresso-based coffee shops is a significant entrepreneurial strategy, a point I will develop further in the next chapter. With the exception of a few restaurants, there had been few places for professional men and women to sit and talk. The new coffee shops are at least in part an acknowledgment of this large gap in Cairo's urban pleasures. According to my interviews with owners and managers, Beano's was started by an Egyptian bakery chain, LePoire, specializing in supplying European-style pastries to hotels and restaurants. A few of these bakeries had small cafeterias attached where customers could get a pastry and a cup of tea. The transformation and expansion of these cafeterias into the Beano's chain was masterminded by a handful of relatively young managers with wide experience abroad who recognized a market niche for places for mixed-gender socializing among the professional class. Cilantro was likewise created as an adjunct to a successful restaurant, La Bodega, by young men who had been customers in similar coffee shops in Europe and North America. The success of the first Cilantro led to the creation of a chain of places where, in the words of one of the partners, "people could hang out with their friends."

An important part of the attraction of these shops is their imitation of key elements of similar coffee shops abroad. The notion of being "out of Egypt" was repeated again and again in my interviews with young women, and it was used in three ways. First, it was used to indicate a customer's physical separation from the phenomenal Egypt outside: the noise, the dust, the heat, the crowds. Separation from crowds leads us to the second meaning of the term, which is one's cultural separation from Egypt. The public gaze is a powerful disciplinary apparatus, felt very strongly by most Egyptians. Inside the coffee shop, women say they feel free from the burden of that gaze. From within, one can easily look out the great glass windows into the Cairene street. But glare and reflection make it difficult for those outside to look in, and in Egypt "seeing without being seen is knowledge, perhaps even power" (Gilsenan 1982: 190). Finally, being outside of Egypt indicates an economic separation, usually described in terms of "luxury" or "elegance." Most young women accepted this luxury as a good, but some older women expressed ambivalent feelings about it. Mrs. Abdel Rahman, a forty-five-year-old professional woman, mused, "These coffee [shop] owners create the illusion that one is in Europe, so you get the atmosphere and convenience for an overpriced cup of coffee. Still, it's a nice place and obviously popular with young people."

"The illusion of being in Europe" points to two other recurrent phrases linked to the coffee shop, "Westernized" and "liberal." Outside of public scrutiny, in a nonconventional space, surrounded by one's young cosmopolitan peers, women can engage in a range of practices that are difficult in less safe environments, including smoking and being with young men. Translocality (the sense that one is in a space both here and not-here) and interlocality (the capacity of a space to point to other, generically similar places) interact powerfully with co-local signifiers to create a sense of openness and newness. As translocal spaces, coffee shops open up new opportunities for social actions. But these actions are generated by understandings of the significance of the space read through sets of cultural logics that precede one's visit to the space.

OUTING AT THE *KAFI SHOB*

OMNEYA: Yeah, it's mostly a girls' place. I mean, look, those two guys are the only men here without a girl.

MARK: Is it strange to see two guys sitting together in here?

OMNEYA: Not strange . . . like, if they are close friends, maybe they want to have a chat without their other guy friends. Maybe his heart is broken, that's why girls want to have chats. [laughs] But a bunch of guys, that's a little strange, guys as an outing, because I associate it with a girls' outing. You're more likely to see girl groups. A girl with a guy, though, that's not strange.

Elsewhere in Cairo, as we've seen, "[u]nchaperoned mixed gender socializing and the presence of single women in leisure venues are generally surrounded by suspicions and restrictions" (de Koning 2006: 222). The coffee shop is one of the safe places in which women can partially resist the traditional gendered divisions of spaces. There are many public spaces that women of the upper classes are taught to avoid from childhood; many of my female students at AUC had never been on the subway, never ridden a bus, never taken a train—not even in a first-class compartment. Indeed, these activities are transgressive acts for most upper-class Egyptian women seeking to be *mu'dab* because they involve a mixing with working-class people that is itself compromising to morals and honor. In a city where women's moral "reputations are the stock subject of whispered gossip and constant concern" (ibid.: 231), Gazbeya, Omneya, and Raghda all agree that the new coffee shops offer a comfortable space in which it is "appropriate" for girls to go on outings together, in mixed-sex groups, or even with young men. They make explicit the problem of the public gaze, that is, the public scrutiny of the middle and working classes, in contrasting coffee shops with *'ahawi*. According to Gazbeya, in an *'ahwa*, "I'm in public, it defeats the whole purpose. I wouldn't be secluded, wouldn't be able to smoke, can't sit comfortably. I'm going to be sitting with everybody else, the people passing by." "It's not as decent to be on the street," adds Omneya. "I don't find anything [morally] wrong in it, but it's not accepted socially, [it's] vulgar, could mean you're rebellious, could mean that you do other things too. It's just the image. Like smoking in public, even though

I'm not against it, even though I smoke, I avoid appearing smoking." "Because it suggests that because you're smoking, you can assume she's been exposed to bad influences, like sinful acts, not in the right crowd, exposed to other incorrect things," says Gazbeya. "But in Beano's, you can smoke because it's a younger crowd, more Western, more liberal." As with the men at the 'ahwa, class and gender are mutually constructed.

And just as the masculinity of the 'ahwa is emphasized by the occasional presence of women, so the behavior of men in a coffee shop can demonstrate its femininity. First, Egyptian men don't frequent coffee shops as women do. I paid nine visits to coffee shops in 2000 to record customer demographics and only once found more than half of the customers to be Egyptian men. This number dropped to under one-quarter for single men or small groups of men unaccompanied by a woman. But the femininity of the coffee shop isn't just a matter of demographics—it is also a matter of how men behave toward and talk about coffee shops. None of the young men with whom I went to the 'ahwa, for example, frequented coffee shops except in mixed-sex groups. I met one of them, Samir, one day on AUC's Greek Campus sitting with a group of other men. He was drinking a cappuccino from Seattle Coffee House, across the street from campus, and in response to my question told me he liked the coffee but not the shop.

MARK: Why not?

SAMIR: Boring atmosphere, it's closed in. Overall, I don't like it, which is why I don't go very often.

MARK: Do you go to any of the coffee shops? To sit, I mean, not just grab a cappuccino and go.

SAMIR: Yes, I've been to Harris [Café] a couple of times with my girlfriend; she likes to go there.

MARK: But you don't go without her?

SAMIR: No, not at all, because when I do something with my friends, it doesn't need to be all talk like with girls. It's amazing how they always find something to talk about and people to gossip about.

MARK: So it's more of a girls' place?

SAMIR: Yes.

MARK: Why do you think so?

SAMIR: *Mish 'arif 'ishtayanni* [I don't know, it just is].

MARK: What do guys do instead of going to coffee shops? I mean, what alternatives—

SAMIR: PlayStation, go to an *'ahwa,* play sports. An *'ahwa* is more social, *shisha* is good, it's in the street. . . . Coffee shop is all closed up, it's too close to a traditional restaurant.

MARK: But a girl can't go to an *'ahwa.*

SAMIR: They could go but [for] *'ishta;* the people are close-minded so it wouldn't be appropriate for them to go. A coffee shop is more liberal, more Westernized.

The very things that make Omneya, Gazbeya, and Raghda feel comfortable are those that make Samir uncomfortable. Samir knows how to comport himself in a coffee shop because he's been to them in Europe and the United States. But in Egypt, the bodily disciplines that make coffee shops appropriate for women make them less attractive to him. Samir expresses this difference as a gendered distinction between active and passive, but also between open and closed. A cosmopolitan woman's outing is to a closed place from which many Egyptians are excluded, where the primary activity is talk. A man's outing is to a place open to men of different classes where the primary activity is play. Samir goes to coffee shops to buy coffee, but he only stays if he is with his girlfriend. Thus, just as women may feel that entering masculine space raises issues about their moral character, men who enter feminine space may feel their masculinity is challenged. Similarly, men who go to hairdressers, a traditionally feminine space, usually don't talk about the experience as women do (Ossman 2002: 89). The association of coffee shops with professional women adds to gender ambiguities; some men may find their masculinity compromised in the eyes of some Egyptian publics by the economic power of the women.

But coffee shops are not inherently feminine, and specific coffee shops can be colonized by men. Noha told me that she used to love to visit the Cilantro coffee shop on the first floor of her apartment building. Then, over the course of just a few weeks, its character changed. It became increasingly inhabited by "men with beards, who look at you like you don't belong there." Egyptian men are traditionally clean-shaven, and a beard is taken by many to be a sign that the man is particularly religious, perhaps a student at Al-Azhar. Noha's story was meant to indicate how the shop had ceased to be a place safe from particular types of masculine gaze, requiring her to shift to another Cilantro branch farther from her home but closer to her place of work.

COFFEE CLASS

> GAZBEYA: Look at the check. I think it says a lot about this place and the people who go here. We had three drinks and a sandwich, and the check amounts to 30 pounds.
>
> MARK: Showing [what]?
>
> GAZBEYA: Showing that this type of coffee shop is aimed at a crowd who can afford to pay substantial amounts of money in outings. By Egyptian standards, this would be considered fairly expensive.

As they are in many settings, the upper-class habitués of coffee shops are uncomfortable directly addressing issues of class that might set them apart from the masses of Egypt. Euphemisms like Gazbeya's "crowd who can afford to pay substantial amounts of money" and Omneya's coy reference to "people of a certain class" abound when the discussion begins to touch on people like themselves, who think nothing of spending on a single snack more than a waiter like Farid makes in a single day. The difference between people of one class and another is a crucial distinction of space and place.

Places are polysemic, just as commodities are. And, of course, places can be commodities. As commodities, they signify particular meanings through the distinctions created by those who enter the commodified space and those who demonstrate a different taste by not consuming the space. An even more fundamental meaning is created by the distinction between those who can indulge in such a choice and those for whom even the possibility of such consumption is inconceivable.

Both *'ahawi* and coffee shops connect Cairo to the global coffee commodity chain, but in vastly different ways. Egyptians during the period of
my fieldwork spent $400 million on tea per year and nearly $500 million
on coffee (Euromonitor 2001: 91). Coffee imports for the *'ahawi* are dominated by the Yemeni Coffee House. The basic import is arabica beans from
Yemen, although other varieties from other places are available. These are
roasted, mixed with cardamom, and ground at small open shops scattered
throughout Cairo.

Coffee shops get their beans from different links in the world coffee
distribution network, and they often make it a point to gather representations of different links in the global coffee commodity chain and display
them. Such efforts include the common practice of naming coffees after
their putative places of origin, or covering the shop walls with photographs
of coffee being grown, harvested, roasted, and shipped from exotic locales,
as did El Greco's in Ma'adi. Alternatively, a coffee shop may emphasize a
particular origin, as did the Seattle Coffee House, which advertised that
all its beans were roasted in and shipped from Seattle, Washington, in the
United States.

This intertwined distinction of place and price between the *'ahwa*
and the coffee shop is not without significance since the spread of coffee,
which can be grown only in the tropics, fits naturally within the colonial
division of labor: "entirely produced in tropical countries, transported on
metropolitan ships, re-exported to countries without colonies of their own,
and mainly consumed in the West" (Topik and Clarence-Smith 2003: 6).
Because, in essence, "poor countries have grown coffee for rich countries"
(2), the translocal coffee shop places one in the rich, receiving world, while
the *'ahwa* is part of a smaller, cheaper regional exchange system. This is
expressed not only through texts and images in the coffee shops but by
the expense of the drinks: the drinks are paying not only for the more
expensive espresso technologies but for the more expensive coffee beans.
The 1000 percent markup one pays to drink coffee in a coffee shop instead
of an *'ahwa* is not only payment for a particular flavor of beverage but pays
one's entrance into one link in the commodity chain rather than another,
less valued link.

Critics in Europe and North America have complained that Star-
bucks-style coffee shops exclude working-class youths. "Their high prices,

understated décor and gourmet products mean that they appeal to affluent young professionals with particular forms of cultural literacy. The 'Seattle speak' which identifies particular coffee types ('mocha,' 'latte,' 'Americano') and sizes ('tall,' 'grande,' 'venti') offer[s] customers a reassuring sense of initiation and exclusivity" (Moran 2006: 567). Similarly, Rose argues that "the boutique economy they have constructed involves a process of class formation, where the accoutrements of the avant-garde are use[d] to distance and distinguish culture workers from more traditional manual workers" (2001: 464). For Cairenes, the capacity to develop these tastes and literacies is simultaneously about distancing themselves from the working classes and about being like their professional counterparts in the United States and the United Kingdom.

COFFEE SHOP COSMOPOLITAN

In Cairo, for upper-class and upwardly mobile Egyptians, Western-style coffee shops are simultaneously three kinds of places. First, coffee shops are gendered spaces which can be construed as more feminine by contrast with the traditionally more masculine 'ahawi. Second, coffee shops are translocal spaces, sites that index other locations to such an extent that to enter one is "almost like not being in Egypt any more." Finally, coffee shops, by virtue of their commodification and their cost in comparison with the distribution of wealth in Egypt, are exclusively places for the upper and upper-middle classes. The coffee shop does not replace the 'ahwa, but coexists beside it, and signifies in part through this coexistence. It opens up new spaces for sociality for professional women and for mixed-sex social gatherings, and thus offers some degree of innovation in public space. Yet its translocality and its place in the local market economy determine that it is an innovation that is available to members of the upper classes alone.

This contrast between the 'ahwa and the coffee shop offers a privileged locus for observing the relationships among gender, morality, class, and consumption among cosmopolitans in global Cairo. The coffee shop offers a public space for elite women because they cannot enter the public spaces that non-elite women enter routinely—government offices, subways, buses, and so forth—without risking both their feminine decency and their cosmopolitan style. Part of what is transgressive in elite women's entrance into these public spaces is precisely the mixing with the lower classes it would entail. Avoidance of the lower classes is crucial for upper-class women's honor. Since the lower classes are necessarily excluded from the coffee shop both by price and by familiarity, upper-class women can be cosmopolitan and honorable at the same time. Indeed, one could argue that they must be cosmopolitan to be honorable; cosmopolitanism (as locally defined) is essential to the construction of femininity of upper-class Egyptian women.

In contradistinction, young Egyptian men of the upper classes go to the 'ahwa to construct their masculinity by mixing with the lower classes. Because they don't actively labor and because they are associated with the cosmopolitan lifestyles so crucial to upper-class women's honor, they are often characterized in popular discourses as effeminate and childish. Slumming at the 'ahwa allows them to perform simultaneously their elite status—expressed through their English-Arabic code-switching and their displays of material goods and Western media commodities—and their masculine comportment (by swearing, insulting each other, speaking loudly, and bullying waiters).

Coffee shops are not unique, but they provide one notable example of the many kinds of places in which upper-class Egyptians can express and construct their cosmopolitan identities. Coffee shops, malls, certain restaurants, selective shops, exclusive clubs, resorts, bars, and discos all offer closed, class-specific sites whose cost and translocality of style create opportunities for the upper class to reproduce itself through the acquisition of cosmopolitan style as expressed in consumption. Consumption is not only a rational means of meeting needs or maximizing individual benefits through market preferences. Consumption is understood as being differently construed by different groups within particular social contexts, and in the current transnational and global milieu, consumption is often an indexical process linking persons not only to local social meanings but simultaneously to transnational categories of meaning.

6

THE GLOBAL AND THE MULTILOCAL: DEVELOPMENT, ENTERPRISE, AND CULTURE BROKERS

In 2005, two rumors spread among upper-class Egyptians regarding Cilantro, the fastest-growing coffee chain in Cairo. The first was that it had been bought by Starbucks, and that the Cilantro logo and decor would soon be replaced by the green-and-white mermaid logo that has become globally ubiquitous from Seattle to Paris to Dubai. The second rumor was that the Cilantro chain had been bought by a prominent Egyptian businessman who was famous for his Islamist views and that the doors were going to be closed to unveiled women. As is often the case, the rumors were exaggerations of actual incidents. In an interview in 2005, one of the founders of the Cilantro chain explained to me that Starbucks had indeed made an offer for the chain, although they ultimately chose not to accept it.[1] The businessman in the second rumor, head of one of the wealthiest families in Egypt, had not bought Cilantro but had invested in the chain as a silent partner, allowing the founders to move ahead with their ambitious expansion plans (without imposing a dress code).

The rumors reflect two central concerns about globalization in Cairo: fears that commercial modernity will be too global, becoming a kind of imperialism, and fears that it will become too local (that is, too middle class), robbing it of the translocal character necessary to serve as elite social capital. Underlying these fears is an important fact known to many of Cairo's elites but often obscured in discourses about globalization produced both by foreigners and by Egyptians: flows of transnational popular culture are not so much cases of foreign imperialism imposing itself on helpless Egyptians as they are processes managed by Cairene entrepreneurs, who are making a buck while creating the kinds of environments they and their families need to socially construct themselves as cosmopolitan.[2]

EGYPT AND THE ENTERPRISE CULTURE

Cilantro was created in 1999 by a group of four friends, three of whom were AUC students and one of whom was educated at a culinary school in the United States. "It all started as an idea," one of them told me in an interview in 2005. "We were traveling . . . in New York and Europe, and we thought, 'why don't we create a restaurant . . . , a place where you can have fun at.'" The result was a trendy, successful, European-style bistro called La Bodega in Cairo's upscale Zamalek area. Underneath the restaurant was a small shop: "We thought we'd take it and do something with it. And at that time we were thinking we'd create a little delicatessen, . . . and that we'd go and buy some gourmet-ish items and sell it here in Egypt where it wasn't available." These gourmet items "got stuck in customs and never made it out. So we had the shop ready and didn't know what to do with it. So we thought, why not start with a coffee machine? And we had a bakery here at the restaurant, and we offer[ed] some croissants and things like that." So Cilantro opened in 2000 not as a delicatessen but as a coffee shop, selling espresso-based beverages, baked goods, fresh sandwiches, and salads. Its success stimulated the partners to open more outlets, and within five years Cilantro had seventeen locations around Cairo. "And now it's a huge corporation with 450 employees where me and my other managing partner are completely devoted to Cilantro. La Bodega is now being taken care of [by] a French manager, she knows her stuff, and it's thriving. We're concentrating on Cilantro because we saw the potential for it to grow as a chain."

In this narrative, enterprising young Egyptians draw on their cosmopolitan experiences to recognize a market niche and exploit it. Their travels and education have made it possible for them to locate foreign models and re-create them in the local context. This story reflects, and contributes to, a larger discourse about entrepreneurship, cosmopolitan character, and development that organizes much of contemporary Egyptian economic activity, at least in those areas we perceive as being about globalization. Of particular significance is the way that Cilantro is described as having emerged not from careful planning but from the exploitation of the particularities of the Egyptian setting. In Egypt, one usually buys a particular building or portion of a building rather than leasing space; as a result, the owners had an empty space to fill, which became Cilantro. The disruption

of their original plans for a deli by Egypt's Byzantine import-export regulations led to a rapid reformulation of plans. Finally, the recognition that
their coffee shop was filling a hitherto unperceived market need and that
it represented a relatively low-investment, high-return project led them to
reconceive their business plan to center not on the original restaurant but
on the rapid growth of the hastily but successfully invented coffee chain.

The founders of Cilantro describe their success by using a master narrative of entrepreneurship currently celebrated in key Egyptian economic
discourses, especially those put forward by proponents of economic liberalization within the government and by international institutions guiding
Egypt's economic development. These young men exhibit the entrepreneurial imagination and thus demonstrate the growth of an Egyptian enterprise
culture that can drive Egypt's current phase of economic development.
Enterprise culture in contemporary economic discourse has two primary
meanings. On one hand, it refers generally to "energetic faith in the forces of
the free market and the corresponding ethos of competitive individualism"
expressed in "active citizenship through forms of consumption, individualism and property ownership . . . along with the massive privatization of
public services and an attack on the so-called 'dependency culture' fostered
by the welfare state" (Franklin 1990: 18–19). This is labeled in the United
Kingdom as "Thatcherism" and in the United States as the "Washington
consensus." But the term enterprise culture is also used by businesspeople
to describe a particular kind of organizational system in which people take
creative and imaginative approaches to problems, thinking outside the box
and taking risks. When these efforts are successful, they are said to exhibit
the entrepreneurial imagination necessary to move the country forward.

Some scholars have argued that this distinction between enterprise
culture as a gloss for neoliberal economic policies and as a description
of a symbolic system that values creative entrepreneurship and risk taking represents an evolution from one set of meanings to another (Keat
1991). In the Egyptian context, the two meanings of enterprise culture
are complementary, and they are both explicated in terms of a third: national development. Egypt has tied its plans for economic prosperity to
liberal capitalism, and the creative problem solving of its cosmopolitan
entrepreneurs is increasingly articulated as one of the keys to the success
of this process.[3] Cosmopolitan entrepreneurs serve as culture brokers,

not only partnering with foreign firms to bring in retailers like Starbucks and McDonald's but drawing on their cosmopolitan knowledge to create the local coffee shops, shopping malls, theaters, and restaurants that index global models but serve local, predominantly upper-class consumers. Cosmopolitan Egyptians participate in "the process by which firm assets take on new meanings in distinct cultural environments" (Brannen 2004: 593). This process places entrepreneurs at the center of meaning making for the kinds of transnational popular culture commodities that shape their class identities. While upper-class Egyptians produce and reproduce their class identities through practices of consumption, upper-class entrepreneurs create the sites of consumption in which these practices take place. Moreover, entrepreneurship burnishes people's cosmopolitan credentials. Successful entrepreneurs who bring in trendy consumer goods or create new sites of consumption demonstrate their capacity to successfully negotiate between modernity and authenticity. This is enabled by the slippage of meanings of *enterprise* from practice to personhood. Successful entrepreneurs are described as possessing the necessary characteristics to help create Egypt's prosperity in the new world order. Successful entrepreneurs exhibit enterprise culture and thus validate their cosmopolitan, upper-class status. Unsuccessful entrepreneurs fail to exhibit the traits necessary not only for personal but for national development. Under the guise of this cultural model of entrepreneurialism, upper-class cosmopolitan entrepreneurs create the venues in and through which the upper class constructs itself as cosmopolitan through practices of consumption.

THE CULTURE OF DEVELOPMENT

Egyptian entrepreneurialism, at least among the upper classes, is embedded in and shaped by a "culture of development," an enormously powerful set of ideas describing and guiding activities, relationships, and exchanges (Gardner and Lewis 1996: 2). Development discourse represents states like Egypt as unfinished countries in comparison to the "developed" economic powerhouses of the West, and holds out the promise that deliberately planned change, guided by powerful transnational or international institutions, can push these developing countries forward on the road of progress until they are the near-equals of the developed nations. This discourse is locally inflected by an understanding that Egypt underwent a profound shift between two visions of modernity, that of the Nasserist, paternalistic, socialist state and that of the market-guided *infitah*. While the actual economic changes over the decades have been slower and less dramatic than this narrative of change would suggest, the tale of the abrupt turn from socialism to capitalism accurately expresses the way most people articulate their economic experiences.

Under President Nasser (1956–1970), Egypt emphasized consolidation of the public sector of the economy as a way to maximize the country's economic potential. The government nationalized all banks and insurance companies, as well as most foreign-owned companies. Those not nationalized were forced into local ownership or into partnerships with local businesspeople or were otherwise incorporated into the Nasserist vision (as in the case of the American University in Cairo). Trade unions and syndicates were largely incorporated as "partners" into the state political system,[4] and the national university system created a steady supply of trained workers to fill managerial roles in the growing state enterprises and in the expanding state bureaucracies. Nasser proposed a "moral economy" (Posusney 1993, 1997) in which the state essentially guaranteed job security and a living wage (accomplished in part through price controls on necessary subsistence items) in exchange for citizens' wholehearted contribution to the national project. Indeed, Nasser famously promised every university graduate a job —a promise more or less kept until well into the Sadat regime. As the number of educated workers expanded and as they were provided state employment, employment redundancy became the norm in Egyptian society.

The regime of President Anwar Sadat (1970–1981) introduced a new language and set of practices for economic development. Three years after his ascension to the presidency, riding on his popularity as the "Hero of the Crossing" after the 1973 war with Israel, Sadat announced the *infitah* policy, which officially shifted Egypt's state policy from Nasserism to both domestic and foreign private economic investment. But, as Timothy Mitchell points out, "the significance of this change in policy should not be exaggerated" (2002: 211). Structurally speaking, it represented little more than another rearrangement of state and private economic processes such as had organized Egypt's political economy since the colonial era. Culturally, however, it produced significant changes in people's social experiences and in the languages through which they articulated these. In particular, it transformed the main sources of transnational cultural flows about economics from the Soviet Union, the Non-Aligned Nations, and the Arab region to flows from Western Europe and North America.

Among the most significant changes was the increasingly important role played by three Washington-based political agencies—the World Bank, the United States Agency for International Development (USAID), and the International Monetary Fund (IMF)—as the source of new models for state-private economic relations. In 1976, Sadat sought debt relief from these organizations as a reward for his economic and political turn toward the West. The World Bank and the IMF predicated the loans on a reduction of Nasserist programs, especially government subsidies of basic necessities, and in January 1977 Sadat announced the elimination of subsidies on flour, rice, and cooking oil. But while Western development agencies had important allies, they also had opponents, both official and non-official, and they met resistance at many levels (Baker 1981). Shouting "*Ya batl al-'ubur, fen al-futur?*" (Hero of the Crossing, where is our breakfast?) and other slogans, hundreds of thousands of Egyptians took to the streets in every major city to protest the cutting of the subsidies. More than 100 buses were burned, nightclubs—symbols of the nouveaux riches profiting from the *infitah*—were attacked, and efforts by police to quell the protests led to more than 800 deaths, forcing the government to reinstate many of the subsidies (Olivier 1994: 56).

The government then turned to the "problem" of employment redundancy. Four years later, Law 137 of 1981 "signified the government's formal withdrawal from the Nasirist 'moral economy'" (Pripstein 1995: 52) by authorizing the right of both private sector employers and public sector managers to hire and fire workers and to set wages and benefits according to their assessments of prevailing market conditions rather than assessments of the needs of the workers. To offset resistance to this law, it also gave workers the right to strike, which had been illegal under Nasserism as detrimental to the national cause.[5]

The Hosni Mubarak regime (1981–present) signified a further shift toward privatization as Egypt became increasingly subject to the "Washington consensus," a set of ten prescriptions for reforming developing countries whose economies had not responded to earlier efforts (Williamson 1994). These reforms have focused on deregulation, privatization, and allowing labor markets to determine wages; governments were pushed to shift their attention from production, labor, and consumption to education and job training (Galbraith 2003). This new approach was expressed in Egypt through a broad government mandate, the Economic Reform and Structural Adjustment Program (ERSAP), which officially began in 1991. This program committed the government to the privatization, restructuring, and, in some cases, liquidation of a large number of its public enterprises. According to the plan's original timetable, one-fifth of Egypt's total public companies, some sixty companies employing about 366,000 workers, were to be restructured or closed by 1994. Law 203 in 1991 reorganized all public sector companies into seventeen profit-seeking "holding companies" and created a public enterprise office (PEO) to act as a liaison in assisting private investors to assume control of parts of these companies. On the advice and with the guidance of foreign donors, especially USAID, the PEO was incorporated into the cabinet-level Ministry for Public Enterprise.

In fact, privatization has been slow and cautious. The Mubarak regime wanted no repeat of incidents like the bread riots of 1981. In spite of ambitious ERSAP goals, privatization did not begin until 1993, when shares of Misr Chemical were offered on the stock exchange. Most of what has been called "privatization" since then has not, in fact, put companies under the control of non–public sector actors or agencies; it has consisted of public offerings of stock (usually limited to no more than 10 percent of the company), opportunities for employees to buy into the company (again, usually limited to 10 percent), and sales of assets. Sixty-four percent of privatization transactions thus did not actually remove companies from government control but rather provided the government holding companies with much-needed infusions of cash (Page 2001). Even with those companies which were sold outright to private investors, the government tried to control anticipated political fallout by first, slating companies for privatization that were not overstaffed, and, second, requiring investors to maintain existing employment levels for periods as long as five years.[6] In spite of these safeguards, privatization led to rising labor unrest, most notably in the Kafr ad-Dawar region, where textile workers took part in a wave of strikes from 2004 to 2007, with more than 7,000 laborers and their supporters participating in mass demonstrations to protest structural adjustments (Beinin 2007).

Liberal economists argue that Middle Eastern and North African governments are trapped in a paradox: overinvestment in public enterprises and redundant workforces drag economic growth, yet only rapid economic growth will produce the rising wages and increased tax revenues necessary to increase privatization and "correct" labor redundancy (Page 2001: 72–73). Having committed to full participation in the world capitalist system, the Egyptian government has three important reasons to increase the privatization of companies: first, to maintain the credibility of its privatization program in the eyes of investors, USAID, the World Bank, and the IMF; second, to generate revenue through the sale of shares or assets of public companies; and third, to reduce the fiscal burden imposed by government companies that lose money. Against this, the government must weigh the potential citizen backlash caused by not only a fear of job losses but also resistance to the overall insecurity of an uncontrolled labor market.

The Egyptian government's articulation of the growing roles of privatization and of entrepreneurial capitalism is thus built around two intertwined discourses. The first constructs private enterprise as a national mandate, focusing on political and economic dangers presumed to face any country that fails to keep competitive in the global marketplace. The second constructs private enterprise as a national opportunity, emphasizing that for-profit expansion serves the larger national objective of sustainable socioeconomic development for all. This perspective, in which private enterprise is both carrot and stick, builds on a model of development in which progress is envisioned as a single evolutionary process whose path has been blazed by the "advanced" countries and which other nation-states must inevitably follow. Privatization is conceived as a magic bullet that promises to deliver socioeconomic development to the country while ensuring profits for entrepreneurs.

Creative entrepreneurship is articulated as an important tool that can overcome the obstacles created by lingering public enterprise structures, and the success stories of entrepreneurs who have managed these obstacles are promoted as evidence of progress. For example, dozens of books, newspapers, and magazines trumpeted the successes of Ahmad Zayat, who purchased the hundred-year-old Al-Ahram Beverage Company (ABC) in

1997. Zayat is celebrated both in Egypt and internationally as an example of the entrepreneurial imagination. The Egyptian-born, U.S.-educated former Wall Street broker managed to buy the moderately profitable ABC for a modest $70 million (less than half the original asking price) in part by promising to leave intact its heavily redundant labor force. Zayat sold a group of investors on the project—something the Egyptian government had been unable to do—and raised enough money for the purchase as well as for investment in improvements. "The company quickly became the model for privatization in Egypt by modernizing production . . . , improving quality and introducing innovative marketing and promotions to build its brands" (Fick 2002: 255). In 1999, ABC acquired the Nile Brewing Company and Gianclis, the state-owned winery. In 2001, it acquired El-Gouna Beverages, giving it a virtual monopoly on the manufacture of beer and wine. Zayat's creativity was rooted in his intimate understanding of his potential markets. Zayat took many of his "superfluous" workers and placed them in a fleet of unmarked white vans. People throughout Cairo could order beer and wine from a toll-free number and have it delivered by these vans without the customers' neighbors knowing, thus avoiding the disapproving social gaze that comes with drinking alcohol. The same creativity is ascribed to Zayat in his handling of the Fayrouz brand of malt beverages. While the brewing process that creates most non-alcoholic beers yields alcohol, the process used by ABC to create its Fayrouz brand does not, enabling Al-Azhar to certify it as *halal*, permitted for consumption by Muslims. Flavored with raspberry, mango, or pineapple, Fayrouz became hugely successful as an export product to Saudi Arabia and other Gulf states (Allam 2003). By 2001, Al-Ahram still employed nearly 4,000 people and had gross sales of more than US$100 million and net profits of more than US$20 million. In the best tradition of globalization, Zayat sold ABC in 2002 to the multinational Heineken corporation for more than $280 million.

The celebration of Zayat offers a measure of the way that contemporary economic discourse constructs entrepreneurship as the engine that drives development. This discourse is carefully constructed by emphasizing how entrepreneurs turn obstacles into opportunities and by erasing prior or subsequent failures, such as Zayat's unsuccessful foray into the bottling industry (Mostafa 2005b). In this new discourse, neither the state nor the international economic system is entirely responsible for the success or failure of a state's economy. Responsibility for development lies with the success or failure of individuals to demonstrate the entrepreneurial imagination. While acknowledging that it remains important for the state to dismantle its overburdened public service sector, stories like that of Ahmad Zayat imply that creative entrepreneurs can not only overcome such obstacles but, as in the cases of Cilantro and ABC, actually use the impediments created by the public sector system to springboard into greater success. True enterprise culture is exhibited by individuals like Zayat, who "spotted potential where others saw only pitfalls," as the *New York Times* reported (Allam 2003). Similarly, rather than ending the 40 percent customs tariffs to promote importation, public discourses praise entrepreneurs who use lower rents and overhead to keep the prices of consumer goods at the same levels as in the Gulf states, where there are no tariffs (Mostafa 2005c). In the face of its massive difficulties in dismantling public sector projects, the state's new role is to help create such successful individuals and to foster a national enterprise culture.

GLOCAL VERSUS MULTILOCAL

Enterprising individuals need not be independent entrepreneurs. Many more will be young men and women working for multinational corporations in ways that draw on their cosmopolitan experience to help these corporations succeed in Egyptian markets. As we have seen, global corporations emphasize that they are constantly looking for locals with the right kinds of character and knowledge to assist them in their local ventures. Heineken's buyout of ABC stock did not lead Heineken to bring in its own European management team; it was precisely the successes of the local management—and especially the development of Fayrouz—that made ABC an attractive acquisition. Heineken had a global distribution capacity that could move Fayrouz from Egypt and the Gulf throughout the Islamic world. Al-Ahram went global as its product entered the international networks of distribution controlled by its new parent company; Heineken in turn had to rely on its capacity to continually find local managers, not only in Egypt but in every node in its distribution market, who understand both the product and local consuming publics so that the company can effectively integrate these products into the marketplace. The global and local are mutually constructed through metacultural, metadeictic discourses that describe these processes and enable corporations to generate practices. Terms like *glocal* and *multilocal* emerge in these discourses as multinational corporations seek ways to talk about this fusion between corporate cultures and practices and the contingencies of local markets.

One of my earliest encounters with the term *multilocal* was at a dinner party in Cairo, where Arvind,[7] a marketing division manager in the local branch of a multinational company who was born and educated in Mumbai, explained the differences between his corporation and its leading rival: "Their strategy is global. Ours is multilocal. They want every package of [every product] to be packaged and marketed in the same way everywhere. They want to establish a global brand identity. When I say we are multilocal, I mean that we select from our family of brands and seek to find the best ways to tie them to local needs and desires." The term *glocal* emerged in a conversation with Donald, an executive with the rival company Arvind described as "global." When I asked him about Arvind's characterization of the differences in their companies, Donald said:

> Well, I don't know how really multilocal any company can ever get. At some point, you have to be who you are or the brand doesn't mean anything. Our experience is that shifting the meaning of your brands in different markets might give you an initial edge over competitors but what if you guess wrong? Then you're stuck with a brand that has the wrong connotations and you have to change gears again. And maybe again. And then who will trust your brand? . . . We're in this for the long haul. We're a hundred-year-old company and we can afford to be thinking about ten years from now and twenty or maybe even fifty years from now.

In a later interview, however, he offered a slightly different version:

> Global branding is an important part of our company's internal organization and it's not something we can or would want to ever change. But the external presentation of brands always has to involve local identifiers. The brand stays the same, the prod-

uct stays the same, but how we interest buyers here in Egypt is
going to be different than how we interest buyers in the U.S. or
France or someplace [else]. So, in a sense, we've invested in glocal brand architectures, consistent with our strategy and our
business model, our company culture.

The terms *glocal* and *multilocal* have a variety of definitions and are
used in a number of contexts to gloss relations between transnational or
multinational phenomena and their local manifestations.[8] As Mazzarella
(2004) has pointed out, marketing in the non-Western world often involves
a series of experiments with modernity, through which the nature of what is
global as well as what is local, traditional, or, in this case, what has "Egyptian character" (a favorite phrase of Egyptian marketing professionals)
becomes at least temporarily reified in commodification. New lexicons
emerge to articulate these changing relations between what is imagined
as global and what is imagined as local. Managers in major corporations
do not simply enact identities, they create them through specific indexical
performances in conjunction with many other members of the corporation.
Here, the managers construct their businesses' identities in terms of how
they handle transnational flows not only of people, goods, and services
but particularly of signs: *brands.* Branding—and marketing in general—is
rooted in Western liberal economic assumptions of the human being as the
locus of an endless series of needs and desires (Sahlins 1972, 1994; Applbaum
1998). Advertising and marketing seek to identify (and to create) wants and
to bring these into alignment with a system of meanings represented as
distinctions between commodities. Marketers, in this view, are not selling
commodities but commodity signs.[9] Branding involves a complex labeling process through which iconic signs—logos, trademark names, color
schemes, and so forth—function as indexes to the companies that produce
them. Ideally, brands provide a level of familiarity that assists consumers in
making choices among a bewildering variety of market goods, but they also
serve as powerful tools by which positive and negative feelings associated
with goods are assigned to the corporation and, by extension, perhaps to
other goods and services provided by that corporation.

Arvind's and Donald's discourses not only involve different descrip-
tions of branding strategies but imply different semiotic visions of how the

commodity sign is constructed. The way Donald tells it, a brand has an essential identity, it is what it is, and this identity is linked to the product and to the company that makes it. Potential markets don't know your brand identity; they must be informed or educated. The purpose of advertising is to articulate your brand in such a way that people come to recognize their need for it. Given such a viewpoint, it is not surprising that, although headquartered in the United States, his company chooses to maintain as much control as possible over local marketing campaigns through managers like Donald, who were born and educated in the United States. Local partnerships do not imply giving control over marketing decisions to local management or subcontractors: one's local partners or employees know the local markets, but they can't know the brand the way the owners do. Arvind's account, on the other hand, constructs brands themselves as flexible and polysemic. The vision conjured by his account presents branded products as a pool of resources upon which the local office draws in creating local markets. One links the product, through local symbols, to local needs and desires. This attention to the local is paralleled in the company's attitudes toward management: Arvind's success in marketing his company's brands locally led to promotion up and out of Egypt, and the appointment of an Egyptian marketing manager to his position. Corporations thus develop particular ways of articulating global-local relations in terms of business practices; these modes of articulation in turn shape decision making about how products will be marketed to local consumers.

Another company that adopts the strategy that Donald calls glocal is the Egyptian branch of an international manufacturer of processed foods whose corporate headquarters is in the United States. The company worked with Egyptian advertising and marketing research firms to transform its advertisements to fit the local market. Sherine, a former AUC student employed as part of a marketing team with one of these agencies, told me this had worked particularly well in positioning the company's brand of ketchup in the local market. Ketchup is a well-known condiment that has been available in Egypt for years, and there are many local brands. The multinational company has traditionally identified its product in its American and European markets as being particularly "rich," "thick," and "flavorful," and local ads emphasizing these characteristics proved successful. The local ads were similar to, indeed modeled on, successful

American ads, with close-ups of ketchup pouring slowly and thickly onto various foods. In these ads, the physical appearance of the actors, the language spoken, the music, and the nature of some of the foods onto which ketchup was poured employed what Donald called "local identifiers," but the narrative and visual structure were nearly identical to similar ads running in the United States and elsewhere.

The success of the marketing scheme in selling "thickness" was particularly interesting, as Sherine pointed out to me, in that it ran counter to what marketing research had pinpointed as one of the central uses of ketchup in Egyptian cooking, which is as a decoration. Many dishes, particularly plates of pale *tahina* (sesame sauce) or *babaganush* (eggplant sauce) are enlivened at middle-class restaurants with decorative borders of bright-red ketchup in filigree patterns. That this use generally requires a thinner ketchup than pictured in the ads (although not, perhaps, thinner than the actual product) does not so much emphasize the gulf that often exists between the commodity sign and the use value of the commodity to consumers as it emphasizes a distinction between different values among different market segments. Sherine and her team assumed from the start that the foreign brand would be an upscale product. As in the case of Chipsy and Lay's, the difference in price between the local and international brands seemed minor to the manufacturer (less than ten cents), but it amounted to a 20–30 percent difference in price. The logical market for the international brand was clearly upper-middle- and upper-class Egyptians like Sherine and her team: educated, possessed of the cosmopolitan taste to appreciate rich, thick ketchup, and having the disposable income not to quibble at the price. The corporation's notion that it could become a market leader in Egypt was privately seen by Sherine as naïve.

The success in replicating a global advertising scheme by making use of local identifiers led to a conflict between the U.S. managers and their Egyptian creative team during a subsequent ad campaign concerning a steak sauce. Although locally produced soy sauces and Worcestershire sauces are available, brand-name sauces for meat are not a common item in Egypt, and Sherine said that company executives told the advertising agency it was understood that they would have to create a new market niche for the product through advertising. The executives insisted, however, that the Egyptian ad campaign draw on an existing international set of advertisements running in slightly different variations in the United States, Europe, and Asia. The ad campaign was built around the English term "zesty" and was intended to be lighthearted and funny. In Egyptian *'ammiyyah* (spoken dialect), there is no real cognate for the word "zesty." Sherine said her team worked very hard to create a campaign that matched the style of the American campaign: "It was lighthearted and funny. We did tests with focus groups and people laughed, and they said the ads would make them likely to try the brand." Unfortunately, she said, when the campaign was shipped to the American office, "they didn't understand it. And they didn't trust us. So they canceled the whole campaign and made us translate an American ad." This included transliterating the word "zesty"—meaningless in Arabic—into Arabic script.

Sherine's account of her experience points up the continuing difficulties of cross-cultural semiotics. Sherine and the rest of her creative team—cosmopolitan, well traveled, and educated at English-language middle schools—assumed that they could understand how a particular sign signifies to American audiences and could create new signifiers that would produce the same effects in Egyptian audiences. The manufacturer of the product—pleased with the results generated by the American ad campaign and completely unfamiliar with Arabic and with Egyptian ways of speaking—was not convinced that signifier and signified could be split in this way. The American executives responded by attempting to impose the signifier on local audiences. Ketchup sold well because translations of the same signifiers produced the same signifieds. Why would a transliteration not work as well? In essence, the company was seeking not only to introduce the product, but to introduce a new word into the language to describe it. The subsequent failure of the product to sell appreciably served as a confirmation to Sherine (and became part of the sales pitch for her expertise to subsequent clients) that multinationals need local but cosmopolitan professionals to function as culture brokers, mediating between the global and the local.

Sherine's story describes exactly the sort of problem that Arvind believes the multilocal approach addresses. He offered an example based on shampoo ads. Since only 6 percent of the Egyptian population used shampoos,[10] Arvind saw it as a wide-open market, in which competitors could work together to bring new consumers to their products rather than competing head to head as they do in saturated markets like the United States:

> The rule of thumb, and our experience in other countries, was that the prime market for shampoo advertising is young women, age eighteen to twenty-four or so, the marriageable age. Women are looking for husbands, or their parents and brothers are looking for husbands for them. And for three years, this was the focus of our advertising. We spent—well, I don't want to tell you but it was hundreds of thousands, dollars not pounds. And in the end, market share was the same.

Arvind explained that his company had long used ethnographers as part of their market research. Since the Egyptian branch of the company had none, he brought in a group from Dubai. Ethnographers, he explained, depart from the quasi-experimental approach of surveys and focus groups used in most consumer research. Instead, they observe and interview people in the act of using products. Ethnography can thus produce new information by answering "questions we never thought to ask," Arvind said. This particular project lasted three months and took the team into people's homes: "And they came back and said we were targeting entirely the wrong market. Instead of young women, we should be targeting mothers of young girls. Mothers here have dreams about their girls. They live vicariously through them, imagining what they will be, who they will become. They want to do things to make them more beautiful, more successful. And we needed to tap into that desire."

The company tested this by taking an existing ad—featuring a young Egyptian woman going through a series of positive experiences from graduation to marriage, shaking her head after each to show off her thick, wavy hair—and adding a prologue and epilogue. The new ad begins with a mother washing her daughter's hair. As she reaches for the shampoo (offering a clear image of the brand), the scene fades into the prior ad. At the end, the scene fades back to a shot of the beaming mother, secure in her knowledge that she has assured her daughter's economic and matrimonial future through her use of the right brand of shampoo. Arvind said that sales boomed from the moment his company launched the revised ad. A new ad campaign was created using this approach, and "we increased our shampoo market share more in the first three months of the new ads than in the three years previous," Arvind said. Shortly after, he was promoted and transferred to a European branch of the company.

For Arvind, the product is the signifier—a partially empty signifier that can be connected to, and filled with, local desires. Arvind's approach to advertising imagines the product as serving psychological functions, meeting psychic needs. Rather than educating the market about one's brand and making consumers want it, one learns what the market wants and ties a preexisting brand to that desire. In this case, it was the desire to do something to improve one's daughter's life chances. Indeed, Arvind argued, the ads were part of the value of the product. Since most shampoos, face creams, and such are largely interchangeable, what makes the brand valuable is precisely the psychological value that accrues to the product because of the advertising. "We're giving them a sense of confidence in the face of an uncertain world, a sense of assurance that they very much want," he told me.

Ultimately, multilocal and glocal refer not only to approaches for selling products but to ways of articulating the nature of the relations between multinational corporations and their local partners. As in most of the world, Egypt's regulation of international investing usually requires foreign corporations to acquire local partners. From a national development standpoint, this is supposed to ensure that Egypt benefits from the relationship and is not merely exploited. However, it involves risks among all parties. Local partners are usually putting up a far greater percentage of their capital than are the international firms; a failure to produce profits is a disappointment to the corporation but can be devastating to the local partners. Multinational corporations, in turn, risk loss of control over operations in the host country, which might not only produce failures but have repercussions for the global brand (for example, product endorsements by local stars who have been previously condemned in Israel for allegedly making anti-Semitic remarks can lead to public protests and calls for boycotts in the more lucrative markets of the United States and Europe). Potential conflicts between the concerns of Egyptian partners focused on profits in the local marketplace and those of the executives with the multinationals, who are focused on shepherding a global brand, are perennial and are managed differently depending on the nature of the social relations between the various partners.

The discourses of glocal and multilocal are articulated within corporations as semi-objective languages for describing the nature of the relations between the multinational corporation and its local Egyptian partners. The corporation brings its global know-how, capital investment, and valuable brands; the local partners provide local knowledge of markets, cultural knowledge, and resources for negotiating political and bureaucratic hurdles. Both are driven by the purely pragmatic objective of making a profit. But these partnerships rarely occur on equal ground because the global partners inevitably retain the capacity to judge the effectiveness of the local partners. In the global-local fusions imagined by corporate discourses about glocal and multilocal, the global inevitably trumps the local. Global, in practice, often becomes a gloss for North American or Western European cultural styles of business, which carry powerful connotations of rational objectivity and autonomy. These become contrasted with the purely cultural logics of the local and become a site for elaborating East-West differences, in which the local must prove its modernity. Egyptians of the cosmopolitan class are uniquely positioned to participate in these struggles as culture brokers between East and West, local and global, cultural and modern.

CULTURE BROKERS

Culture brokers, in this sense, are people who position themselves as able to recognize cultural differences, interpret between these differences, appropriate or create symbols that will travel across differences, and render these as implementable practices, whether in production, management, or marketing. Culture brokers create the hybridities noted by observers of transnational cultural flows. Many of the global-local partnerships touted as most successful involve subcontracting or franchising cultural products entirely to successful local businesses that act as culture brokers.

In 2005, for example, Nahdet Misr acquired *Miki* (*Mickey*), a comic book featuring the adventures of Mickey Mouse and other Disney characters. As Judith MacDougall and David MacDougall have noted, the appropriation of Disney characters by local artisans, entrepreneurs, and others represents "not simply an instance of cultural hybridity but an example of the ability of local artisans to invest the products of international capitalism with new meanings drawn from their own experience and cultural traditions" (2003: 1). What is rarely noted is the extent to which Disney's international experience has taught it over the decades to trust its culture brokers to be able to localize commodities so as to create such possibilities. Nowhere is this truer than in the case of Mickey Mouse comics. Much has been made of the fact that Disneyland Paris has not been the unqualified success Tokyo Disneyland has been; less commonly noted is that *Le Journal de Mickey* has been France's top-selling comic for decades (Brannen 2004). Published consecutively in the United States by Dell, Gold Key, and Gladstone, Disney comics have never been one of Disney's top intellectual properties in North America, and in 2008 the company discontinued their publication. Overseas, however, comics are one of the primary media through which millions of people encounter the Mickey Mouse universe and the Disney brand.[11]

In the Middle East, *Miki* had long been the bestselling Arabic-language comic book in the region. Although published for many years by a Gulf firm, Nahdet Misr successfully bid for the contract in 2004.[12] The prior publisher had employed Egyptian writers to render *Miki* in Egyptian dialect, the vernacular of regionally successful comedy films. The first and most significant change made by the new Egyptian publisher was to put the comics into modern standard Arabic.

"They've absolutely ruined them," said Butros, who grew up reading *Miki*. He is a computer programming and software solutions manager with a European-based international corporation. Educated in private schools in Cairo, Butros received his degrees from a Canadian university and worked in Canada for several years. He returned to Egypt for family reasons and stayed when he realized that his skills and experience were at a premium in the Egyptian labor market. In his early thirties, Butros has a collection of old *Miki* comics dating back to his childhood. "They're just not funny any more," he lamented of the new editions.

In the summer of 2005 when I spoke with the editor of *Miki* and with Dalia Ibrahim, head of the licensed publications division of Nahdet Misr, they were adamant they'd made the right decision. "We've increased sales 30 percent," Ibrahim said proudly when I shared the concerns of Butros and other *Miki* fans who'd offered similar complaints. What Ibrahim and her staff understood about *Miki*'s market was similar to the lesson Arvind learned from his ethnographers: the larger market is not those who will buy comics for their own and their children's pleasure, but those who want to improve their children's social futures.

Ibrahim emphasized at several points in our interview that the primary mission of Nahdet Misr remained the publication of high-quality scientific and educational materials, "not only comics or things that are funny and frightening." Nahdet Misr was established in 1938 when Dalia's grandfather, bookseller Ahmed Ibrahim, added a print shop, and began to publish books for the Egyptian Ministry of Education. In 1968, Nahdet Misr launched the Al-Adwa, educational series for which it is most well known. Now running more than 150 titles, the series covers all grades and subjects, and at least some titles are available from nearly every bookseller in Cairo. The company also bought the Arabic rights to American, British, German, and French educational materials.[13] In 1998, Nahdet Misr began offering multimedia titles—combining animation, video, photos, music, and sound effects—on religious, educational, and cultural topics.

But there is also "our market for people who don't try to read scientific books. Just little stories they like, fiction, very much strange fiction, and very famous fiction," said Ibrahim. Given a choice between "giving them what they want" and "telling them what they should have," Nahdet Misr chose selections from bestselling international popular print culture and brought them out in the same modern standard Arabic it promotes in its educational materials. It first experimented with translating global children's popular culture in 1990, when it successfully published the *Teenage Mutant Ninja Turtles* comic book. With the acquisition of the Disney titles *Miki, Super Miki, Miki Geib,* and *Winnie the Pooh* added to its successful *Superman* and *Batman* comics, the company established in 2004 a division specifically to manage foreign licensed publications, which Ibrahim heads.

Hybridity here is a conscious entrepreneurial choice driven both by assessments of the market and by a preexisting corporate culture deeply shaped by the histories of "national development" even while successfully positioning itself as the market leader in the post-*infitah* Arabic market. And it is extremely successful. In 2005, Nahdet Misr was the largest publisher in Egypt and the second largest in the Arab world. One of the company's techniques is to hire well-known Arab authors to do the translations. Under the pen names of the texts' original authors, these writers earn valued supplemental income translating, often very freely, J. K. Rowling's *Harry Potter* series and the *Goosebumps* books by R. L. Stine as well as comics and other materials. This has ensured that the books are written in the elegant modern standard Arabic which Nahdet Misr wants associated with its brand. The story plots remain those of the original texts, and names are not altered but placed between angle brackets to alert readers that these are non-Arabic words.

Contemporary graphic art technologies allow not only words but images to be transformed. In previous eras, the comics' balloons could contain translated text, but words drawn as part of the picture—exit signs, fight noises, signs, titles—were inviolable. Now, all can be re-rendered in Arabic. Choosing where to draw the line involves conscious editorial decisions. Once the *Daily Planet*'s sign is re-rendered in Arabic, why not replace U.S. flags with Egyptian flags? "We change things to fit them to the Egyptian culture," said Ibrahim. "If the main character woman is wearing something very tight, we change it. If she's wearing something that shows too much, we change that. . . . Batwoman, she wears very tight clothes and we just take something else and make it not so tight." But "Harry Potter, we didn't make it Egyptian. If you change Harry Potter, [if] you make it Egyptian culture, you will destroy it. The same thing with Superman and Batman."

People buy these products in part because they are *not* Egyptian, because products that index specific foreign culture popular fads are part of people's social capital. Hybridity involves finding a balance; pushing the translation process too far will destroy people's desire for the product. But there are other constraints. "We couldn't make these [books and comics] Egyptian even if we wanted to," said Ibrahim, because global popular culture is so deeply intertextual. If an editor pushes localization too far, "it will not match, and if you watch the movie on TV or in the cinema, it is the same comic, same everything. We just change it a little bit."

Hybridity does not just happen; it involves conscious choices by specific culture brokers in entrepreneurial settings seeking to avoid the kinds of errors that led to the Pokémon moral panic while maintaining the market attraction of the "foreign odor" (Iwabuchi 2002). There is no single uniform scheme for pulling it off; decisions are contingent and shaped by different productive concerns. In purchasing the publication rights to *Winnie the*

Pooh, for example, Ibrahim said she and her staff were extremely unhappy with the Arabic names attached to the characters. They would not have changed the names from the English originals, or if they did they would have done it differently. "The people who made the first translation of the names into the Arabic language, they suggested very bad names just because the lip-sync was closer to the lip-sync of the English one. . . . Eeyore is Hawar. What is Hawar? It is a very bad name but is just close to Eeyore."

MARKETING McDONALD'S

But describing multilocal enterprises only as successes or failures, as many narratives do, robs these tales of their complex contingencies. Global and local are constantly being negotiated and renegotiated among multiple constituencies, including the publics from which customers may be drawn. The story of McDonald's Egypt is an excellent illustration of this. Egypt was the seventy-fourth country to open McDonald's restaurants. The franchise was licensed as a corporation owned by two sister companies: Manfoods Company, owned by Yassin Mansour, which initially licensed the Giza and Alexandria stores, and Orascom Foods Company, owned by Nassef Sawiris, which licensed the Cairo stores. While Egyptian business-people had many times approached McDonald's, the company waited until 1983 before entering into a partnership. As part of McDonald's multilocal practice of buying as much as possible locally, it spent eleven years putting the infrastructure in place, so that the lettuce, tomatoes, onions, and potatoes were grown and processed in Egypt, the buns were baked in Egypt, and yet all met the corporation's international quality standards. The first two restaurants in Egypt opened on October 20, 1994, in Mohandiseen and Heliopolis in Cairo.

For the first three years of McDonald's existence in Egypt (1994–1997), little effort was made to define McDonald's for Egyptian consumers (Peterson 1998). In 1998, for example, McDonald's chief advertisement was a full-color flyer that was distributed in all McDonald's restaurants and as an insert in the English-language weekly edition of the *Al-Ahram* newspaper. The flyer displayed the pictures, names, and prices of all of the major McDonald's foods. Of the eighteen items shown, only three were not transliterations of the English names (hamburger, French fries, etc.). Of generic products, only "soft drink" was translated, as *mashruubaat* (drinks). The other two were trademarked names: Filet-o-Fish became the curiously blended Mak Feeleeta *samak,* while Happy Meal was translated rather literally into the Arabic *Wagba Mafraha.* Both were trademarked in Egypt under these local names. This practice of transliteration in advertising extended even to generic words. Milk shake, apple pie, ice cream sundae, and cheeseburger were all transliterated rather than translated. *Laban* (milk), *tuffah* (apple), *lahma* (meat)—these Arabic words never appeared in the flyer or in any other ad. What they created was, in essence, McDonald's in transliteration, incapable of communicating to Arabic literates who did not already know what McDonald's offers. The rest of the advertising materials were even less geared toward outreach than this flyer, consisting largely of materials imported from the United States (and hence in English) rather than printed in Egypt.

This campaign made sense in the local context. While Americans visit McDonald's primarily for its low price, convenience, speed, and efficiency (Ritzer 1993), this cannot be true of Egyptians. McDonald's is far more expensive and usually slower than many shops and carts serving local "fast foods," such as *koshary, fitiir,* and *shawarma.* In 1998, I could feed my entire family of six on *koshary* for the price of a single McDonald's value meal. What McDonald's is selling in Cairo is not "hot, tasty food, quickly, at a low price," as Ray Kroc is supposed to have once summed up the company's message. What it is selling is the McDonald's experience, a multilocal space partially disassociated from the Egyptian context in which cosmopolitan consumers—tourists and wealthy Egyptians—can participate in a particular form of commodified modernity.[14]

Local marketing experts recognized this. Heba, a marketing executive at McDonald's, explained the transformation to me over lunch one day:

> We had this ready-made market: cosmopolitan, well-traveled
> people who have eaten at McDonald's in London and Los An-
> geles and Jiddah.[15] And they know what the food is, basically,
> so the ads just needed to remind them, to prompt them. And
> we have the tourists. They are in a foreign land, surrounded by
> strange foods, strange language. They want the McDonald's to
> be a refuge. They want it to be very American . . . with maybe
> just a touch of exotic Egypt.

Transliteration also helped to train the staff, she said. An Arabic-literate employee hearing "apple pie" can usually locate *abilbai* (written in Arabic script) on the cash register with little difficulty.

The vision of the local partners, then, was of a limited number of restaurants in select locations, targeting the tourist trade and upscale local consumers. McDonald's International, by contrast, envisioned a viral expansion of stores reaching out to middle-class consumers. At first, the McDonald's Egypt partners left many of the decisions about sales and expansion to the corporation. "And they came up with the idea that Egypt has 70 million people . . . so we are going to sell [millions of burgers] on that basis," a Manfoods official told me in 2005. While the local partners grew increasingly nervous about their investment, they "left it up to the experts in the corporation." However, in 1998, after nearly three years of financial losses, Egyptian partners Orascom and Manfoods decided to stop the ambitious expansion plan they had worked out with McDonald's International. To keep the plan alive, the multinational stepped in with a huge investment and built nine more restaurants. Marketing changed to keep step with the plans to reach out to the middle classes. In mid-1999, I noticed banners going up at the McDonald's in Tahrir Square, across the street from the American University in Cairo. These banners offered two pounds off the regular price of *wagba lahma* (meat lunches), the Arabic term for prepackaged sets of sandwiches, fries, and drinks. In early 2000, I took my youngest daughter to the McDonald's in New Ma'adi, where we found advertisements for *fitiir tuffah*. We were both delighted by the appropriateness of the name. The McDonald's pastry bears as little resemblance to the Egyptian *fitiir* as it does to the American apple pie—the similarity being merely that all three involve crusts and fillings—yet the name gives those who've eaten *fitiir* an immediate sense of what they will be getting if they've never had the McDonald's dessert before.

In a 2000 follow-up interview, Heba told me that "Chicago," as she referred to McDonald's corporate headquarters in Oak Brook, Illinois, had insisted that the transliteration campaign, which simply informed people where the products were and how much they cost, would limit its plans for local expansion. Egyptians in the company who agreed with Chicago pointed to other elements in Egyptian society that could be targeted as consumers, particularly the "new" middle class whose money comes from fathers and husbands working in the Gulf states. These families have money, and they have the desire to emulate the affluent classes, Heba said. What they lack is the English literacy and easy familiarity with things foreign of the cosmopolitan class. The shift in advertising campaigns involved educating them into the McDonald's experience. When I asked her if McDonald's in Egypt planned to go the way of India, adapting the menu to local tastes and flavors,[16] she shook her head, answering in a way that echoed Ibrahim's discussion of comics:

> HEBA: I don't see McKoshary coming. People don't come here for what they can get somewhere else. They come here for McDonald's, and that includes hamburgers and French fries. If we started serving koshary and shawarma, we could lose our core market. They would say it isn't really McDonald's any more.
>
> MARK: So maybe you are seeking two ways of experiencing the same McDonald's?
>
> HEBA: Yes, maybe you could say that. If you are class A, or a tourist, you're in the one McDonald's. It has all the things that are familiar to you and the English menu and the register man who speaks English. And if you are class B or C, you know, Arabic-speaking, there is the Arabic menu and the advertisements and the register man speaks Arabic. But they are still the same McDonald's.[17]

But Heba turned out to be wrong. Encouraged by its international partners, in May 2001 McDonald's Egypt offered McFalafel, a fried patty of beans and vegetables (mostly parsley) on a burger bun, with lettuce, tomatoes, pickles, and a spicy *tahina* sauce. This was the McDonaldization of a traditional regional food called in Egypt *ta'miyya*, but better known in the West by its Syrian/Lebanese/Palestinian name, *falafel*. Although it cost three times what *ta'miyya* cost in nearby Egyptian restaurants, this first localized McDonald's product sold briskly for a few weeks, frightening a few local *ta'miyya* shops enough that they also began to offer *ta'miyya* patties on a Western-style bun, alongside the more usual, and less expensive, *baladi* pocket bread. Sales declined rapidly as the novelty wore off, however, and most people decided that *ta'miyya* was better at local restaurants, served on *baladi* bread with a less spicy tahina sauce, for less money.

The local interest in McFalafel went beyond consumer desire for the product as a food, however. McFalafel fired local imaginations with the idea that an Egyptian food could become a contribution to global modernity. Local newspaper columnists waxed eloquently on the idea that the McFalafel might spread from Egypt to McDonald's counters throughout the world. "Is Egypt the test market for what may become the latest global fast-food phenomenon?" asked columnist Tarek Atia in *Al-Ahram Weekly* (2001: 14). "Does globalization sometimes go in the opposite direction?" Globalization is widely understood by Egyptians as something that happens *to* them, rather than as something to which they can contribute. Atia was publicly articulating—and no doubt adding fuel to—a rumor sweeping Cairo that McFalafel was going to be offered in McDonald's restaurants throughout the world.

Rumors that Egypt might offer its own franchises of local foods to foreign countries are not uncommon. Just prior to McFalafel, for example, rumors circulated that the trendy, upscale Studio Misr, an Egyptian film-themed restaurant chain, was going to open branches in New York, Los Angeles, and Dearborn, Michigan. In the case of McFalafel, the rumor was in part a result of McDonald's Egypt's advertising campaign for the sandwich, which played on just such global-local relations. The sandwich was advertised in English with the slogan "A Taste of Egypt Comes to the World," certainly implying that it was being offered worldwide, rather than exclusively in franchises in Cairo and Alexandria. "They must be going to market it abroad or why would they name it Mc*Falafel* [instead of Mc*Ta'miyya*]?" insisted one of my students in the face of my skepticism.

The McFalafel effort is an exemplar of McDonald's in Egypt selling the experience of modernity, rather than mere food. McFalafel is the local modernized, a metaphor for the neoliberal promise in Egypt. This interpretation was pounded home by the advertising campaign, in which the McFalafel value meal, which includes fries and a soft drink with the sandwich, was given the slangy name *al-Mu'allim* (The Boss). The juxtaposition of this "vulgar" language with the clean, efficient image of McDonald's caught customers' attention through its surprise, while at the same time signifying the ways modernity can overturn local rules that tie together wealth and distinctions of language and taste.[18] And in case anyone missed the point, McDonald's Egypt showed how the traditional Egyptian food had become *al-Mu'allim* through its McDonald's incarnation in a jingle sung on television by the popular rags-to-riches star Sha'ban Abdel-Rahim.

From a local standpoint, the choice of Sha'ban to sing the advertisement was brilliant. Because of its status as an American icon, McDonald's had fared poorly in several boycotts of American businesses. Stimulated by the *intifada al-Aqsa* in September 2000, then by the Israeli invasion of Ramallah in 2001, boycott petitions with lists of companies were circulated, urging Egyptians to stop supporting "the Zionist project" through pro-Western consumption. Unlike the largely informal effort to boycott Pokémon, these boycott campaigns brought together a diverse set of actors, including the leftist Egyptian Anti-Globalization Group; the pro-business Egyptian Federation of Chambers of Commerce; conservative sheikh Muhammed Sayed Tantawi, head of Al-Azhar; and tele-sheikh Yusuf al-Qaradawi (Amr Khaled's early mentor), and were quite successful in spite of opposition to the boycott from President Hosni Mubarak and Prime Minister Atef Ebeid. While several companies managed the boycott quite well (see Kehrer 2006), the September 2001 issue of *Business Week Egypt* reported a 20 percent loss in sales revenue for McDonald's—and this at a time when the company had yet to show a profit. McDonald's Egypt was a prime target of the boycott in spite of a public relations campaign aimed at educating people that a boycott would hurt the Egyptian management and employees more than it would the multinational. Rumors of links between American food chains and Israel focused particularly on McDonald's. One false message circulating on the internet claimed, "McDonald's will donate its Saturday income to Israel."[19]

Putting Sha'ban into a marketing campaign was particularly clever because McDonald's was a key target of the boycott, and Sha'ban was part of the boycott's guiding spirit. After years on the *sha'bi* circuit,[20] Sha'ban rose to unexpected success with a series of vulgar, patriotic, and sometimes witty tunes that captured the mood of much of the public. His song "Ana Bakrah Israil" (I Hate Israel) became a theme song of the boycott, with lyrics insisting, "I'd refuse foreign wool but wear my country's burlap." Linking Sha'ban with McDonald's Egypt thus dramatically localized the restaurant, politically and socially. But the link also reinforced the image of the lowly made great through modernity. A middle-aged working man and amateur crooner, Sha'ban rose to sudden success after he appeared on a television talk show. His rags-to-riches story is analogous to the lowly *ta'miyya* reinvented as the trendy, upscale McFalafel. The equation of the vulgar singer made wealthy and successful through the modern technology of television and the lowly food made modern and upscale became part of the promise of the McDonald's experience.

Globally, however, the choice of Sha'ban was a disaster. The New York–based American Jewish Congress issued a public statement condemning McDonald's for hiring the singer, whom they called a "sponsor of hate" (Associated Press 2001). The local and international offices of McDonald's attempted to manipulate their transnational relationship to have it both ways: McDonald's International apologized and expressed shock in American newspapers, while McDonald's Egypt insisted that it was pleased with its campaign in Egyptian newspapers. But media are no longer so easily localized: Egyptian newspapers reported on the American controversy, juxtaposing Egyptian and American corporate voices and raising the question of whether McDonald's Egypt was American and pro-Israel, or local and anti-Israel. When McDonald's Egypt stopped airing the advertisement after only three weeks, most Egyptians who were paying attention were convinced it had capitulated to pressure from its American partner. No one believed denials by both U.S. and Egyptian corporate officers that the ads were never intended to run more than three weeks, including, apparently, Sha'ban, who gave interviews to members of the local media. "If I had ever known that McDonald's was related to or would benefit anything Jewish or American, I would never have done the ad," he told the *Cairo Times* (Dabbous 2001; also see Grippo 2006). In distancing himself from McDonald's, he connected the company to both America and Israel, specifically undermining the very localization that McDonald's Egypt was trying to introduce into local imaginations through its creation of McFalafel and its use of him to promote the product.[21]

But the boycotts and the embarrassment over Sha'ban were minor compared to the consequences of McDonald's International's successful plan to expand the clientele of the restaurants to middle-class consumers. From the Egyptian perspective, a key problem was that McDonald's multilocal approach to marketing and food supply did not extend to localization of the business plan, and McDonald's ultimately opened more than fifty restaurants in Egypt, with thirteen in Cairo alone. Because class distinctions are predicated in many sites as class separation, the influx of middle-class consumers led upper-class Egyptians to largely abandon the restaurants in many locations. While certain locations, like the McDonald's in the Hilton Ramses mall, are in class-selective venues, many of the company's restaurants have traded upper-class Egyptians who can afford to eat at McDonald's on a regular basis with customers for whom "[g]oing to McDonald's is meant to be an outing on a Friday, feast days or holidays" (Abaza 2006: 181).

In the face of continual struggles over the definition of local markets and the value of expansion, with no profits even after five years of investment and expansion, the Sawiris family in 2001 sold its 20 percent interest to its local and international partners as part of a package of divestments of companies that Naguib Sawiris described as producing "lots of headaches, no thanks and no money" (Mostafa 2005a). The Mansour family considered dumping its holdings in McDonald's as well but held on in part, a company executive told me, because the family could not believe that McDonald's International really did not know what it was doing. Owners of one of the greatest corporations in Egypt, the local partners of such multinationals as Microsoft and General Motors, the Mansours still tended to defer to the global partner that asserted the rationality of its business model over the Mansours' understandings of the local markets. At the same time, the Manfoods company made a number of efforts to build revenues in its McDonald's division. For example, because it owns many of the companies supplying food to McDonald's Egypt, it has taken advantage of its low labor costs to sell burger buns and other goods to restaurant chains in Greece and elsewhere in the Mediterranean.

But what has really saved McDonald's Egypt—if it has been saved—is delivery. This innovation was not implemented by McDonald's Egypt as a corporate decision but arose out of the entrepreneurial imaginations of individual restaurant managers in the early days of the company. In Egypt, every fast-food company delivers to customers. Shortly after McDonald's opened, several restaurant managers added delivery service, and delivery quickly spread throughout the chain. When company officials found out, McDonald's International strongly resisted this innovation. Company policy held that home and office delivery allowed deterioration of the food's flavor and contradicted the company's international standards. But by the time they learned of it, company officials told me, "more than 20 percent of our revenues came from delivery."[22]

McDonald's Egypt had pioneered the image of the restaurant as a child-friendly space and introduced into Cairo "the novel habit of celebrating birthdays by renting public places" (Abaza 2006: 181). With the abandonment of many of the restaurants by upper-class families, the company increased its party catering operations, sending food, music, and costumed characters to rooftop and backyard gardens. Delivery and catering have allowed consumers to indulge in their cosmopolitan taste for McDonald's without having to associate with the kinds of people who may enter a public restaurant. Similarly, it has allowed customers to indulge in McDonald's food at home, free from the disapproving gaze of those who support a boycott, although it is an economic indulgence: a typical delivery charge runs a pound and a half—the price of a single serving of *koshary* or two *ta'miyya* sandwiches at a food stand in Cairo. A Manfoods executive told me in 2005 that while the McDonald's operations were not yet out of the red, the company could at least now imagine that day arriving. More recent public statements describe small, steady profits.

ENTERPRISING EGYPTIANS

The public face of Cairo's globalization—the commodification of leisure spaces, the creation of public parks, the growth of shopping malls, and the emergence of branded chain retailers, from all of which working-class locals are excluded (Abaza 2006)—is largely the result of cosmopolitan entrepreneurs creating a global style for Cairo by drawing on international models while seeking local profits. In 1999, Tahrir Koshary, one of the most famous traditional eateries in the center of Cairo, closed its doors during Ramadan—the slow month for food sales since most people fast during the lunch hours and eat dinners with their families—and began renovating its shop. It became a pattern: every Ramadan, the shop would close, and every Shawwal it would reopen with structural changes to its facility and operation. First, the food operation, in which cooks scoop spoonfuls of rice, lentils, pasta, chickpeas, tomato sauce, and fried onions into plastic bags, was moved from the window to behind a counter. The next year, plastic buckets replaced the bags. Then, the payment counter moved from right next to the door (so that one could pay, receive a ticket, and redeem it from the cooks) to the end of the counter (so one could pay after receiving the meal). It was clear that Tahrir Koshary was becoming, year by year, more and more like Kentucky Fried Chicken, one of the first and most successful international fast-food franchises lining Muhammed Mahmoud Street a block away. By 2005, Tahrir Koshary had added a distinctive logo, a fleet of delivery motorcycles, and franchises in outlying parts of the city.

The transformation of Tahrir Koshary represents an example of a phenomenon noted by Watson and his contributors (1997) in their studies of McDonald's in Asia: the appropriation by local entrepreneurs of specific signifiers from McDonald's (and other foreign franchises) and their integration into local consumer markets. These have included smiling employees, new standards for clean restrooms, the use of uniform color schemes, and so forth. While the authors attribute this evolution to the agency of "changed customer expectations," they offer no mechanism describing how these customer expectations get translated into transformations of local businesses. I think it more reasonable to recognize that the owners and managers exercising their entrepreneurial imagination by reorganizing production and marketing are not separate from the consumption system but are co-participants in a complex field of values. At the same time, entrepreneurs enter the field of consumption with a different set of practices: they experience their own consumption more reflexively, observe consumer behavior carefully, imagine consumers like and unlike themselves, and make judgments about what these imagined consumers will and will not like to consume.

Mohammed Tawfiq imagined that upscale Egyptian consumers would take to pizza. He first encountered pizza at a Greek bakery popular with students at the University of Alexandria, where he was studying, but he did not have an American-style—now global-style—pizza until he went to a pizza restaurant while in France on a business trip. The simplicity of the menu and layout and the efficiency with which the food and customers were processed caught Tawfiq's interest, and he became certain he could open a successful pizza parlor in Egypt.

Tawfiq is from a family of prosperous builders who buy land and build on it. As developers, they sell shops in their buildings to prospective entrepreneurs. Occasionally, one defaults, leaving them with an empty space. "And you can't have an empty shop in your building," he told me. "It looks very bad." So the family's pattern was to open a shop: "We might buy a load of furniture and put it in the shop, and hire a couple of guys to sit in there. And once or twice a year, they might sell something."

Mohammed and his brother were among the first to imagine that there might be money to be made in putting these accidental shops on a solid business footing. Their first experiment was the Doulmo Bakery, which sold bread, cakes, sweets—and pizza. The popularity of pizza with their customers confirmed their sense that a pizza chain was possible.

Tawfiq went to the United States with the intention of purchasing a franchise and relying on the expertise of the chain. All the major companies wanted far too much money, however, for what was essentially a risky proposition. So Tawfiq began visiting as many pizza restaurants as he could, introducing himself to their managers and learning what brands of ovens they used, what arrangements of cooking space worked best, and what didn't work and why.

Carefully selecting a location in Nasser City, Tawfiq opened Pizza Plus, a beautifully designed hyperspace (Kearney 1995) that could have been dropped into France or the United States as easily as Cairo. He quickly faced an unexpectedly high volume of sales, and the first several months were spent tinkering with the system to be able to handle the quantities of pizzas customers were buying. One of the principles Tawfiq developed involves a recognition that, in Egypt, labor is the lowest cost in a retail business. Instead of seeing labor redundancy as a negative, he hired more people than were necessary for the work, trained them all, and treated them well so that they would not want to lose the job. Thus, however high the demand, there were always enough employees to handle it. In his discussions with U.S. pizza retailers, the managers had always named employee turnover as the biggest problem, and his approach resolved that. But his decision to employ so many people was also inspired by a traditional ethic in which successful Arab men help and support less-successful people. "No one has ever asked me for a job, that I have not provided one," he said. Like most jobs in Egypt, the restaurant offers no benefit packages.

But Tawfiq and his brother spend most of their *zakat*—the charity equal to 2.5 percent of one's wealth that every Muslim owes to the poor—on caring for their employees' and their families' illnesses, weddings, and other needs. Just as Amr Khaled has yoked religious charitable obligations to social development goals, so businesspeople like Tawfiq yoke charitable obligations to entrepreneurial success.

Pizza Plus ran into immediate, significant competition. A well-capitalized group of businesspeople had partnered with Pizza Hut to bring the franchise to Egypt. In 1995, the same year Pizza Plus opened, the first Pizza Hut opened. Because of its international brand, Tawfiq knew Pizza Hut would necessarily be more attractive to the upscale, cosmopolitan class whose taste for pizza was whetted by its international indexicality. Pizza Plus, like Cilantro, Beano's, and other sites serving cosmopolitan desires, represent hyperspaces, spaces that are global because they could exist in roughly the same form anywhere in the world. Places like Pizza Hut, McDonald's, and Starbucks are experienced rather as multilocal spaces, spaces that while distributed throughout the world are somehow always the same place. For upper-class Egyptians whose tastes are strongly shaped by the brand identification that makes the multilocal experience possible, a Pizza Hut is more immediately attractive, the brand rendering it more authentically global.

But "there is another group of customers," said Tawfiq, those who grow up with cosmopolitan tastes but more limited means. In addition, there are upwardly mobile middle-class people whose tastes recognize the cosmopolitanism of pizza although they haven't internalized the sophisticated distinctions of international brands. The crucial difference between these groups of consumers, Tawfiq understands, is disposable income. Like the coffee houses, Pizza Plus is a cosmopolitan place where mixed couples can gather. The trick is to bring in couples who would find Pizza Hut expensive. "So I looked at my menu and [found that] pizza was the lowest cost item [to produce]." He introduced a two-for-one pizza deal.

Although "buy one, get one free" is one of the oldest devices in the Western marketing repertoire, it was quite novel in Egypt. Nearly any Egyptian to whom I mentioned Pizza Plus, whether or not they had ever eaten there, would nod and say, "Two for One." The slogan became synonymous with the restaurant. It was highly effective, and the restaurant

204 CONNECTED IN CAIRO

handled an extremely high volume of traffic. Pizza Plus quickly expanded
to a five-restaurant chain over four years. Pizza Hut, meanwhile, intend-
ing (like McDonald's) to attract both upper- and middle-class consumers,
embarked on an ambitious expansion plan and opened fifteen restaurants
in the same period.

After five years, however, revenues for both chains began to drop pre-
cipitously. Like McDonald's, Pizza Hut had expanded beyond the number
of restaurants that could be sustained by its core audience of well-heeled
upper-class Egyptians, and it also faced competition from such new international franchises as Domino's. Pizza Plus, meanwhile, suffered from
a number of imitators springing up throughout Cairo. Pizza became a
food trend, and many restaurants quickly added it to their menus. In addition, hundreds of new pizza parlors of varying quality were started by
entrepreneurs to take advantage of this fad. Pizza Plus stopped expansion,
and Pizza Hut was forced to close some stores. By 2005, Tawfiq estimated,
there were some 400 pizza outlets in Cairo. All but one of his restaurants
continued to turn a steady profit, but the high volume and cash flows of
the first five years were over.

THE LIMITS OF MULTILOCALIZATION

In the summer of 2005, I sat in the shade of a cabana, drinking fruit juice,
discussing entrepreneurialism with Rami, and watching people splash
and play in the swimming pool of the health club he built with two partners. An AUC graduate in engineering, Rami was widely read in North
American entrepreneurial literature and had attended workshops that
explained the secrets of business success in liberal economies. The club
he and his partners had built was designed around a core concept: that of
being a sports school rather than an ordinary health club. They had recognized this as a market niche, exploited their own knowledge as sports
enthusiasts, and developed a "health academy." Racquetball, swimming,
and tennis lessons, along with diet and nutrition workshops, were offered
as a way to set the club apart from its competitors and became the focus of
its marketing. So far, the club was profitable, but Rami was worried. Plans
for expansion—the construction of a second club under the same brand

name and approach—were well under way and would stretch the partners' capital and credit to the maximum. If either or both clubs failed, now or down the road, his financial resources could be exhausted. Again and again in our conversation, he spoke determinedly of the need for "aggressive expansion" and "the need to take risks" if one "wants to be a success" as explanations for this perilous enterprise.

Risk and uncertainty are central in economic theories of entrepreneurialism, especially in the so-called Austrian school that dominates entrepreneurial theory (Chiles et al. 2007). Schumpeter (1934, 1993) was a critic of the mainstream economic assumption that people always behave rationally, and his account of the boom-bust cycle, both at the micro level of individual businesses and at the macro level of economic sectors, is driven by entrepreneurs unable to make rational choices because of inadequate information. People must act in uncertainty, which requires risk at every level of the economy. The more stable the economy, the more willing people are to take risks (which may lead to destabilizing innovations); the less stable the economy, the less willing people are to take risks. In this vision of the economic world, entrepreneurial imagination involves the capacity of successful entrepreneurs to innovate in relative uncertainty through "the capacity of seeing things in a certain way which afterwards proves to be true, even though it cannot be established at the moment, and of grasping the essential fact, discarding the unessential, even though no one can give an account of how this is done" (Schumpeter 1934: 85). In terms of public discourses about entrepreneurship, this romantic notion contributes to the celebration of successful entrepreneurs, the erasure of their errors, and the unceremonious dumping of failed enterprises into the dustbin of history. For actual Egyptian entrepreneurs, though, their actions have consequences. Entrepreneurial success is tied to cosmopolitan identity, so that economic risk is also social risk.

One way entrepreneurs attempt to handle uncertainty is by imitating prior successful models, which may lead to overexpansion. Overexpansion, whether by specific companies (like McDonald's or Pizza Hut) or by entire retail sectors seeking to exploit particular market fads (like pizza), is a constant theme in stories about business in Egypt. In tourism, for instance, for every international success like Stella di Mare in Ain Sukna, there are a half-dozen hotels and resorts unable to turn a profit. In 2000,

Osman, a Cairene businessman in his late forties, told me he had picked up two hotels for a song. Since he had not assumed the original investors' debt, he was in a good position to "turn the hotels around" with "aggressive marketing" that would pull in tourists from Italy, Germany, and elsewhere in Europe. Osman said the hotels were first-class, with restaurants, snorkeling, and boating, and he blamed the failure of the hotels on the "poor management" and "inadequate marketing strategies" of the investors who built them—on a lapse, that is, of entrepreneurial imagination. When I met him again in 2005, however, the hotels were continuing to fail. "The location is not good," he explained. "Even with aggressive marketing and management, and the low value of the pound against the euro, we can't bring in enough tourists to maintain [the hotel facilities]." He was renting the rooms at extremely low prices and slowly allowing the physical structure to degenerate. "Only if I could find a partner to put in some capital, perhaps we could turn it around."

Osman's story reveals an important element of the notion of the entrepreneurial imagination as a feature of identities: it re-allocates the responsibility for success and failure from infrastructural conditions and the regulatory environment and places it on the character of the individual entrepreneurs. If the secret of successful development, on both individual enterprise and national scales, lies in the capacity of the entrepreneurial imagination to creatively discover ways to overcome infrastructural and regulatory obstacles, then it is the imagination that fails.

Osman's narrative positions the original builders as poor managers, and himself as someone who can come in and use his enterprise to turn things around. When things don't turn around, Osman positions himself as the victim of the original builders' failure of imagination—to choose a better location, for example. At one level, this is a classic example of the tendency of people to attribute their own failures to external situational causes and those of others to internal dispositional causes (Gurevitch 1989). But there is a defensive note to his narrative, for others will talk about Osman as a failure, and the model of enterprise culture limits the effectiveness of blaming, for example, the underregulated development and environmental situation of the Red Sea.

Although it is deeply entwined with current models of state-guided development, enterprise culture is not merely some kind of false consciousness imposed by a state ideology. It is a cultural model, a system for organizing knowledge about the world, making sense of experience, and generating meaningful action. As a cultural model, it is self-consistent and largely immune to verification, since it contains within itself explanations for its own lapses and failures. This kind of model serves many functions, not the least of which is to encourage the continuation of the entrepreneurial impetus of risk taking and innovation in the wake of failure after failure. The discourses of enterprise culture maintain the promise that, no matter how poorly a business performs, there is someone out there with the imagination to turn it around and make it work: an Ahmad Zayat to turn overemployment into a resource, a Mohammed Tawfiq to undercut multinational competition, entrepreneurs like the founders of Cilantro to find opportunity in Byzantine import regulations. But for my argument about cosmopolitanism and class reproduction, the important thing to note is the way that discourses of entrepreneurial imagination can be mobilized as exclusionary practices for constructing class distinctions.

"The problem, you know, is that Egyptians don't have an enterprise culture," Rami told me over our cabana lunch at his club. I looked at him, dumbfounded, and disagreed. I offered dozens of examples of creative enterprise among shopkeepers and others I'd witnessed over the years: the vegetable vendor who sold prewashed and cut produce, the taxi driver who learned Japanese and tripled his income, the shopkeeper who parlayed a 200-pound micro loan into a refrigerated section, the whole informal economy of *sawwayis,* guys who park your car for you in overcrowded Cairo. He frowned a bit, then shook his head dismissively. These are not serious enterprises, he said. They do not risk nor produce significant capital. Rami thus excluded more than 85 percent of the Egyptian population from his discussion on the grounds that their enterprises do not engage upscale consumers.

This notion that Egyptians lack an enterprise culture was apparently the main point that was hammered home at a two-day workshop on entrepreneurialism held at one of Cairo's five-star hotels during the summer of 2005, which Rami had attended with one of his partners. According to Rami, the essence of the workshop was that foreign investors didn't understand local conditions sufficiently to prosper without local partners. But Egypt lacked an indigenous enterprise culture. It was therefore people of Rami's class—Egyptian but Western-educated, at home in both Arabic and European languages, and knowledgeable about modern business practices—who were the bright hope of Egypt's future in the global economy.

This denial of enterprise culture to Egypt is not limited to high-priced workshops designed to stimulate Egyptian entrepreneurs worried about risky or overextended investments. Within the expatriate community and among the foreign managers of multinational companies, dinner party conversations frequently slide at some point to the problems of doing business in Egypt. Some of these American, British, Canadian, Indian, South American, and other members of the global corporate managerial class discuss "local culture" almost entirely in terms of the obstacles it presents to the smooth operation of a presumably rational and "culture-free" business system. The following four excerpts from interviews with corporate officers demonstrate the framework through which foreign management conceives local labor.

For Phil, an American consultant involved in the start-up of a major agribusiness, the problems are the local partners and the hierarchical nature of the workplace.

> They are all so afraid to spend any money unless the big boss
> okays it. And he's always traveling. Then, he needs to think
> about it, and by the time he makes a decision it's too late. In ag-
> riculture, the seasons change, timing is everything. . . . Everyone
> is so afraid to make a mistake, we can't get anything done. You
> should see them all when the big boss walks in. He's some kind
> of retired minister. The whole mood of the office changes. They
> all just freeze up until he leaves.

The project Phil heads is funded by Saudi investors and run by the American management company of which he is an officer. Under Egyptian law, the investors must have a local partner who is often, as in this case, a retired government official. Phil describes this situation as one in which the project would move ahead smoothly under untrammeled American management, but it grinds to a halt because of the obstacles posed by the presence of the Egyptian partner who is, he points out, the product of a socialist bureaucracy.

For Girgis, the Egyptian-born, American-educated director of the Cairo office of a major multinational manufacturer, the problems involve work ethics.

> [Egyptian employees] ask me, why doesn't the company believe
> in promoting Egyptians? These guys come into the office right
> on the dot, or maybe fifteen minutes late. Never early. They're
> *never* early. Then, they have to walk around the room and say
> hello to every single person. And then, they have to get a cup of
> coffee, and by the time they sit down it's forty-five minutes into
> the workday. They say Americans are anti-Arab, and I tell them,
> hey, what am I? I tell them when I was bucking for promotion, I
> found out what time my boss got to work. And I made it a point
> to be at my desk working before he got there every morning and
> after he left every night. And my visibility went up and so did
> my productivity. And I got the promotion. I can tell them this
> in Arabic or in English, [but] it's like I'm speaking a different
> language.

Girgis offers himself here as a local boy made good, the living embodiment of the promise of multinational employment that has attracted the Egyptians he is now supervising. With hard work and adherence to the Western corporate work ethic, which puts productivity ahead of family and social relationships, anyone can escape the stigma of the local and rise in the global corporation. Girgis portrays himself as frustrated because, in spite of his facility in both the global and local languages, he cannot translate this message across the social gap between him and his employees.[23]

For Maggie, an Anglo-American consultant supervising a feasibility study for a British manufacturer interested in coming into the region, the problem is the peculiar "bureaucratic mindset" of the Egyptians created by their educational system.

> They go out and do a second-rate assessment and come back
> [and] tell me about how much money they've saved. And I tell
> them, spend the money and do the job right. We're *supposed*
> to spend the money. . . . The universities here all train them to
> work in the government bureaucracy, where if you come in un-

der budget you're rewarded, no questions asked. Nobody asks about quality. And I don't know how to train them out of that mindset.

Knowing how to spend money to make money is a crucial aspect of liberal economics. Employees who attempt to apply frugality as a universal principle to every situation are unacceptable for Maggie's project. Maggie is looking for fiscal cosmopolitans who can move smoothly from context to context, recognizing when to spend and when to save in order to further the project's goals.

For Carlos, the Peruvian-born director of the Middle East regional office of a major oil company subsidiary, a key issue is corruption.

You know, in Latin America and India, all these places [that] are famous for being corrupt, I don't think we had these problems. Our company, it's one of the principles of our company, we don't pay bribes, we don't pay kickbacks. Anywhere. I've been here four years, and I've put in for a transfer. I told them I can't do any more. I told them it's time to bring in somebody else. I was only supposed to be here two years, finishing up the work of the guy before me. But we're nowhere near ready to give control of the office over to the local managers.

Collectively, these accounts by Rami, Phil, Girgis, Maggie, and Carlos construct Egypt as an anti-enterprise culture. Rather than acknowledging that, in any enterprise culture, many projects will fail, these Western and Westernized managers posit the failure of projects as caused by the supposed collective characteristics of the Egyptian people. Each of these stories involves an assumption that local knowledges and competences are not boons but obstacles to successful production, distribution, and sales. These stories all assert two ways of business, an Anglo-European, global, correct way and a local way that impedes global entrepreneurship. In this discourse, local knowledge and competence may be necessary for comprehending the needs of local audiences toward which goods and services can be directed, but they are not regarded as appropriate for managing production and distribution. Similarly, Kehrer in an otherwise exemplary study of how transnational corporations adapt to the Egyptian market milieu, seems to be taking her managerial consultants at face value when they claim that multinational corporations have "shown much more ability than local corporations to respond to special local conditions" (2006: 155). Foreign businesspeople are assumed in these accounts to be the Schumpeterian entrepreneurs who are instinctively correct, while local entrepreneurs have to prove themselves. The cases of Pizza Plus, Cilantro, and Tahrir Koshary show that local entrepreneurs can be quite savvy about adapting to local, shifting market conditions, and the case of McDonald's clearly illustrates that transnationals don't always get it right when they override the misgivings of local managers. Moreover, as with celebrations of entrepreneurial imagination generally, these informants exclude failures in constructing their accounts. Phil, for example, neglects to mention that the U.S. company he works for had gone bankrupt and been acquired by its largest competitor. The California-based company knew how to make the desert bloom but perhaps not how to do so profitably even in Western markets. Girgis's story erases his own difficulties when he returned to Egypt and violated his company's policy by hiring relatives and friends in accordance with local networks of favors and status (*wasta*). His own success at corporate social relations may thus be tied more to social contexts than to an ability to "transcend" local culture. Clearly, these foreign managers are not disinterested analysts; their stories about the problems posed by Egyptian culture partially absolve them of responsibility for the failures of projects they are paid to oversee and bring to success. The real question then, is not what to do about local culture, but rather what these discourses of distinction between the global and the local—and the successful hybrids—accomplish in regard to constructing cosmopolitan identities.

Thus, however "true" these stories may be as explanations for the failures of these specific projects, the use of such stories creates an exclusionary discourse that helps to maintain the class distinction by which cosmopolitan style justifies improved life chances. Taken together, these stories construct an opposition of persons. On one side are Egyptians of the working and middle classes who are represented as lacking any real enterprise culture, which can only come to them through the kinds of Western educations and patterns of consumption that are the patrimony of the upper class. On the other side are the Western or Western-educated administrators, businesspeople, and managers who come to Egypt to operate international companies. From this dialectical opposition comes the synthetic identity that successful entrepreneurs adopt and new entrepreneurs aspire to: the enterprising Egyptian entrepreneur who both understands capitalist business ethos and the local system and so can create local economic success in the changing global economy.

In so doing, the cosmopolitan class simultaneously constructs itself as apart from the Egyptian masses, while at the same time serving as the pivotal engine of the Egyptian economy. Within this idiom, to speak of foreign investment, of privatization, of international marketing is to speak of the need for a class of cosmopolitan Egyptians to manage and reimagine these processes, and so benefit from them as producers, managers, and consumers in ways that exceed the benefits that accrue to middle- and working-class Egyptians. Yet, as with other aspects of cosmopolitan identity—consumption of global branded goods, private school educations, faith, gender—this one is fraught with tension. Where foreigners can blame their failures on the Egyptian culture, cosmopolitan culture brokers' failures almost inevitably suggest that they have failed to strike that balance between Egyptian and modern—that they are too Egyptian or too Westernized—to successfully create the kind of enterprise culture that would validate their class identity.

It is increasingly clear that the strengthening of local and national identities and the spread of global market capitalism are not contradictions but two aspects of the same dynamic process (Miller 1997; Wilk 1999; Mazzarella 2004). Notions of the McDonaldization of local culture, involving the equalization of consumption and an associated transfer of values that weakens local domains of meaning, are ubiquitous, but do not well reflect the reality of the changes in the economic sphere that are occurring as a result of transnational flows of consumer goods. By partnering with local cosmopolitans—members of the class that consumes many of these goods as status-bound tastes—foreign investors and transnational corporations "are in fact extremely well-equipped to respond to the diversity of local cultural spheres of meaning within their diverse markets" (Kehrer 2006: 152). While analysis that sees contemporary globalization as a product of an increasingly uniform Western capitalism has increasingly given way to accounts of "glocalization," "hybridity," and "mélange" (Appadurai 1996; Hannerz 1992; Nederveen Pieterse 2004), there has been little effort to describe the ways in which hybrids are constructed, and to ask what is hybrid to whom, under what circumstances, and in what ways. In particular, the question of who is doing the producing of transnational consumer goods and their social relations to consumers requires explication.

In Egypt, members of the cosmopolitan class facilitate these processes by acting as the agents of hybridity. As culture brokers, cosmopolitan entrepreneurs produce, manage, and market most of the enterprises that have been transforming Egypt in the twenty-first century, giving Cairo its increasingly cosmopolitan face and enabling the processes collectively glossed as "globalization." They do so within a complex social field. Egypt's current models of development are predicated in part on the implementation of Western management techniques for production and marketing whose premises contradict many preexisting national economic institutions. The notion of the entrepreneurial imagination offers a way to overcome this contradiction by yoking the dynamics of capitalism to the capacities of individuals and teams of producers, managers, and marketers to creatively overcome infrastructural obstacles and, indeed, even turn them to advantage.

But establishing cosmopolitan Egyptian professionals in these roles has important implications for identity. Western management techniques masquerade as universally efficient, maximally applicable practices. Because they are seen as culturally neutral, managerial failure is often understood not as a clash of different cultures but as caused primarily by the impediments of local culture. As culture brokers, members of Egypt's cosmopolitan class walk a thin line between being "too Egyptian" or "too Western" to successfully manage these supposed cultural obstacles. Entrepreneurial success becomes the ultimate arbiter of whether one has achieved the essential balance between fully Egyptian and fully modern.

Finally, as they negotiate this razor's edge, Egyptian capitalists, managers, and marketers contribute to the ongoing reproduction of the cosmopolitan class by continually producing and distributing the goods and sites necessary for their own and their children's acquisition and display of cosmopolitan style.

EPILOGUE

Everyone grows up global, and everyone does so in locales. There is a tendency in much public discourse everywhere modernity has penetrated to see the traditional as the realm of culture and the modern as wiping culture away, or at least reducing it from its role in organizing shared public realms to a matter of individual psychology. Many of the cosmopolitan Egyptians I knew saw the world in this way. "Egypt used to have a culture that all people shared," wrote Ingy in a class paper. "But now we all eat at McDonald's and have lost our culture." Similar sentiments were expressed over the years by many students, who complained that mobile phones, cable television, computers, or Coca-Cola were rendering Egyptian life increasingly inauthentic. Part of my job was to demonstrate, as I have tried to do in this book, that in spite of their iconicity and indexicality with their counterparts abroad, McDonald's, computers, and other transnational goods and technologies do not replace local culture with global but become part of local culture by becoming situated in an infrastructural and social matrix that transforms them. Moreover, the "we" who eat at McDonald's are a tiny percentage of the people of Egypt. Because that fact is known both by the people who eat there and by those who cannot, eating at McDonald's, ownership of computers, and similar forms of consumption take on symbolic importance as indicators of inclusion and exclusion. Human beings, modern and otherwise (if an otherwise is even possible), can no more stop symbolizing than they can stop eating. At some level, cosmopolitans know this; successful entrepreneurs rely on it in their work of creating the very social fields in which Ingy's naïve statement can be uttered in sincerity.

There are many kinds of cosmopolitanisms in the contemporary literature on globalization and transnationalism, including a humanist ideal (Nussbaum 1996, 1997), a concept of global professionals practicing transnational trades (Hannerz 2004), a philanthropy that looks beyond the local (Miller 2006), and a view of those "victims of modernity" forced to live tenaciously in the fraught terrains of globalization (Breckinridge et al. 2002). In this book, I have dealt with cosmopolitanism not as an idea but as a grounded social category situated in a particular time and space and constituted by concrete social practices. I have argued that, among Egypt's upper class and upwardly mobile middle class, modernity has become a cosmopolitan style, an expression of education, experience, and taste that valorizes their greater control over the country's resources. This style is generated through indexical signification, signifying practices that mean something locally because their referents are foreign, transnational, or global. The meanings of these signs and signifying practices are worked out in various metadeictic discourses, in which the indexical meanings of the signs are asserted, resisted, and negotiated. Through these practices, Egyptian cosmopolitans construct local notions of the global and integrate these into broader systems of social relations. Yet their cosmopolitan identities are always fraught as they seek to find a balance between being fully modern and fully Egyptian. This balance is difficult to find because the communities that define modern and global deem Egypt to be backward, while the communities that define local and traditional deem many of the styles adopted by cosmopolitans to be inauthentic.

This account has implications for a social theory that understands globalization in terms of the linking of locales. While most theories give lip service to claims that localization is the obverse of globalization, the tendency has been to focus on anecdotal accounts of apparent hybridities and to make generalizations about commonalities in an effort to grasp the global rather than examining local places. In this view, all locales are "contact zones" (Pratt 1991) in which people encounter, appropriate, manage, resist, and negotiate cultural flows. An adequate theory of globalization needs to begin with a theory of localization, an account of how different social and cultural groups create the processes we gloss as globalization as they actively take part in social change by incorporating transnational flows of goods, people, and symbols into their lives and localities. In particular, I draw four key lessons from this study for a broader understanding of these processes.

First, "local," "foreign," and "hybrid" are not objective facts about peoples, practices, ideas, or objects but are local interpretations of experience. People produce the local and the global as they ascribe meanings to goods, events, and activities. It is the anthropologist who sees such things as Pokémon and McDonald's in Egypt as hybrid. Both the elite classes who were McDonald's original audience and the working classes who are excluded from it see McDonald's as a foreign institution.

This book has claimed that what is important about cosmopolitanism is not participation in transnational flows, for such participation at some level or other is ubiquitous and inevitable in the twenty-first century. Rather, what is important is the style through which participation is imagined and expressed, and the webs of social relations created through this. Localization is a metacultural process involving metadeictic discourses that select which connections to pay attention to, define these connections, and link these to social relations.

The production of globalization takes place within a political-economic context partially shaped by the government and by international financial institutions. Yet the shape and style of globalization in Cairo are not controlled by these institutions. The kinds of changes the Egyptian government makes in response to USAID, World Bank, and IMF strictures do not really usher in the kinds of privatization those institutions seek to create. And the magic bullet that will accelerate economic development, whether tax-free zones, information technology villages, or enterprise culture, continues to elude government planners. Ultimately, while Cairo is connected to the world economy through processes of entrepreneurialism, production, marketing, and consumption, it is locals who make it happen as entrepreneurs, managers, investment partners, culture brokers, and consumers. And the logics by which they pursue these activities are not necessarily those predicted by the managers and economic advisors at financial institutions, government bureaucracies, marketing research firms, and multinational corporations. People in Egypt may pursue their own interests in rational ways, but the forms of rationality are shaped by local histories and systems of social relations.

Which brings me to my final point: Localization produces persons. Far from being instances of some universalizing process, such as the differentiation of global elites and local masses (J. Friedman 1997, 2002a), the realization of essential cultural difference (Huntington 1993), or the collapse of cultural difference into a flattened world (T. L. Friedman 2007), consumption, management, and entrepreneurship are all economic activities pursued in part according to market logics and with real economic consequences, but they are also performances that produce persons by linking local identities and cultural notions of selfhood in practices that mobilize symbols of the foreign "other." In addition, market logics are strongly inflected by this symbolic dimension, since both what constitutes risk and rewards, and how people pursue rewards and manage risk, are culturally patterned. The social, economic, and political processes we gloss as globalization take place as people pursue their personal goals to create particular kinds of selves, including, but not limited to, economically successful selves.

DRAMATIS PERSONAE

Many, many people helped me understand Cairo's cosmopolitan class. This is a list of the small group that made it into the final text, alphabetically by pseudonym.

Mrs. Abdel Rahman. Forty-five-year-old translator and interpreter for a multinational corporation; divorced. Son attends ASC; daughter attends AUC. The children live with her, but their father pays their fees.

Ahmed. Male engineering major at AUC; attended the French-language Choueifat International School and spent two years at Cairo University's School of Medicine before switching to AUC. Hopes to find work in the United States or Canada or, barring that, with a multinational in Egypt. Fond of *shisha*.

Aida. Female AUC junior majoring in anthropology. Grew up in California until she was twelve and wished to study sports medicine at UCLA.

Aline. Ten-year-old female student at ASC. Egyptian father and French mother are co-owners of a successful international development company. Has an ample trust fund; plans to pursue education in Europe.

Amin. General manager of a large pharmaceutical firm. Married with four children, including Ismail.

Amira. Female sophomore at AUC, majoring in modern history. Took the veil after listening to Amr Khaled tapes with a friend.

Arvind. Director of marketing research for the Egyptian branch of a major European household goods and processed foods manufacturer. Born and educated in Mumbai, India.

Ashraf. Male tenth-grade student at ASC. Huge fan of Arabic, European, and North American pop music. Hopes to form a band while in high school but says his parents will make him major in engineering or medicine when he goes to college.

Bilqis. Female tenth-grade student at ASC. Has attended ASC since first grade; spends summers with cousins in Riyadh and New York.

Butros. Computer programming and software solutions manager with a European-based international corporation. In his early thirties, educated at a Canadian university, worked in Canada for several years, returned to Egypt for family reasons and stayed.

Carlos. Peruvian-born director of the Middle East office of a major oil company subsidiary. Married to an American woman; four children.

Dalia. AUC undergraduate student in communications, graduate student in sociology/anthropology. Mother of two.

Dina. Teacher at ASC with B.A. and M.A. from AUC. Married with two children, both of whom attend ASC.

Donald. Vice president of marketing for Egyptian branch of a major U.S. household goods manufacturer.

Eiman. Female tenth-grader at ASC. Attended a less expensive, private, English-language school until her freshman year, then switched to ASC to prepare for college at AUC or abroad. Her younger brother (by five years) attended ASC since first grade.

Farid. Waiter at an *'ahwa* in Tahrir Square near AUC; lives in the *sha'abi* neighborhood of Abu Khalifa in Ghamra. Nicknamed Maru'a (Generous).

Gazbeya. Female student at AUC, majoring in political science. Father is in the diplomatic service, and she would like to follow in his footsteps, as part of the growing number of women in the diplomatic corps.

Girgis. Egyptian-born, American-educated director of the Cairo office of a major multinational manufacturer.

Hassan. Fifteen-year-old student at ASC. Hopes to attend Boston University and pursue a business career abroad.

Hawass. AUC computer science graduate who obtained a job with a German firm and was preparing to relocate to Bonn.

Heba. Account executive for advertising agency that handled McDonald's Egyptian marketing. AUC graduate with a double major in business and psychology.

Hedayat. Female graduate student in sociology/anthropology at AUC. Attended Choueifat International School, then took her undergraduate degree at Alexandria University. Accepted to a U.S. graduate program, she switched to AUC when she got engaged to a local doctor.

Hosni. In his late thirties, degree from the School of Law, Cairo University. He has a minor position in the post office, runs the cash register and handles the books at a store owned by a family connection, and drives a friend's taxi. Most of his income pays school fees for his children, an investment he felt was gloriously repaid when his son received the highest score in the nation on the *i'dadiyya 'amma*.

Ingy. Daughter of a New York businessman of Egyptian origin. She and her mother lived in Cairo during her education at AUC. After her father was injured, she moved to New York, changed her name to Angie, and finished college in the United States.

Ismail. Ten-year-old student at MLS in Ma'adi Gadida.

Jim. Oil executive living in Ma'adi. One eight-year-old son, one ten-year-old daughter.

Karim. Male student at AUC, majoring in engineering. Major *shisha* fan; has a bumper sticker on his car that reads, "I Only Smoke *Shisha* on Days Ending in Y."

Khaled. Male student at AUC, majoring in mechanical engineering. Took his international baccalaureate at the German school in Cairo. Son of Osman.

Maged. Taxi driver who took me to Giza to see the First Mall. In his early fifties, Maged argues that it is the corrupt practices of the rich that are destroying the country.

Maggie. Anglo-American consultant supervising a feasibility study for a British investor interested in coming into the region. Born and educated in Britain, she took her M.B.A. at a U.S. university.

Marwa. Twenty-five-year-old journalist; born to Egyptian parents, raised in Kuwait. Educated at Ain Shams University in Egypt, she has worked as a journalist in Cyprus, Jordan, and Egypt.

Maryam. Principal of MLS. Daughter of a military officer, she studied English at Cairo University. Married a doctor, who encouraged her to continue her education. Received an M.A. in child psychology from Cairo University and a Ph.D. in comparative education from the School of Education, Eötvös Loránd University, Budapest.

Mina. Female undergraduate at AUC, majoring in mass communications. Raised in Egypt until her early teens, her mother sent her to boarding school in England after her father died. After six years, she returned to Egypt, very much against her will, to study at AUC and, her family

hoped, find a husband. Her mother's death in her second year of college left her in the custody of her paternal uncles, but she intends to
head for the United States at the earliest opportunity.

Mona. Tenth-grade student at ASC. Mona's father and uncles own a business facilitating Egyptian exports and locating new markets. She lived
three years in the United States and four in Canada before returning
to Egypt for high school and college.

Mustafa. Teacher at a private school. Married, in his early thirties. Received his undergraduate degree at Delhi University and an M.A. in
sociology from AUC.

Nadia. Director of a human resources consulting firm that serves mostly
foreign clients doing business in Egypt. Graduated from AUC, then
took a degree in human resources management at a U.S. university.

Nireen. Female AUC undergraduate, majoring in psychology. Adopted a
more pious lifestyle after a series of accidents; began to consider veiling after listening to Amr Khaled but worried about whether it would
affect her graduate studies in the United States.

Noha. Attended ASC and AUC (degree in communications). Journalist for
English-language lifestyle and business magazines.

Nora. AUC mass communications undergraduate, she returned to AUC
for graduate school after the birth of her first child.

Omneya. Female political science major at AUC. Active in pro-Palestinian
causes on campus.

Osman. Businessman in his late forties. He and his brother own a successful German-Egyptian import business. With another partner, he is
engaged in real estate and development, including majority ownership
of two Red Sea resorts.

Phil. American consultant involved in the start-up of a major agribusiness
intended to produce fruit for the export market.

Raghda. Female sociology student at AUC. Born to Egyptian parents in
Morocco, studied in a French school, received a French baccalaureate.
Attended a French university but the financial and emotional cost of
living abroad proved to be too much for her and her family, and she
completed her education at AUC. While proud that she is fluent in
English and French, she is sometimes teased by her friends for the
"French" accent that creeps into her Arabic and English.

Rami. Co-owner of a Cairo health club. Graduated from AUC with a degree in engineering.

Dr. Reem. In her late thirties, a graduate of Cairo University School of Medicine. Married to another doctor whose practice supports the family, she founded and operates the free women's clinic at a large downtown mosque. Mother of Yussuf; led an anti-Pokémon campaign at MLS.

Saad. Thirty-four-year-old project manager for an international development agency. Father of two children at MLS.

Sabry. Male business student at AUC, twenty-two years old. Educated in English-language "American" schools in Egypt except for two years of high school in an affluent Los Angeles suburb.

Salma. Female computer science major at AUC. Engaged to another AUC student, hopes they can both find work abroad.

Samir. Male student at AUC, majoring in engineering. Runs a nightclub with his brother.

Sherif. Son of an Egyptian politician, graduated from Cairo University School of Medicine, but then went to AUC for a graduate degree in sociology while he considered what to do with his life. A nonpracticing Muslim for most of his undergraduate life, he underwent a religious reconversion, which led him to begin attending Amr Khaled lectures.

Sherine. Received B.A. in psychology from AUC and joined an advertising agency several months after graduating.

Soraya. Public relations officer for a multinational corporation. Mother of Yasseen.

Stephen. Twelve-year-old American student at ASC, originally from Oklahoma. Father is a former petroleum engineer now working in middle management for an oil company; mother does not work outside the home.

Yasmin. Undergraduate at AUC, majoring in psychology. Father is one of the investors in the First Mall in Giza.

Yasseen. Ten-year-old son of Soraya and her husband, who owns a small electronics business. Pokémon fan and computer/internet buff.

Yussuf. Eleven-year-old student at MLS. Son of Dr. Reem.

NOTES

1. Toward an Anthropology of Connections

1. If my students are right, perhaps Zaynab's decision to refuse her children food she has not prepared is motivated in part by a sense of what may be lost to her and her children when food becomes a commodity. Based on fieldwork in Florence, Italy, Carole Counihan has argued that many professional modern women have less input into their children's socialization than their mothers had because they no longer control what they eat, which is equated with the ingestion of the mother's cultural values. "Women are losing the manipulative power of food, and perhaps the world is losing it as well" (Counihan 1999: 60). People of my students' class grow up largely fed by maids, yet I noted that, in most families, mothers cooked at least one meal a week, often some regionally significant dish like *mulukhiyah* (a thick vegetable soup).

2. By "managerial class," I mean the educated upper-middle-class families from which are drawn the people who run the nation's institutions: upper-level bureaucrats, school administrators, and corporate management. One study showed that 54.4 percent of fathers and 17.8 percent of mothers of AUC students worked in managerial and administrative positions (Russell 1994).

3. Class is an older and more established concept than globalization, but no less problematic. That people live in hierarchically stratified systems is obvious, not only to anthropologists but to Egyptians. What is problematic is the nature of the boundaries between the classes. Classes are forged in everyday performances. I will follow Bourdieu in acknowledging that class is thus mutable, but in patterned ways.

4. Writing of the rise of Westernized elites under colonial regimes, Keith David Watenpaugh emphasizes that class was "defined not just by the wealth, professions, possessions, or levels of education of its members, but also *by the way they asserted their modernity*" (Watenpaugh 2006: 8; emphasis mine). On the history of consumption and assertions of cosmopolitan modernity in Egypt, see Ryzova 2005; Shechter 2006.

5. *Bi'a* is a slang term of uncertain origin. Abaza (2001b) suggests that it derives from a euphemism for "smelly" and is associated with the culture of the *'ashwa'iyyat* (slums). And as both Abaza and Ghannam (2002) point out, the characterization of an area as a "slum" is itself an important ideological construction crucial to the production of modern counterspaces in Cairo.

2. Making Kids Modern

1. Founded in 1945, just as Unity had passed its heyday, the school has occupied its present ten-acre site since 1963.

2. In 2004, a branch of the trendy Cairo coffee-house chain Cilantro opened a small café in its basement (see chapters 5 and 6).

3. Indeed, at the beginning of the twenty-first century, Egypt had only 17 daily and 30 weekly newspapers—a sharp decline from the turn of the twentieth century, when it had 114 newspapers (Essoulami 2000).

4. For example, according to the office of the U.S. trade representative, Egypt's imports from the United States (its largest trading partner) totaled $3.3 billion in 2000, while Egypt's exports to the United States totaled only $888 million.

5. There are also small Korean and Japanese schools, but they do not seek Egyptian students nor do Egyptians seem to desire to attend. At least as far as education is concerned, cosmopolitanism in Egypt is largely about knowing "the West." In 2008, a Chinese school for Egyptians opened to much fanfare, but it is not yet clear how it will fit into the local cultural system.

6. *Majid* is less expensive in Cairo than in the oil-rich states. "Since the Egyptian prices do not cover costs, they are effectively subsidized by profits from the richer petroleum states" (Douglas and Malti-Douglas 1994: 150).

7. Created in the 1930s by Ernie Bushmiller and Carl Anderson, respectively, *Nancy and Sluggo* and *Henry* have been in continual syndication ever since. Part of their popularity for foreign publishers seems to be that both are extremely visual comic strips that often use only a minimum of dialogue.

8. In 2002, less than a year after my research period ended, *Alaa Eldin*'s founding editor, Ezzat El-Saadan, retired. The new editor told me she has made it a point to privilege hand-drawn art over computer-generated texts.

9. Flash is a significant player in the domain of children's popular culture in the Egyptian market. Flash offers dubbed Arabic versions of a variety of American and European video productions, including those featuring Pokémon and Batman.

10. Indeed, when I asked her to describe a story or article that had influenced her, she was unable to think of one.

11. On the creation of children's networks among magazine readers, see Imada 2002.

12. By "region," I mean the geographic and demographic area represented in the map that appears weekly in *Majid:* North Africa and the Gulf states, from Morocco to the Indian Ocean, including Sudan. Building on commonalities of language and Muslim traditions is a common media strategy for extending the viability of content across national boundaries into the rest of the region (Hawkes 1997: 24–25; Sreberny 2001).

13. The portrayal of girls in Western dress is a decades-old technique for portraying generational change and modernity. One of *Majid*'s most popular comic strips in Marwa's day was *Zakiyya al-Dhakiyya* (*Zakiyya the Clever*), whose protagonist was a girl in Western dress, complete with saddle shoes and huge spectacles, who knew everything and was frequently seen lecturing her *higab*-wearing mother (Douglas and Malti-Douglas 1994). Interestingly, while the *Zakiyya* strip no longer runs regularly, the character Zakiyya is still found in the pages of the magazine introducing websites and computer features.

14. This does not mean that Christians do not read the magazine, only that they are unlikely to articulate their identities as Christians in correspondence. Subbarao, the creator of India's *Tinkle* magazine, reported a similar problem in India, where Muslim children acquiesced to the dominance of the Hindu culture in the magazine, even sending

in stories in which all the characters had Hindu names. Subbarao successfully created a specifically Muslim character called Anwar not so much to increase Muslim readership as to increase Muslim readers' identity with the magazine (Rao 2001: 45–46).

15. Palestine is by no means the only political issue that finds its way into these magazines. In 1996, *Alaa Eldin* ran a seventeen-week cartoon series on the work of the Red Cross. And the degree to which political stories run varies not only from magazine to magazine but may change over time. When I returned to Cairo in 2005, for example, the editorship of *Alaa Eldin* had been transferred, and the new editor told me she much preferred to emphasize art and culture over politics.

16. On the difference between *jinn* and genies, see Peterson 2007.

17. I do not know if it is significant that these boys read magazines that are not edited and published in Egypt. The boys themselves seemed unaware that the magazines are not Egyptian, and I was unable to determine from my interviews whether this meant anything to their parents.

18. Soraya certainly has a point. While many middle-class men may well expect their wives to stay home, in upper- and upper-middle-class families women's professional work is the norm. In a 1993 survey at Egypt's (then) only private university, the American University in Cairo, less than 30 percent of students reported their mothers as exclusively engaged in unpaid household labor (Russell 1994: 128). A survey of customers at computer matchmaking services showed that men with upper-middle-class aspirations were actively seeking wives with professional careers (Abu-Hashish and Peterson 1999).

3. Pokémon Panics

1. On the role of MSA in Egyptian society, see Haeri 2003; Mellor 2005: 109–121.

2. Also see O'Dougherty's argument that the hegemony of places like the United States and Japan "make their middle classes the international standard" (O'Dougherty 2002: 4).

3. *Captain Majid* is an Arabic-dubbed and -edited version of the Japanese animated series *Captain Tsubasa,* which is about a football (soccer in the United States) team and its adventurous captain. Based on a Japanese *manga* series by Yoichi Takahashi, the animated television show and video games have been enormously popular under various names in most of South America, Europe, and the Middle East. The *manga* began in 1961 and the animated series has run in Japan since 1983. It has been carefully "de-odorized" (Iwabuchi 2002) for export. *Captain Majid* has aired in the Middle East at least since the late 1980s, and many people speak of having grown up watching it. Many viewers are unaware that the programs are not locally produced somewhere in the Middle East.

4. A Ramadan staple since 1998, *Bakar* is an animated cartoon about a Nubian boy and his pet goat, which was created by Egyptian animator Mona Abul-Nasr and her Cairo Cartoon Production Company.

5. Much of the "evidence" for these claims can be refuted by the visual representation. For example, one article claimed that the Pokémon Stario, a bejeweled starfish, was a six-pointed Star of David, in complete contradiction to the fact that Stario is drawn with five points. The charge that a Mogen David ("symbol of international Zionism," the report explains) appears on Pokémon cards likewise requires a considerable exercise of imagination since the six-pointed figure actually resembles an asterisk.

6. Ironically, many Pokémon licensees felt caught in the same web of indexicality that defines Pokémon. A manager at Lay's Egypt told me that his company would have preferred to Arabicize the characters before using them to market the chips, but felt constrained by the fact that the characters were already known by their American names because of the television show. The government agency that licensed Pokémon for television did not have the money to adapt Pokémon for local audiences nor had it imagined any need to. The great value of phenomena like Pokémon to merchandisers is their synergy: every product is an advertisement for every other product. This value is weakened if licensees fail to maintain mimetic uniformity throughout the market. Thus, early users can set binding parameters on later licensees, despite the latter having more savvy about cross-cultural marketing.

7. A rare exception was a column in the UAE newspaper *Al Bayan* whose author put responsibility for resisting globalization squarely on the shoulders of good mothers: "I believe that no home or student's notebook or child's bed does not have a picture of this strange creature, until it becomes a member of the family. But it is an undesirable member, and any housewife can get rid of it if she wants. . . . But will she do that?" (Darwish 2000: 26).

8. Although Turkey was the first country in the world to ban Pokémon, albeit temporarily, the ban was motivated by health concerns rather than moral anxieties. In November 2000, following two separate incidents of young children leaping from balconies after watching the show, apparently in emulation of flying characters, the Radio and Television High Council ordered the private television station ATV to stop airing the program. The show was returned to the air pending an appeal and was never again restricted. The temporary ban only affected the TV show, not the related commodities.

9. Only a handful of children owned Game Boys, so they do not figure prominently in this analysis.

10. Because students wear uniforms, Pokémon apparel was not an issue.

11. The accusation of wasting food is not simply an economic accusation but, at least potentially, a religious or moral one. Wasting food is sinful behavior to most Muslims and many Christians in the Middle East. It is not uncommon for upscale consumers to bring their uneaten slices of pizza or last few French fries out of the Pizza Hut or McDonald's and distribute them to street children so they don't have to throw food in the garbage. Schoolchildren I asked about the uneaten chips claim denied it ever happened. "You can always find someone to eat the chips," one young man pointed out reasonably.

12. I was unable to get copies of these articles from Dr. Reem, who said she had discarded them.

13. The largest foreign group after Americans is Canadians (seventy-three students), followed by Koreans (forty-nine), then Swedes, Indians, Israelis, and Britons (all between twenty and twenty-five students).

14. These figures are imprecise as they refer to one specific moment in time in an extremely fluid and changing population. The figures are also somewhat misleading, since dual passport holders often declare their foreign citizenship rather than their local citizenship. It is not uncommon for members of wealthy Egyptian families, for example, to travel to the United States or Canada to give birth, since children born within national boundaries are automatically recognized by these countries as citizens. Egypt, on the other hand, recognizes citizenship as passed down through fathers. Many such

students, although raised in Egypt, declare themselves to be Americans. The school is complicit in this activity.

15. Bourdieu has been mischaracterized on this point; Bourdieu is not reinventing Gramsci's notion of hegemony. Rather, symbolic violence "presupposes on the part of those who are subjected to it a form of complicity which is neither a passive submission to an external constraint nor a free adherence to values. . . . The specificity of symbolic violence resides precisely in the fact that it requires of the person who undergoes it an attitude which defies the ordinary alternative between freedom and constraint" (Bourdieu and Wacquant 1992: 168).

16. But see Schaub 2000; Warschauer, El Said, and Zohry 2002.

4. Talk Like an Egyptian

1. The filmmakers are apparently giving their imagined AUC an examination-based system like that at the national universities. Because AUC uses a course-grade system, it would be impossible for a student who had one or two dismal semesters to subsequently achieve the top rank by hard work.

2. The film cannot be described as anti-Semitic unless one takes this term to include any political anti-Israeli speech. There *are* unambiguously anti-Semitic films in Egypt, but most have done poorly at the box office. Armbrust's 2000 essay strongly influenced my interpretation of the film.

3. There's even an interesting parallel to Khalaf's unexpected receiving of the flag. As part of the 1996 protests, a group of students held up a large Palestinian flag. One of the protest leaders was called to speak with a journalist and he handed his corner of the flag to one of his professors, an American, who was just passing by, and asked him to hold it for a minute. The professor, who sympathized with the students, was holding the flag as a photographer snapped a picture, and soon he found himself on the front pages of several Egyptian newspapers. Although he had lived in Cairo and taught at AUC for fifteen years, he said this incident changed his status entirely. He told me that people he barely knew, from high-ranking officials to workers in his neighborhood, began greeting him warmly and he found himself welcomed into the Egyptian community in an entirely new way.

4. As an American viewer, my own enjoyment of the film was marred by the representations of black Egyptians in the film, which raised specters of the stereotypes of bygone U.S. cinema. On Egyptian "blackness," see Fabos 2008. On representations of Nubians in Egyptian cinema, see Smith 2006; Shafik 2007: 64–77.

5. Nor can families send their children for just a year or two of cosmopolitan polish; high school students are required to enter ASC as freshmen.

6. My understanding of these issues and even many of the questions I posed to students at MLS and ASC were strongly influenced by the work of Shearin Abdel-Moneim, an AUC graduate student who undertook two fascinating ethnographic projects at schools quite similar to MLS, and inspired me to do the same.

7. One of the most interesting aspects of this was the tendency of students to engage in code-switching between Arabic and English in their interviews with me about these issues. Ten-year-olds at ASC almost never used Arabic, but many adolescents found they could not talk about their Egyptianness without code-switching. I have therefore paid special attention to these terms and offer extended glosses in what follows.

8. On articulations of high and low culture in Egypt, see Armbrust 1996a.

9. On *adab,* see also Starrett 1998: 5, 100, 148; Farag 2001; Hirschkind 2006a: 46–48.

10. Among eighth-graders at ASC, "boyfriend" and "girlfriend" do not usually indicate a dating relationship. Rather, one's boyfriend or girlfriend is a designated member of the opposite sex who signifies a person's attractiveness to the wider school community. To accept the position of boyfriend or girlfriend thus bestows status but at a cost in cross-sex interactions: boys who talk to girls other than their girlfriends are subject to public reproaches from their girlfriends, and vice versa. By high school, the terms do come to indicate dating relationships.

11. The adjectival form, *baladi,* can be used positively to indicate something traditional: beloved foods, codes of honor, virtue. It can also be employed pejoratively, to refer to something poorly conceived, crude, unsophisticated, and "inevitably 'premodern'" (Armbrust 1996a: 26).

12. Armbrust argues that many of the negative connotations of *ibn az-zawat* have been absorbed by the term *infitahi.*

13. Almost always said in French rather than the Arabic *al-aghniyya al-gudad.*

14. Locally, Hakim was notorious for being late for concerts. Indeed, less than a year earlier, he was featured in an amusing ad for Mobinil, the concert's sponsor, singing into a cell phone held to a microphone as he raced to a concert.

15. Again, these dichotomies between Western and Arab artists are constructed by the students as part of their effort to make sense of their own experiences and are not the only ways these categories can be construed. Hakim is a globe-trotting musician who by the time of this concert had already completed two world tours and released a series of successful albums in the United Kingdom and the United States. Since then, he has recorded with James Brown, Olga Tanon, and Stevie Wonder, and performed alongside Joan Baez, Mick Fleetwood, and Gloria Gaynor. Ashraf's "these guys" would also seem to tar with the same brush Algerian rai musician Cheb Mami and Lebanese pop star Elissa, who both performed that night but were not late.

16. This notion that the social structure ("system") constrains moral agency pops up again and again in many different contexts. For example, a colleague of mine had, during a lengthy stay abroad, become accustomed to drinking a glass of wine each evening after his children were in bed. Lately, he had taken up reading the Qur'an at this time. When I questioned him about the impropriety of this, he laughed and said, "Of course I shouldn't, but what can I do? This is how things are nowadays." Charles Hirschkind reports a very similar experience with a student smoking while listening to cassette sermons (Hirschkind 2006b: 69).

17. On the changing place of the American University in Cairo in Egyptian society, see Ibrahim 1982; Murphy 1987; Sharkey 2008.

18. AUC's preparatory school, the Lincoln Academy, closed in 1951. Its functions were absorbed by the school I'm calling ASC.

19. Officially, the faculty balance is supposed to be 45 percent Egyptian, 45 percent U.S. citizens, and 10 percent other internationals, but this makeup varies from year to year as a result of hiring conditions.

20. In 1993, the Egyptian government passed a law authorizing the establishment of private universities. The first three of these, the Modern Sciences and Arts University, Misr University for Science and Technology, and Sixth of October University, opened

in 1996. "International" universities on the AUC model began opening about five years later, beginning with the Université Française d'Égypte in 2002.

21. Ahmed had attended a French-language school, the Choueifat International School. He entered the national university because his scores were high enough to get him into the prestigious School of Medicine. AUC does not have a pre-med program.

22. Since then, AUC has begun offering a diploma in human resources.

23. Again, we find a construction of Westernization as style. The self-styled "Islamist-Egyptian" Sidahmed focuses on Westernization simply as style or as political ties to nation-states, rather than offering a thorough critique of Western modernity, which would force him to note the substantive structural similarities between the national universities and AUC. His criticism of AUC, in other words, is entirely concerned with how AUC indexes the United States.

24. Amr Khaled was an accountant when he began preaching in 1995, and did not leave his profession until 1998. He apparently has no formal religious education but was a protégé of Dr. Yusuf al-Qaradawi, an Egyptian religious leader living in exile in Qatar, disseminating his view via Al-Jazeera television and his website, www.qaradawi. net. On Amr Khaled, see Bayat 2002; Wise 2003; El-Katatney 2007; Sparre and Petersen 2007; van Nieuwkerk 2007.

25. Weeping is associated with Amr Khaled's style of preaching. According to Sherif, after a particularly powerful sermon Amr Khaled simulates weeping, which in turn "makes people really emotional until most of them start crying and asking God to forgive them. Most people start [to cry] because they remember the bad deeds and sins they have committed and feel guilty about." But this also generates communitas (Turner 1995) as "the big mass of people is united doing something that is supposedly private or personal like crying," Sherif said. On simulation and sincerity in Muslim prayer, see Mahmood 2001b.

26. Not everyone interprets Amr Khaled's discussions of gender as equitable. Bayat points out that Khaled has based "the integrity of society" on "the integrity of women" and the latter on her *higab* because "one woman can easily entice one hundred men, but one hundred men cannot entice a single woman." This would seem to establish male sexual desire as natural and female sexual desire as unnatural. Bayat argues that this casts women as promoters of sin in ways men are not.

27. Three of the four interview subjects attributed to Khaled much of the credit for their profound conversion to a more active Islamic piety. A fourth came from a devout family and credited the preacher with helping him to find the balance between personal piety and the pressures and possibilities presented by the university.

28. That Khaled could leave Egypt to continue his ministry in defiance of religious authorities emphasizes the point made by Eickelman (2002), Starrett (1998), Anderson (2003b), and others that the objectification and functionalization of Islam over the past century and a half and the movement of public Islam into new mediated realms of communication have undermined the authority of the *'ulama* as exclusive specialists in religious knowledge.

29. For example, she initially dismissed the notion (when I raised it) that Amr Khaled's words might resonate with women like her maid. She recanted a moment later to say that obviously God's message is the same for all of us but "different kinds of people need different *da'wa.*" This may be an illustration of Salvatore's claim that, in contemporary public Islam, "the older, firmer notion of a consensus of the community of believers may

be turning into a more precarious 'consensus of communication'" (Salvatore 2000: 15; Salvatore 1997: 81–96).

30. It is important to note that precisely because AUC stands for a particular kind of modernity that contrasts with many discourses of authenticity, AUC was specifically targeted for censorship. During the months of the book-banning controversy, one could find copies of one of these books, Maxime Rodinson's *Muhammad: Prophet of Islam,* in the library at the national Cairo University, and buy another, the English edition of Alifa Rifaat's *Distant View of a Minaret,* in bookstores around the university. It was only AUC whose limits had to be publicly established. For an interesting (and highly personal) account of the censorship during this period at AUC, see Mehrez 2008.

31. AUC is by no means alone among Egyptian institutions banning various forms of veiling. In 2001, a French school in Alexandria suspended a student for wearing the *higab* (she sued, and won her right to continue). In 2002, the privately owned Egyptian-Kuwaiti Shorouk Airlines fired a pilot for donning the *higab.* In October 2009, the Egyptian government banned the *niqab* for students taking exams, after multiple reports that students were taking exams for other candidates, using the face covering as a disguise. A court challenge in April 2010 upheld the government's decision.

32. El-Shabrawy eventually withdrew from AUC and entered a national university.

5. Coffee Shops and Gender in Translocal Spaces

1. Not all malls are exclusively for the wealthy. Abaza describes the ways different malls are aimed at different classes of Egyptians. Yet nearly all employ security guards to regulate who can and cannot move about freely. "The obsession of the rich of Cairo today is to push away the unwanted poor as far as possible. All these malls, be they the Yamamah Centre, the WTC or the Ramses Hilton annexe [*sic*] mall, maintain strict security measures and video cameras monitor the public" (Abaza 2001b: 102).

2. This is not to imply that the salespersons at these establishments do not benefit from their positions. Abaza points out that "malls could be viewed as offering social mobility and access to cash for lower-class, young saleswomen" (Abaza 2001b: 102).

3. Compare this to Eric Denis's account of the well-to-do Mr. Al-Mansur whose driver, using the elevated beltway, "skimmed over that unknown world where peasants are packed into an inextricable universe of bricks, refuse, self-made tenements, and old state housing projects" (Denis 2006: 47).

4. Contrary to the usual anthropological practice, I have not changed the names of the cafés and *'ahawi* described here. On the contrary, the owners of the *'ahawi* at which I conducted interviews all insisted that I mention their shops by name so that if any of my distinguished readers visited Cairo, they would stop by for a visit. Although it is impossible to account for every *'ahwa* and coffee shop I visited over five years, there were a number in which I conducted more formal research, including interviews, assessing demographics, and so forth. In fulfillment of my promise, I offer this list of *'ahawi* that contributed to my research: Dardasha near the Roxy theater downtown, El Erouba in Zamalek, El Haya in El Korba, Misk in Tahrir Square, Sadek in Mohandiseen, El Sohba in 'Ard al Golf, Talib Café on Mohamed Farid Street in downtown Cairo, and Zahrit on El Nakhil Street. Coffee shops that I visited include Beano's in El Malaky and Tahrir; Cilantro in Ma'adi, in Zamalek, and on Muhammed Mahmoud Street; Coffee Roastery in Ma'adi and Zamalek (across from the AUC dormitories); Harris Café and Coffeeology

101 in Zamalek; El Greco in Ma'adi; and Seattle Coffee House across from AUC's Greek Campus. (As of 2005, Seattle Coffee House had ceased operations, but both a Beano's and a Cilantro had opened on Muhammed Mahmoud Street, which connects AUC's two urban campuses.)

5. Except that he doesn't really say "please" (*min fadlak*) but "for the sake of the Prophet," a local idiom that means "please" but connotes a kind of cheery familiarity. Compare this to later in the discourse, where I am mocked for being too polite (and perhaps stodgy) when I say *min fadlak*.

6. This is not a large amount in itself, but it was about 20 percent of the total spent—a significant tip in a place where tipping is not customary but rather another aspect of the cosmopolitan style.

7. At the time of my fieldwork, Egyptians consumed 0.76 kilograms of tea per person and 0.7 kilograms of coffee. However, they spent more on coffee (Euromonitor 2001: 227–228).

8. *Maru'a* is another word that has no perfect cognate in English. Like *shahama*, it designates masculine self-respect. It is most often used in Egyptian Arabic to connote the positive masculine characteristic of generosity, but may also be glossed as strong, dignified, courteous, and virile, depending on context.

9. I thank Jessica Winegar for first drawing my attention to this point.

10. Similarly, Stokes describes Turkish Arabesk films as dividing male characters into two categories: macho and effete (Stokes 1994: 28).

11. This particular use of *'ishta* is itself a class marker, since the upper and lower classes use the term differently. Where it is ubiquitous among the upper classes to refer metonymically to cream's "sweetness" and "coolness" (and as a cognate to the U.S. slang terms "cool" and "sweet"), among the working classes it is cream's "thickness" that is invoked. In working-class neighborhoods like Shubra, men shout *'ishta* (thick) at plump, attractive, unaccompanied women.

12. Samir told me in a subsequent interview that the *mabasim* are to prevent their getting tuberculosis, citing an Egyptian Ministry of Health decree. When I tracked down a news report on the decree, I found that it actually warned that *mabasim* do *not* prevent the spread of TB, since the bacteria is likely to exist in the tube or the water rather than the mouthpiece (Wassmann 2004). The mobilization of this text by Samir in contradiction to its actual content in order to explain and justify a ritual of class exclusion—for TB, as Samir points out, is a disease of the poor and dirty—emphasizes the importance of class differentiation in the practice of *shisha* smoking.

13. Jessica Winegar suggests (personal communication) that the severe disapproval of women smoking *shisha* is linked to the transgressive act of sucking that the water pipe entails.

14. Abaza argues that one of the social functions of Islamic attire is to allow young women to transgress public norms while evading public criticism. "Islamic attire becomes here a protective mechanism, allowing youth to smoke cigarettes or water pipes in public, and allowing flirtation in the intimate spaces of the coffee houses" (2001b: 119).

15. Karim's claim is naïve. In my experience, most of these young women are perfectly capable of editing their performances if they acquire new boyfriends or fiancés.

16. Shechter (2006: 140–145) details how early twentieth-century media representations in Egypt—literature, film, and advertising—held out smoking as a sign simultaneously of women's modernity and of sexual vice. On one hand, public smoking with men

could represent a liberated woman devoted to the idea of companionate marriage; on the other hand, it was associated with actresses, dancers, and "women of vice" (145).

17. I emphasize the plurality of this form of reference because such sites are never actual replicas. However much a site may "quote" elements the designer has seen in other coffee shops elsewhere, indexical signification involves an imagined resemblance to imagined places elsewhere. In this sense, they are simulacra, copies that have no original (Baudrillard 1983; Deleuze 1983; Kearney 1995).

18. Of the five coffee shops in the upscale Zamalek neighborhood in 2000, only one —Coffeeology 101—offered *shisha* on the menu.

6. The Global and the Multilocal

1. The first Starbucks opened in Cairo in December 2006, a year and a half later. It is owned by Alshaya Egypt, a branch of the Kuwaiti Alshaya Group which runs more than 200 Starbucks in eleven Middle Eastern countries. Alshaya operates franchises of almost fifty global brands, including the Body Shop, Foot Locker, and Peugeot, in the Middle East, Russia, and Poland.

2. A related open secret is that, among those who bring international brands to Egypt, including Starbucks and Mango's, their partners are more often than not companies from the emirates, Kuwait and Saudi Arabia, which already hold regional distribution rights for the Middle East, Africa, Eastern Europe, and western Asia.

3. Enterprise culture as a term for creative entrepreneurship need not be tied to liberal economics, however. Williams (2007) points out that, even in the United Kingdom, fully one-third of entrepreneurs describe their activities as other than profit-motivated. This is consistent with Elyachar's observation that, in Egypt, young college-educated entrepreneurs engaging in competitive, profit-driven businesses and using government micro loans generally fare less well than traditional craftspeople engaged in socially cooperative forms of entrepreneurship, even when these tradespeople have been uprooted by government programs from their networks of local suppliers and clienteles (Elyachar 2005).

4. Syndicates collect fees from members, which are often supplemented by tariffs on products produced through the labor of their members. For example, the Syndicate of Engineers collects tariffs on the production of iron and cement, the Syndicate of Farmers collects fees on fertilizers and some agricultural products, and the bar association collects tariffs on all court cases. These fees enable them to offer services such as health insurance, pensions, and training programs.

5. I am dealing primarily with urban and industrial privatization. The history of agricultural privatization follows a somewhat different trajectory.

6. In addition, the holding companies often seek to improve their own performances by offering for sale only those companies that are losing money.

7. As many of my informants spoke to me in confidence, I have changed personal names and concealed the names of some of the companies in order to protect them from any possible criticism.

8. Indeed, *glocal* is often said to be a gloss for "think globally, act locally," a phrase coined in 1969 as the motto of the Friends of the Earth environmental group; it has since been appropriated into corporate and security discourses, among others. *Multilocal* may have originated as a medical term to describe genetic features that are distributed

throughout regions of organisms but act together. Both are ubiquitous in international business discourses in the twenty-first century.

9. The idea of the *commodity sign* derives from Adorno, Baudrillard, and others, and is discussed by Featherstone (1990) and Applbaum (1998, 2000). It expresses the fact that, in a capitalist consumer society, the value of goods is mainly symbolic. Commodities derive value from their symbolic associations—romance, beauty, prestige, fulfillment, etc.—rather than from any use value the items may possess.

10. I am taking the word of Arvind's company's marketing research department for this.

11. And, as Dorfman and Mattelart (1984) argue, comics are one of the first places many children encounter the cultural logic of capitalism, of which Disney is a powerful agent.

12. An official at Nahdet Misr told me that the publisher was asked to bid for it by the corporation, which was unhappy with the previous publisher's capacity to maintain and expand sales.

13. For example, they are the Arabic publishers of the U.S. *Magic Schoolbus* series and many of the British *Dorling Kindersley* books.

14. An American sociology graduate student doing research in Cairo, commenting on an earlier paper of mine about McDonald's in Egypt, said in exasperation, "Why do you read so much into it? Why can't people just go to McDonald's because it's clean and air conditioned and they know their kids will eat the food?" But it is precisely such distinctions between McDonald's and many other eating places that create the notion of McDonald's as a global topos: no matter where you are in the world, you know what the experience will be before you even enter the restaurant.

15. The first McDonald's restaurant opened in Jiddah, Saudi Arabia, in 1992, two years before one opened in Egypt.

16. Many McDonald's around the world have adapted the menu to local tastes. India, where the chain serves only chicken and vegetarian products, has perhaps gone the furthest with this process.

17. The terms "class A," "class B," and "class C" refer to categories of consumers. In this terminology, which seems to be widespread among marketing professionals in Cairo, class A refers to multilingual, cosmopolitan, well-to-do consumers. I believe the system bottoms out at class D (at least, I've never heard anyone speak of a class E or F), a group that has no college education, speaks only regional Arabic dialects, and has very limited disposable income.

18. For a nuanced discussion of Egypt's "split vernacular" and its relationship to modernity, see Armbrust 1996a.

19. This was a particular strike at McDonald's efforts to build its image by supporting such charities as the Friends of the National Cancer Institute, Caritas Egypt, Red Crescent, Awladi, and Association Dar al-Hanan.

20. *Sha'bi*, "popular," refers in this case to the struggling musicians singing at weddings and selling cheaply produced cassettes at performances and to (and through) taxi drivers and sidewalk vendors.

21. Although once kept distinct, "Jew," "Israeli," and "Zionist" are used almost interchangeably in contemporary Egyptian media. The complexity of the relationships among these three categories, such as the existence of anti-Zionist Jews, non-Jewish Israelis, non-Jewish Zionists, and so forth, is usually invisible to the regional media.

22. Ironically, McDonald's International has since initiated delivery service in dozens of countries and describes Egypt as the place where the concept was "pioneered" (Arndt 2007).

23. Indeed, my interviews with Girgis were the result of his asking me at a social event if I knew "as an anthropologist" how to cross this cultural divide. My answers did not entirely please him since what I know "as an anthropologist" is that something is lost, as well as gained, in adopting the kind of enterprise culture he was promoting.

REFERENCES

Abaza, Mona. 2001a. Perceptions of 'urfi Marriage in the Egyptian Press. *ISIM Newsletter* 7(1): 20–21.

———. 2001b. Shopping Malls, Consumer Culture and the Reshaping of Public Space in Egypt. *Theory, Culture and Society* 18(5): 97–122.

———. 2006. *Changing Consumer Cultures of Modern Egypt: Cairo's Urban Reshaping.* Leiden: Brill.

Abu-Hashish, Shereen, and Mark Allen Peterson. 1999. Computer *Khatbas*: Databases and Marital Entrepreneurship in Modern Cairo. *Anthropology Today* 15(6): 7–11.

Abu-Lughod, Lila. 1986. *Veiled Sentiments: Honor and Poetry in a Bedouin Society.* Berkeley: University of California Press.

———. 1997. The Interpretation of Culture(s) after Television. *Representations* 59: 109–134.

———. 1998a. Television and the Virtues of Education: Upper Egyptian Encounters with State Culture. In *Directions of Change in Rural Egypt,* ed. Nicholas Hopkins and Kirsten Westergaard. Pp. 147–165. Cairo: American University in Cairo Press.

———. 1998b. The Marriage of Feminism and Islamism in Egypt: Selective Repudiation of Postcolonial Cultural Politics. In *Remaking Women: Feminism and Modernity in the Middle East,* ed. Lila Abu-Lughod. Pp. 243–269. Cairo: American University in Cairo Press.

———. 2005. *Dramas of Nationhood: The Politics of Television in Egypt.* Chicago: University of Chicago Press.

Adams, Abigail. 1993. Dyke to Dyke: Ritual Reproduction at a U.S. Men's Military College. *Anthropology Today* 9(5): 3–6.

Agar, Michael. 1986. *Speaking of Ethnography.* Beverly Hills, Calif.: Sage.

———. 1994. *Language Shock: Understanding the Culture of Conversation.* New York: William Morrow.

Alam, Muzaffar, and Sanjay Subrahmanyam. 2004. The Making of a Munshi. *Comparative Studies of South Asia, Africa and the Middle East* 24(2): 61–72.

Allam, Abeer. 2003. Making Near Beer Acceptable in Near East. *New York Times,* Jan. 4: http://query.nytimes.com/gst/fullpage.html?res=9A03E7DF1F3FF937A35752C0A9 659C8B63&sec=&spon=&pagewanted=all (accessed Sept. 8, 2008).

Allison, Anne. 2003. Portable Monsters and Commodity Cuteness: Pokémon as Japan's New Global Power. *Postcolonial Studies* 6(3): 381–395.

Al-Qurani, Ali Ben Shewil. 2000. Will the Japanese Pokémon Become the Character of the 21st Century? *Al Jazeera* (Saudi Arabia), Sept. 25: 11.

Al-Rubai'. 2000. Our Children Are Gambling!!! *Al-Rubai'* (Saudi Arabia), Dec. 9: 25.

American University in Cairo. 2000. *Catalog.* Cairo: American University in Cairo Press.

Anderson, Benedict. 1991. *Imagined Communities: Reflections on the Origin and Spread of Nationalism,* rev. ed. London: Verso.

Anderson, Jon W. 2003a. The Internet and Islam's New Interpreters. In *New Media in the Muslim World,* ed. Dale Eickelman and Jon W. Anderson. Pp. 45–60. Bloomington: Indiana University Press.

———. 2003b. New Media, New Publics: Reconfiguring the Public Sphere of Islam. *Social Research* 70(3): 887–906.

Appadurai, Arjun. 1996. *Modernity at Large: Cultural Dimensions of Globalization.* Minneapolis: University of Minnesota Press.

Applbaum, Kalman. 1998. The Sweetness of Salvation: Consumer Marketing and the Liberal-Bourgeoisie Theory of Needs. *Current Anthropology* 39(3): 323–350.

———. 2000. Crossing Borders: Globalization as Myth and Charter for American Transnational Consumer Marketing. *American Ethnologist* 27(2): 257–282.

Armbrust, Walter. 1996a. *Mass Culture and Modernization in Egypt.* Cambridge: Cambridge University Press.

———. 1996b. Terrorism and Kabab: A Capra-esque View of Modern Egypt. In *Images of Enchantment: Performance, Art, and Image of the Middle East,* ed. Sherifa Zuhur. Cairo: American University in Cairo Press.

———. 2000. An Upper Egyptian in the American Press. *SAIS Review* 20(2): 207–216.

———. 2003. Bourgeois Leisure and Egyptian Media Fantasies. In *New Media in the Muslim World,* ed. Dale Eickelman and Jon W. Anderson. Pp. 106–132. Bloomington: Indiana University Press.

———. 2006. When the Lights Go Down in Cairo. In *Cairo Cosmopolitan,* ed. Diane Singerman and Paul Amar. Pp. 415–444. Cairo: American University in Cairo Press.

Arndt, Michael. 2007. Knock, Knock, It's Your Big Mac. *Bloomberg Businessweek,* July 12: http://www.businessweek.com/globalbiz/content/ju12007/gb20070712_387164 .htm.

Associated Press. 2001. McDonald's Dumps "I Hate Israel" Singer. July 5.

Atia, Tarek. 2001. Goodnight, Mr. Hamburger. *Al-Ahram Weekly* 540: 14.

Augé, Marc. 1995. *Non-Places: Introduction to an Anthropology of Supermodernity.* London: Verso.

———. 1999. *An Anthropology for Contemporaneous Worlds.* Stanford, Calif.: Stanford University Press.

Badawi, Muhammed Mustafa. 1992. Introduction to *Modern Arabic Literature,* ed. M. M. Badawi. Pp. 1–22. Cambridge: Cambridge University Press.

Badawi, Muhammed Mustafa, and Martin Hinds. 1986. *A Dictionary of Egyptian Arabic.* Beirut: Librairie du Liban.

Baker, Raymond William. 1981. Sadat's Open Door: Opposition from Within. *Social Problems* 28(4): 378–384.

Barsoum, Ghada. 1999. Female Graduates in Egypt: The Jobs Dilemma. In *Human Development for the 21st Century: Proceedings of the Sixth American University in Cairo Research Conference,* ed. Mohamed Farag. Cairo: American University in Cairo.

———. 2004. The Employment Crisis of Female Graduates in Egypt: An Ethnographic Account. *Cairo Papers in Social Science* 25(3): 1–121.

Battaglia, Debbora. 1995. Problematizing the Self. In *Rhetorics of Self-Making,* ed. Debbora Battaglia. Pp. 1–15. Berkeley: University of California Press.

Baudrillard, Jean. 1983. *Simulations.* New York: Semiotext(e).

Bautista, Julius. 2008. The Meta-Theory of Piety: Reflections on the Work of Saba Mahmood. *Journal of Contemporary Islam* 2: 75–83.

Bayat, Asef. 1997. Cairo's Poor—Dilemmas of Survival and Security. *Middle East Report* (Winter): 2–8.

———. 2002. Piety, Privilege and Egyptian Youth. *ISIM Newsletter* 10(2): 23.

Beinin, Joel. 2007. The Militancy of Mahalla al-Kubra. *Middle East Report Online,* Sept. 29: http://www.merip.org/mero/mero092907.html (accessed Nov. 7, 2008).

Bestor, Theodore C. 2001. Supplyside Sushi: Commodity, Market and Global City. *American Anthropologist* 102(1): 76–95.

Bieber-Roberts, Peggy, and Elisa Pierandrei. 2002. Cafe Riche: Memory in the Formation of Egyptian National Identity. Paper presented at International Association for Media and Communication Research (IAMCR), July 22: http://www.portalcomunicacion.com/bcn2002/n_eng/programme/prog_ind/papers/b/pdf/b005_biebe.pdf (accessed Sept. 20, 2009).

Bielo, James. 2007. "The Mind of Christ": Financial Success, Born-Again Personhood, and the Anthropology of Christianity. *Ethnos* 72(3): 316–338.

Boktor, Amir. 1936. *School and Society in the Valley of the Nile.* Cairo: Elias Modern Press.

Bourdieu, Pierre. 1977. *Outline of a Theory of Practice.* Cambridge: Cambridge University Press.

———. 1979. The Kabyle House; or, The World Reversed. In his *Algeria 1960.* Cambridge: Cambridge University Press.

———. 1984. *Distinction: A Social Critique of the Judgment of Taste.* Cambridge, Mass.: Harvard University Press.

———. 1990. *Homo Academicus.* Oxford: Polity.

Bourdieu, Pierre, and Jean-Claude Passeron. 1977. *Reproduction in Education, Society and Culture.* Beverly Hills, Calif.: Sage.

Bourdieu, Pierre, and Monique de Saint-Martin. 1974. Scholastic Excellence and the Values of the Educational System. In *Contemporary Research in the Sociology of Education,* ed. J. Eggleston. Pp. 338–379. London: Methuen.

Bourdieu, Pierre, and Loic Wacquant. 1992. *An Invitation to a Reflexive Sociology.* Chicago: University of Chicago Press.

Bowen, Donna Lee. 2002. Abortion and the Ethics of Life. In *Everyday Life in the Muslim Middle East,* 2nd ed., ed. Donna Lee Bowen and Evelyn Early. Pp. 169–179. Bloomington: Indiana University Press.

Brannen, Mary Yoko. 2004. When Mickey Loses Face: Recontextualization, Semantic Fit and the Semiotics of Foreignness. *Academy of Management Review* 29(4): 593–616.

Breckinridge, Carol A., Sheldon Pollock, Homi K. Bhabha, and Dipesh Chakrabarty, eds. 2002. *Cosmopolitanism.* Durham, N.C.: Duke University Press.

Bucholtz, Mary, and Kira Hall. 2005. Identity and Interaction: A Sociocultural Linguistic Approach. *Discourse Studies* 7(4–5): 585–614.

Buckingham, David, and Julian Sefton-Green. 2003. Gotta Catch 'em All: Structure, Agency and Pedagogy in Children's Media Culture. *Media, Culture and Society* 25(3): 379–399.

Burkhart, Grey E., and Susan Older. 2003. *The Information Revolution in the Middle East and North Africa*. Santa Monica, Calif.: Rand.

Butler, Judith. 1990. *Gender Trouble*. London: Routledge.

Chiles, Todd H., Allen C. Bluedorn, and Vishal K. Gupta. 2007. Beyond Creative Destruction and Entrepreneurial Discovery: A Radical Austrian Approach to Entrepreneurship. *Organization Studies* 28: 467–493.

Chock, Phyllis Pease. 1987. The Irony of Stereotypes: Toward an Anthropology of Ethnicity. *Cultural Anthropology* 2: 347–368.

Chun, Allen. 2002. Global Dissonances: Bringing Class and Culture Back In. *Social Analysis* 46(2): 1–10.

Cockburn, Laura. 2002. Children and Young People Living in Changing Worlds: The Process of Assessing and Understanding the "Third Culture Kid." *School Psychology International* 23(4): 475–485.

Cohen, Stanley. 1972. *Folk Devils and Moral Panics*. London: MacGibbon and Kee.

Cole, Donald, and Soraya Altorki. 1998. *Bedouin, Settlers, and Holiday Makers: Egypt's Changing Northwest Coast*. Cairo: American University in Cairo.

Conermann, Stephan. 1996. *Mustafa Mahmud und der Modifierte Islamische Diskurs*. Berlin: Klaus Schwarz.

Cook, Daniel Thomas. 2001. Exchange Value as Pedagogy in Children's Leisure: Moral Panics in Children's Culture at Century's End. *Leisure Sciences* 23: 81–98.

———. 2002. Introduction: Interrogating Symbolic Childhood. In *Symbolic Childhood*, ed. Daniel Thomas Cook. New York: Lang.

Cope, Bill, and Mary Kalantzis, eds. 2000. *Multiliteracies: Literacy Learning and the Design of Social Futures*. New York: Routledge.

Counihan, Carole M. 1999. *The Anthropology of Food and Body: Gender, Meaning and Power*. New York: Routledge.

Crapanzano, Vincent. 1992. *Hermes' Dilemma and Hamlet's Desire*. Cambridge, Mass.: Harvard University Press.

Critcher, Chas. 2003. *Moral Panics and the Media*. Buckingham, England: Open University Press.

Dabbous, Dalia. 2001. Sing a Song of Conflict. *Cairo Times* 5(20): 19–25.

Danielson, Virginia. 1998. *The Voice of Egypt: Umm Kulthum, Arabic Song, and Egyptian Society in the Twentieth Century*. Chicago: University of Chicago Press.

Darwish, Adel. 2007. The Surge in Egyptian Nationalism. *Middle East* (Oct.): 22–25.

Darwish, Hussein. 2000. A Pokémon in Every Home. *Al Bayan* (UAE), no. 42 (Dec. 15): 26.

de Beauvoir, Simone. 1972. *The Second Sex*. New York: Vintage.

de Koning, Anouk. 2006. Café Latte and Caesar Salad. In *Cairo Cosmopolitan*, ed. Diane Singerman and Paul Amar. Pp. 221–233. Cairo: American University in Cairo Press.

Deleuze, Gilles. 1983. Plato and the Simulacrum. *October* 27: 52–53.

Denis, Eric. 2006. Cairo as Neoliberal Capital? From Walled City to Gated Communities. In *Cairo Cosmopolitan*, ed. Diane Singerman and Paul Amar. Pp. 42–76. Cairo: American University in Cairo Press.

Dissanayake, Wimal. 1994. Introduction: Nationhood, History and Cinema: Reflections on the Asian Scene. In *Colonialism and Nationalism in Asian Cinema*, ed. Wimal Dissanayake. Pp. ix–xxix. Bloomington: Indiana University Press.

Dorfman, Ariel, and Armand Mattelart. 1984. *How to Read Donald Duck: Imperialist Ideology in the Disney Comic.* New York: International General.

Douglas, Allen, and Fedwa Malti-Douglas. 1994. *Arab Comic Strips: Politics of an Emerging Mass Culture.* Bloomington: Indiana University Press.

Douglas, Mary, and Baron Isherwood. 1981. *The World of Goods.* New York: Basic.

Drotner, Kirstin. 1992. Modernity and Media Panics. In *Media Cultures: Reappraising Transnational Media,* ed. Michael Skovmand and Kim Christian Schroder. Pp. 42–62. London: Routledge.

Dwyer, Kevin. 1987. *Moroccan Dialogues: Anthropology in Question.* Prospect Heights, Ill.: Waveland.

Eco, Umberto. 1979. *A Theory of Semiotics.* Bloomington: Indiana University Press.

Eickelman, Dale. 2002. Inside the Islamic Reformation. In *Everyday Life in the Muslim Middle East,* 2nd ed., ed. Donna Lee Bowen and Evelyn A. Early. Pp. 246–256. Bloomington: Indiana University Press.

Eickelman, Dale, and Jon W. Anderson. 1997. Publishing in Muslim Countries: Less Censorship, New Audiences and the Rise of the Islamic Book. *Logos* 8(4): 192–198.

El-Aswad, El-Sayed. 2002. *Religion and Folk Cosmology: Scenarios of the Visible and Invisible in Rural Egypt.* Westport, Conn.: Praeger.

El-Ghobashy, Mona. 2005. Egypt Looks Ahead to Portentous Year. *Middle East Report On-Line.* http://www.merip.org/mero/mero020205.html (accessed Sept. 18, 2010).

El-Hamamsy, Laila Shukry. 1982. The Assertion of Egyptian Identity. In *Ethnic Identity: Cultural Communities and Change,* ed. George De Vos and Lola Romanucci-Ross. Pp. 276–306. Chicago: University of Chicago Press.

El Husaami, Nabih. 2000. Pokémon: Legendary Characters Sneak into Arab Children's Bedrooms (in Arabic). *Al-Sharq Al Awsat* (London), Oct. 17: 15.

El-Katatney, Ethar. 2007. A Religious Rock Star. *Egypt Today,* Oct.: http://www.egypt today.com/article.aspx?ArticleID=7718 (accessed Mar. 22, 2008).

El Kholy, Heba Aziz. 2003. *Defiance and Compliance: Negotiating Gender in Low-Income Cairo.* New York: Berghahn.

Ellis, Markman. 2004. *The Coffee House: A Cultural History.* Cambridge: Cambridge University Press.

El-Messiri, Nur, James Deemer, and Djenane Kamil-Sirry. 1992. Profile of Students. In *Report of Task Force for Academic Excellence.* Cairo: American University in Cairo.

El-Messiri, Sawsan. 1978. *Ibn al Balad: A Concept of Egyptian Identity.* Leiden: Brill.

El-Shakry, Omnia. 2007. *The Great Social Laboratory: Subjects of Knowledge in Colonial and Postcolonial Egypt.* Stanford, Calif.: Stanford University Press.

Elyachar, Julia. 2005. *Markets of Dispossession: NGOs, Economic Development and the State in Cairo.* Durham, N.C.: Duke University Press.

Englund, Harri. 2004. Cosmopolitanism and the Devil in Malawi. *Ethnos* 69 (3): 293–316.

Ennaji, Moha. 2002. Comment. *International Journal of the Sociology of Language* 157: 71–83.

Epstein, Arnold L. 1967. The Case Method in the Field of Law. In *The Craft of Social Anthropology,* ed. A. L. Epstein. Pp. 153–180. London: Tavistock.

Eriksen, Thomas Hylland. 1996. *Small Places, Large Issues.* Sterling, Va.: Pluto.

Essoulami, Said. 2000. *The Press in the Arab World: 100 Years of Suppressed Freedom.* Casablanca, Morocco: Center for Media Freedom.

Euromonitor. 2001. *Consumer Middle East 2001*. London: Euromonitor International.

Ewen, Stuart. 1976. *Captains of Consciousness: Advertising and the Social Roots of Consumer Culture*. New York: McGraw-Hill.

Exertzoglou, Haris. 2003. The Cultural Uses of Consumption: Negotiating Class, Gender, and Nation in the Ottoman Urban Centers during the 19th Century. *International Journal of Middle East Studies* 35: 77–101.

Fabos, Anita. 2008. Resisting "Blackness": Muslim Arab Sudanese in the Diaspora. *ISIM Review* 21: 24–25.

Farag, Iman. 2001. Private Lives, Public Affairs: The Uses of *Adab*. In *Muslim Traditions and Modern Techniques of Power*, ed. Armando Salvatore. Pp. 93–120. Munster, Germany: Lit Verlag.

Favero, Paolo. 2003. Phantasms in a "Starry" Place: Space and Identification in a Central New Delhi Market. *Cultural Anthropology* 18(4): 551–584.

Featherstone, Michael. 1990. *Consumer Culture and Postmodernism*. London: Sage.

Fellman, Jack. 1973. Language and National Identity: The Case of the Middle East. *Anthropological Linguistics* 15(1): 244–249.

Ferguson, Charles. 1971[1959]. Diglossia. In *Language Structure and Language Use: Essays by Charles Ferguson*. Stanford, Calif.: Stanford University Press.

Ferguson, James. 2002. Global Disconnect: Abjection and the Aftermath of Modernism. In *The Anthropology of Globalization*, ed. Jonathan X. Inda and Renato Rosaldo. Pp. 136–153. Oxford: Blackwell.

Fernandez, James. 1986. *Persuasions and Performances: The Play of Tropes in Culture*. Bloomington: Indiana University Press.

Fernea, Elizabeth. 2002. The Veiled Revolution. In *Everyday Life in the Muslim Middle East*, 2nd ed., ed. Donna Lee Bowen and Evelyn A. Early. Pp. 151–157. Bloomington: Indiana University Press.

Fick, David S. 2002. *Entrepreneurship in Africa: A Study of Successes*. Santa Barbara, Calif.: Greenwood.

Fine, Benjamin, and Ellen Leopold. 1993. *The World of Consumption*. London: Routledge.

Fisherkeller, JoEllen. 1997. Everyday Learning about Identities among Young Adolescents in TV Culture. *Anthropology and Education Quarterly* 28(4): 467–492.

Fong, Vanessa. 2004. Filial Nationalism among Chinese Teenagers with Global Identities. *American Ethnologist* 31(4): 631–648.

Foucault, Michel. 1979. *Discipline and Punish*. New York: Vintage.

Franklin, Sarah. 1990. The Values of Enterprise Culture. *Anthropology Today* 6(1): 18–20.

Friedman, Jonathan. 1997. Global Crises, the Struggle for Cultural Identity, and Intellectual Porkbarrelling: Cosmopolitans versus Locals, Ethnics and Nationals in an Era of Dehegemonization. In *Debating Cultural Hybridity: Multicultural Identities and the Politics of Antiracism*, ed. Pnina Werbner and Tariq Modood. Pp. 70–89. London: Zed.

———. 2002a. Champagne Liberals and the New "Dangerous Classes": Reconfigurations of Class, Identity and Class Production in the Contemporary Global System. *Social Analysis* 46(2): 33–55.

———. 2002b. From Roots to Routes: Tropes for Trippers. *Anthropological Theory* 2(1): 21–36.

Friedman, Thomas L. 2007. *The World Is Flat 3.0: A Brief History of the 21st Century*. New York: Picador.

Gaffney, Patrick D. 1994. *The Prophet's Pulpit: Islamic Preaching in Contemporary Egypt*. Berkeley: University of California Press.

Gal, Susan. 2005. Language Ideologies Compared: Metaphors of Public/Private. *Journal of Linguistic Anthropology* 15(1): 23–37.

Galbraith, James K. 2003. *What Is the American Model Really About?* Annandale-on-Hudson, N.Y.: Levy Economics Institute.

Gardner, Katy, and David Lewis. 1996. *Anthropology, Development and the Post-Modern Challenge*. Sterling, Va.: Pluto.

Geertz, Clifford. 1973. Thick Description. In his *The Interpretation of Cultures*. Pp. 3–30. New York: Basic.

———. 1998. Deep Hanging Out. *New York Review of Books* 45(16): 60–72.

Gereffi, Gary, and Miguel Korzeniewicz, eds. 1994. *Commodity Chains and Global Capitalism*. Westport, Conn.: Praeger.

Ghannam, Farha. 2002. *Remaking the Modern Space: Relocation and the Politics of Identity in a Global Cairo*. Berkeley: University of California Press.

Giddens, Anthony. 1990. *The Consequences of Modernity*. Cambridge: Polity.

Gilsenan, Michael. 1982. *Recognizing Islam: Religion and Society in the Modern Arab World*. New York: Pantheon.

Golia, Maria. 2004. The Debilitating Impact of Egypt's Emergency Law. *Daily Star* (Lebanon), Mar. 30: http://www.dailystar.com.lb/article.asp?edition_id=10&categ_id=5&article_id=1340 (accessed Apr. 25, 2006).

Goode, Erich, and Nachman Ben-Yehuda. 1994. *Moral Panics: The Social Construction of Deviance*. Oxford: Blackwell.

Goodwin, Charles, and Marjorie Harness Goodwin. 1992. Assessments and the Construction of Contexts. In *Rethinking Context: Language as an Interactive Phenomenon*, ed. Alessandro Duranti and Charles Goodwin. Pp. 147–189. Cambridge: Cambridge University Press.

Goodwin, Marjorie Harness. 1990. *He-Said-She-Said: Talk as Social Organization among Black Children*. Bloomington: Indiana University Press.

Gordon, David C. 1971. *Self-Determination and History in the Third World*. Princeton, N.J.: Princeton University Press.

Gordon, Joel. 2002. *Revolutionary Melodrama: Popular Film and Civic Identity in Nasser's Egypt*. Chicago: University of Chicago Middle East Center.

Grippo, James R. 2006. The Fool Sings a Hero's Song: Shaaban Abdel Rahim, Egyptian Shaabi, and the Video Clip Phenomenon. *Transnational Broadcasting Studies* 16: http://www.tbsjournal.com/Grippo.html.

Guano, Emanuela. 2002. Spectacles of Modernity: Transnational Imagination and Local Hegemonies in Neoliberal Buenos Aires. *Cultural Anthropology* 17(2): 181–209.

Gupta, Akhil, and James Ferguson. 1992. Space, Identity, and the Politics of Difference. *Cultural Anthropology* 7(1): 6–23.

Gurevitch, Michael. 1989. Comparative Research on Television News: Problems and Challenges. *American Behavioral Scientist* 33(2): 221–229.

Gutmann, Matthew. 1997. The Ethnographic (G)Ambit: Women and the Negotiation of Masculinity in Mexico City. *American Ethnologist* 24(4): 833–855.

Habermas, Jürgen. 1989. *The Transformation of the Public Sphere.* Cambridge, Mass.: MIT Press.

Haeri, Niloofar. 1997. The Reproduction of Symbolic Capital: Language, State and Class in Egypt. *Current Anthropology* 38(5): 795–816.

———. 2003. *Sacred Language, Ordinary People: Dilemmas of Culture and Politics in Egypt.* New York: Palgrave.

Hafez, Sherine. 2003. The Terms of Empowerment: Islamic Women Activists in Egypt. *Cairo Papers in Social Science* 24(4): 1–122.

Hall, Stuart. 1990. Cultural Identity and Diaspora. In *Identity: Community, Culture, Difference,* ed. Jonathan Rutherford. Pp. 235–246. London: Lawrence and Wishart.

Hannerz, Ulf. 1990. Cosmopolitans and Locals in World Culture. *Theory, Culture and Society* 7: 237–251.

———. 1992. *Cultural Complexity: Studies in the Social Organization of Meaning.* New York: Columbia University Press.

———. 1996. *Transnational Connections: Culture, People, Places.* London: Routledge.

———. 2004. *Foreign News: Exploring the World of Foreign Correspondents.* Chicago: University of Chicago Press.

Haour-Knipe, M. 1989. International Employment and Children: Geographical Mobility and Mental Health among Children of Professionals. *Social Science Medicine* 28(3): 197–205.

Hattox, Ralph S. 1985. *Coffee and Coffeehouses: The Origins of a Social Beverage in the Medieval Near East.* Seattle: University of Washington Press.

Hawkes, Rebecca. 1997. The Zilo Interview. *Middle East Broadcast and Satellite* 5(3): 28.

Heineken Press Centre. 2002. Heineken Bid for Al-Ahram Shares Successful. http://www .heinekeninternational.com/alahram.aspx (accessed Sept. 3, 2008).

Held, David, and Anthony McGrew. 2000. The Great Globalization Debate. In *The Global Transformations Reader,* ed. David Held and Anthony McGrew. Pp. 1–49. Cambridge: Polity.

Heyworth-Dunne, James. 1968. *An Introduction to a History of Education in Egypt.* London: Cass.

Hinnebusch, Raymond. 1982. Children of the Elite: Political Attitudes of the Westernized Bourgeoisie in Contemporary Egypt. *Middle East Journal* 36(4): 535–561.

Hirschkind, Charles. 2001. The Ethics of Listening: Cassette-Sermon Audition in Contemporary Egypt. *American Ethnologist* 28(3): 623–649.

———. 2006a. Cassette Ethics: Public Piety and Popular Media in Egypt. In *Religion, Media and the Public Sphere,* ed. Birgit Meyer and Annelies Moors. Pp. 29–51. Bloomington: Indiana University Press.

———. 2006b. *The Ethical Soundscape: Cassette Sermons and Islamic Counterpublics.* New York: Columbia University Press.

Hoffman-Ladd, Valerie J. 1987. Polemics on the Modesty and Segregation of Women in Contemporary Egypt. *International Journal of Middle East Studies* 19: 23–50.

Hoodfar, Hoda. 1997. *Between Marriage and the Market.* Berkeley: University of California Press.

Huntington, Samuel. 1993. The Clash of Civilizations. *Foreign Affairs* 72(3): 22–49.

Ibrahim, Saad Eddin. 1982. Social Mobility and Income Distribution in Egypt, 1952–1975. In *Political Economy of Income Distribution in Egypt,* ed. Gouda Abdel Khalek and Robert Tigner. Pp. 375–434. New York: Holmes and Meiers.

———. 1996. *Egypt, Islam and Democracy.* Cairo: American University in Cairo Press.

Imada, Erika. 2002. The Establishment and Dissolution of "Girl's Networks" in a Girl's Magazine: As Seen from the Readers' Column of a Girl's Magazine in 1931–1945. *Kyoiku-shakaigaku Kenkyu/Journal of Educational Sociology* 70(1): 185–202.

Inhorn, Marcia. 1995. *Infertility and Patriarchy: The Cultural Politics of Gender and Family Life in Egypt.* Philadelphia: University of Pennsylvania Press.

———. 2003. *Local Babies, Global Science: Gender, Religion and In Vitro Fertilization in Egypt.* London: Routledge.

Iwabuchi, Koichi. 2002. *Recentering Globalization: Popular Culture and Japanese Transnationalism.* Durham, N.C.: Duke University Press.

Jameson, Fredric. 1984. The Postmodern Condition; or, The Culture of Late Capitalism. *New Left Review* 146: 53–92.

Jankowski, James. 1986. *Egypt, Islam and the Arabs: The Search for Egyptian Nationhood, 1900–1930.* New York: Oxford University Press.

Jankowski, James, and Israel Gershoni. 1995. *Redefining the Egyptian Nation, 1930–1945.* Cambridge: Cambridge University Press.

Jenks, Chris. 1996. *Childhood.* London: Routledge.

Jordan, Tim. 2004. The Pleasures and Pains of Pikachu. *European Journal of Cultural Studies* 7(4): 461–480.

Joyce, Cynthia. 1999. Give Pokémon a Chance. *Salon,* July 6: http://www.salon.com /entertainment/tv/int/1999/07/06/pokemon_primer/index.html.

Kahane, Henry. 1986. A Typology of the Prestige Language. *Language* 62(3): 495–508.

Katsuno, Hirofumi, and Jeffrey Maret. 2004. Localizing the *Pokémon* TV Series for the American Market. In *Pokémon's World Adventure,* ed. J. Tobin. Pp. 81–107. Durham, N.C.: Duke University Press.

Kearney, Michael. 1995. The Local and the Global: The Anthropology of Globalization and Transnationalism. *Annual Review of Anthropology* 24: 547–565.

Keat, Russell. 1991. Introduction: Starship Britain of Universal Enterprise? In *Enterprise Culture,* ed. Russell Keat and Nicholas Abercrombie. Pp. 1–20. London: Routledge.

Kehrer, Michaela. 2006. Transnational Consumer Goods Corporations (TNCs) in Egypt: Reaching toward the Mass Market. *Research in Economic Anthropology* 25: 151–172.

Klaus, Elisabeth, and Susanne Kassel. 2005. The Veil as a Means of Legitimization: An Analysis of the Interconnectedness of Gender, Media and War. *Journalism* 6(3): 335–355.

Kline, Stephen, Nick Dyer-Witheford, and Greig de Peuter. 2003. *Digital Play: The Interaction of Technology, Culture, and Marketing.* Montreal: McGill-Queen's University Press.

Koehne, Norma. 2005. (Re)Construction: Ways International Students Talk about Their Identity. *Australian Journal of Education* 49(2): 104–119.

Larkin, Brian. 1997. Indian Films and Nigerian Lovers: Media and the Creation of Parallel Modernities. *Africa* 67(3): 406–440.

Lau, Jenny Kwok Wah. 2002. Introduction to *Multiple Modernities: Cinemas and Transcultural Media in East Asia,* ed. Jenny Kwok Wah Lau. Philadelphia, Pa.: Temple University Press.

Leclerc-Madlala, Suzanne. 1996. Here's the Beef: The Grand Opening of McDonald's First Fast-Food Restaurant in South Africa Heralds Bad News for the Health of the

Nation. *New Internationalist,* June: http://www.newint.org/features/1996/06/05/ endpiece (accessed Sept. 9, 2010).

Lemish, Dafna, and Linda Renee Bloch. 2004. Pokémon in Israel. In *Pokémon's World Adventure,* ed. J. Tobin. Pp. 165–186. Durham, N.C.: Duke University Press.

Levinson, Bradley, and Dorothy Holland. 1996. The Cultural Production of the Educated Person: An Introduction. In *The Cultural Production of the Educated Person: Critical Ethnographies of Schooling and Local Practices,* ed. Bradley A. Levinson, Douglas E. Foley, and Dorothy C. Holland. Pp. 1–55. Albany: State University of New York Press.

Livia, Anna, and Kira Hall. 1997. "It's a Girl!" Bringing Performativity Back to Linguistics. In *Queerly Phrased: Language, Gender and Sexuality,* ed. Anna Livia and Kira Hall. Pp. 3–18. New York: Oxford University Press.

Low, Setha, and Denise Lawrence-Zúñiga. 2003. Locating Culture. In *The Anthropology of Space and Place: Locating Culture,* ed. Setha Low and Denise Lawrence-Zúñiga. Pp. 1–47. Oxford: Blackwell.

MacDougall, Judith, and David MacDougall. 2003. Blind Ducks in Borneo. *Visual Anthropology* 16(1): 1–14.

MacLeod, Arlene. 1991. *Accommodating Protest: Working Women, the New Veiling and Change in Cairo.* New York: Columbia University Press.

Mahmood, Saba. 2001a. Feminist Theory, Embodiment, and the Docile Agent: Some Reflections on the Egyptian Islamic Revival. *Cultural Anthropology* 16(2): 202–236.

———. 2001b. Rehearsed Spontaneity and the Conventionality of Ritual Disciplines of Salat. *American Ethnologist* 25(4): 827–853.

Margolis, Eric. 2007. Guest Editor's Introduction. *Visual Studies* 22(1): 11–12.

———. 2005. *Politics of Piety: The Islamic Revival and the Feminist Subject.* Princeton, N.J.: Princeton University Press.

Mato, Daniel. 1998. On the Making of Transnational Identities in the Age of Globalization: The U.S. Latina/o–"Latin" American Case. *Cultural Studies* 12(4): 598–620. Reprinted in *Identities: Race, Class, Gender and Nationality,* ed. Linda Alcoff and Eduardo Mendieta. Pp. 281–294. Oxford: Blackwell.

Mauss, Marcel. 1985[1935]. A Category of the Human Mind: The Notion of Person, the Notion of Self. In *The Category of the Person: Anthropology, Philosophy and History,* ed. Michael Carrither, Steven Collins, and Steven Lukes. Pp. 1–25. New York: Cambridge University Press.

Mazzarella, William. 2004. *Shoveling Smoke: Advertising and Globalization in Contemporary India.* Durham, N.C.: Duke University Press.

Medalag, Hafez el. 2000. The Responsible and the Responsibility!!! *Al Riyad* (Saudi Arabia), Dec. 16: 27.

Mehrez, Samia. 2008. *Egypt's Culture Wars: Politics and Practice.* London: Routledge.

Mellor, Noha. 2005. *The Making of Arab News.* Lanham, Md.: Rowman and Littlefield.

Merton, Robert K. 1957. *Social Theory and Social Structure.* New York: Free Press.

Miller, Daniel. 1994. *Modernity: An Ethnographic Approach.* New York: Berg.

———. 1997. *Capitalism: An Ethnographic Approach.* New York: Berg.

Miller, Daniel, ed. 1995. *Acknowledging Consumption: A Review of New Studies.* London: Routledge.

———. 2001. *Home Possessions: Material Culture and the Home.* Oxford: Berg.

Miller, Eugene. 2006. Philanthropy and Cosmopolitanism. *Good Society* 15(1): 51–60.

Mitchell, Timothy. 1988. *Colonising Egypt*. New York: Cambridge University Press.

———. 1999. Dreamland: The Neoliberalism of Your Desires. *Middle East Report* (Spring): 28–33.

———. 2002. *Rule of Experts: Egypt, Techno-Politics, Modernity*. Berkeley: University of California Press.

Moeran, Brian. 2004. Women's Fashion Magazines: People, Things and Values. In *Values and Valuables: From the Sacred to the Symbolic*, ed. Cynthia Werner and Duran Bell. Pp. 257–280. Walnut Creek, Calif.: AltaMira.

Moerman, Michael. 1993. Ariadne's Thread and Indra's Net: Reflections on Ethnography, Ethnicity, Identity, Culture, and Interaction. *Research on Language and Social Interaction* 26(1): 85–98.

Moore, Roy L., and George P. Moschis. 1983. Role of Mass Media and the Family in Development of Consumption. *Journalism Quarterly* 60(1): 67–73.

Moran, Joe. 2006. Milk Bars, Starbucks and the Uses of Literacy. *Cultural Studies* 20(6): 552–573.

Mostafa, Hadia. 2005a. Business Secrets of the Sawiris Family. *Business Today Egypt*. http://www.businesstodayegypt.com/article.aspx?ArticleID=4361 (accessed May 14, 2010).

———. 2005b. Bottlenecked. *Business Today Egypt*. http://www.businesstodayegypt.com /article.aspx?ArticleID=6072 (accessed Sept. 8, 2008).

———. 2005c. Top Dollar. *Egypt Today* 26(12): http://www.egypttoday.com/article.aspx ?ArticleID=6176 (accessed Feb. 25, 2010).

Murphy, Lawrence R. 1987. *The American University in Cairo: 1919–1987*. Cairo: American University in Cairo Press.

Nagi, Abdel Sattar. 2000. Pokémon (in Arabic). *Al Anbaa'*, Oct. 2: 23.

Nash, Manning. 1989. *The Cauldron of Identity*. Chicago: University of Chicago Press.

Nederveen Pieterse, Jan. 2004. *Globalization and Culture: Global Melange*. Lanham, Md.: Rowman and Littlefield.

Nicol, Alan. 1991. The Labor Pains of Privatization. *Business Monthly* 7(10): 6–8.

Nussbaum, Martha. 1996. *For Love of Country: Debating the Limits of Patriotism*. Boston: Beacon.

———. 1997. Kant and Cosmopolitanism. In *Perpetual Peace: Essays on Kant's Cosmopolitan Ideal*, ed. James Bohmann and Matthias Lutz-Bachmann. Pp. 25–57. Cambridge, Mass.: MIT Press.

Ochs, Elinor. 1992. Indexing Gender. In *Rethinking Context: Language as an Interactive Phenomenon*, ed. Alessandro Duranti and Charles Goodwin. Pp. 335–358. Cambridge: Cambridge University Press.

———. 1993. Constructing Social Identity: A Language Socialization Perspective. *Research on Language and Social Interaction* 26(3): 287–306.

Ochs, Elinor, and Lisa Capps. 2001. *Living Narrative: Creating Lives in Everyday Storytelling*. Cambridge, Mass.: Harvard University Press.

O'Dougherty, Maureen. 2002. *Consumption Intensified: The Politics of Middle Class Life in Brazil*. Durham, N.C.: Duke University Press.

Okker, Patricia. 2003. *Social Stories*. Charlottesville: University of Virginia Press.

Oldenburg, Ray. 1989. *The Great Good Place: Cafes, Coffee Shops, Community Centers, Beauty Parlors, General Stores, Bars, Hangouts and How They Get You through the Day*. New York: Paragon.

Olivier, Roy. 1994. *The Failure of Political Islam*. Cambridge, Mass.: Harvard University Press.

Ortner, Sherry. 1995. Resistance and the Problem of Ethnographic Refusal. *Comparative Studies of Society and History* 37(1): 173–193.

Osman, Osman M. 1998. *Development and Poverty Reduction Strategies in Egypt*. Cairo: ERF.

Ossman, Susan. 2002. *Three Faces of Beauty: Casablanca, Paris, Cairo*. Durham, N.C.: Duke University Press.

Öztürk, Serdar. 2008. The Struggle over Turkish Village Coffee Houses (1923–45). *Middle Eastern Studies* 44(3): 435–454.

Page, John. 2001. Getting Ready for Globalization: A New Privatization Strategy for the Middle East? In *State-Owned Enterprises in the Middle East and North Africa: Privatization, Performance and Reform*, ed. Merih Celasun. Pp. 63–88. London: Routledge.

Peterson, Mark Allen. 1998. Languages of Globalization. In *Globalization: Blessing or Curse?* ed. Mohammed Farag. Pp. 119–127. Cairo: American University in Cairo.

———. 2003. *Anthropology and Mass Communication: Media and Myth in the New Millennium*. New York: Berghahn.

———. 2007. From Jinn to Genies: Intertextuality, Media, and the Rise of Global Folklore. In *Folklore/Cinema: Popular Film as Vernacular Culture*, ed. Mikel J. Koven and Sharon Sherman. Pp. 93–112. Logan: Utah State University Press.

Peterson, Mark Allen, and Ivan Panovic. 2004. Accessing Egypt: Making Myths and Producing Web Sites in Cyber-Cairo. *New Review of Hypermedia and Multimedia* 10(2): 199–219.

Pollard, Lisa. 2003. Working by the Book: New Homes and the Emergence of the Modern Egyptian State under Muhamed Ali. In *Transitions in Domestic Consumption and Family Life in the Modern Middle East*, ed. Relli Shechter. Pp. 13–36. New York: Palgrave Macmillan.

Posusney, Marsha Pripstein. 1993. Irrational Workers: The Moral Economy of Labor Protest in Egypt. *World Politics* 46(1): 83–120.

———. 1997. *Labor and the State in Egypt: Workers, Unions, and Economic Reconstruction*. New York: Columbia University Press.

Prandi, Michele. 1994. Meaning and Indexicality in Communication. In *Pretending to Communicate*, ed. Herman Parret. Pp. 33–47. Berlin: de Gruyter.

Pratt, Mary Louise. 1991. Arts of the Contact Zone. *Profession* 91: 33–40.

Pripstein, Marsha. 1995. Egypt's New Labor Law Removes Worker Provisions. *Middle East Report* 194–195: 52–53, 64.

Ram, Uri. 2007. Liquid Identities: Mecca Cola versus Coca-Cola. *European Journal of Cultural Studies* 10(4): 465–484.

Rao, Aruna. 2001. From Self-Knowledge to Super Heroes: The Story of Indian Comics. In *Illustrating Asia*, ed. John Lent. Pp. 37–63. Honolulu: University of Hawaii Press.

Reid, Donald M. 1977. Educational and Career Choices of Egyptian Students, 1882–1922. *International Journal of Middle East Studies* 8: 349–378.

Renard, John. 2007. *Al-Jihad al-Akbar*: Notes on a Theme in Islamic Spirituality. *Muslim World* 78(3–4): 225–242.

Ritzer, George. 1993. *The McDonaldization of Society*. Thousand Oaks, Calif.: Pine Forge.

Robertson, Roland. 1992. *Globalization: Social Theory and Global Culture*. London: Sage.

Rock, Aaron. 2010. Amr Khaled: From *Da'wa* to Political and Religious Leadership. *British Journal of Middle Eastern Studies* 37(1): 15–37.

Rodenbeck, Max. 1999. *Cairo: The City Victorious*. Cairo: American University in Cairo Press.

Rodman, Margaret C. 2003. Empowering Place: Multilocality and Multivocality. In *The Anthropology of Space and Place: Locating Culture*, ed. Setha Low and Denise Lawrence-Zúñiga. Pp. 204–223. Oxford: Blackwell.

Rosaldo, Michelle. 1984. Toward an Anthropology of Thought and Feeling. In *Culture Theory: Essays on Mind, Self and Emotion*, ed. Robert A. Levine and Richard A. Schweder. Pp. 137–157. Cambridge: Cambridge University Press.

Rosaldo, Renato. 1980. *Ilongot Headhunting, 1883–1974*. Stanford, Calif.: Stanford University Press.

Rose, Jonathan. 2001. *The Intellectual Life of the British Working Classes*. New Haven, Conn.: Yale University Press.

Rosenberg, Justin. 2000. *The Follies of Globalization Theory*. London: Verso.

Russell, Michael E. 1994. *Cultural Reproduction in Egypt's Private University*. Unpublished Ph.D. diss., University of Kentucky.

Russell, Mona. 2003. Modernity, National Identity and Consumerism: Visions of the Egyptian Home 1805–1922. In *Transitions in Domestic Consumption and Family Life in the Modern Middle East*, ed. Relli Shechter. Pp. 37–62. New York: Palgrave Macmillan.

———. 2004. *Creating the New Egyptian Woman: Consumerism, Education and National Identity 1863–1922*. New York: Palgrave Macmillan.

Ryzova, Lucie. 2005. Egyptianising Modernity: Social and Cultural Constructions of the Middle Classes in Egypt under the Monarchy. In *Re-envisioning the Egyptian Monarchy*, ed. Arthur Goldschmidt, Amy Johnson, and Barak Salmoni. Pp. 124–163. Cairo: American University in Cairo Press.

Sahlins, Marshall. 1972. The Original Affluent Society. In his *Stone Age Economics*. New York: Aldine-Atherton.

———. 1994. Cosmologies of Capitalism: The Trans-Pacific Sector of "the World System." In *A Reader in Contemporary Social Theory*, ed. Nicholas Dirks, Geoff Eley, and Sherry B. Ortner. Pp. 412–456. Princeton, N.J.: Princeton University Press.

Salamandra, Christa. 2004. *A New Old Damascus: Authenticity and Distinction in Urban Syria*. Bloomington: Indiana University Press.

Salvatore, Armando. 1997. *Islam and the Public Discourse of Modernity*. Reading, England: Ithaca.

———. 2000. Social Differentiation, Moral Authority and Public Islam in Egypt: The Path of Mustafa Mahmud. *Anthropology Today* 16(2): 12–15.

Samper, Mario K. 2003. The Historical Construction of Quality and Competitiveness: A Preliminary Discussion of Coffee Commodity Chains. In *The Global Coffee Economy in Africa, Asia, and Latin America, 1500–1989*, ed. William Gervase Clarence-Smith and Steven Topik. Pp. 120–153. Cambridge: Cambridge University Press.

Sassen, Saskia. 2001. *The Global City: New York, London, Tokyo*. Princeton, N.J.: Princeton University Press.

Sassen, Saskia, ed. 2002. *Global Networks, Linked Cities*. London: Routledge.

Schaub, Mark. 2000. English in the Arab Republic of Egypt. *World Englishes* 19(2): 225–238.

Schumpeter, Joseph A. 1934. *The Theory of Economic Development.* Cambridge, Mass.: Harvard University Press.

———. 1993. The Creative Response in Economic History. In *Evolutionary Economics,* ed. Ulrich Witt. Pp. 3–13. Brookfield, Vt.: Elgar.

Scott, Joan. 1992. Experience. In *Feminists Theorize the Political,* ed. Judith Butler and Joan Scott. Pp. 22–40. New York: Routledge.

Sell, Ralph. 1990. International Affinities in Modern Egypt: Results from a Social Distance Survey of Elite Students. *International Journal of Middle East Studies* 22: 59–84.

Shafik, Viola. 2007. *Popular Egyptian Cinema: Gender, Class and Nation.* Cairo: American University in Cairo Press.

Shahine, Gihan. 2002. Preacher on the Run. *Al-Ahram English Edition* 616: 7.

Sharkey, Heather. 2008. *American Evangelicals in Egypt: Missionary Encounters in an Age of Empire.* Princeton, N.J.: Princeton University Press.

Shechter, Relli. 2006. *Smoking, Culture and Economy in the Middle East: The Egyptian Tobacco Market 1850–2000.* London: Tauris.

Shechter, Relli, ed. 2003. *Transitions in Domestic Consumption and Family Life in the Modern Middle East.* New York: Palgrave Macmillan.

Shiraz, Faegheh. 2001. *The Veil Unveiled: The Hijab in Modern Culture.* Gainesville: University Press of Florida.

Sidahmed, Rifa'at. 1985. *Ikhtiragh al Agl al Misry: Al-Gama'a al-Amrikiyya wal Buhuus al Mushtaraka* [Invasion of the Egyptian Mind: The American University and Joint Research]. Cairo: n.p.

Siddiqi, B. H. 1960. *Ilm al-Akhlaq:* A Brief Survey. *Pakistan Philosophical Journal* 3(3): 58–66.

Sidnell, Jack. 2003. Constructing and Managing Male Exclusivity in Talk-in-Interaction. In *The Handbook of Language and Gender,* ed. Janet Holmes and Miriam Meyerhoff. Pp. 327–352. Oxford: Blackwell.

Silverstein, Michael. 2003. Indexical Order and the Dialectics of Sociolinguistic Life. *Language and Communication* 23: 193–229.

Singerman, Diane. 1995. *Avenues of Participation: Family, Politics and Networks in Urban Quarters of Cairo.* Princeton, N.J.: Princeton University Press.

Singerman, Diane, and Paul Amar. 2006. Introduction: Contesting Myths, Critiquing Cosmopolitanism, and Creating the New Cairo School of Urban Studies. In *Cairo Cosmopolitan,* ed. Diane Singerman and Paul Amar. Pp. 3–43. Cairo: American University in Cairo Press.

Smith, Elizabeth A. 2006. Place, Class and Race in the Barabra Café: Nubians in Egyptian Media. In *Cairo Cosmopolitan,* ed. Diane Singerman and Paul Amar. Pp. 399–414. Cairo: American University in Cairo Press.

Sparre, Sara Lei, and Marie Juul Petersen. 2007. Youth and Social Change in Jordan and Egypt. *ISIM Review* 20: 14–15.

Springhall, John. 1998. *Youth, Popular Culture, and Moral Panics: Penny Gaffs to Gangsta-Rap, 1830–1996.* New York: St. Martin's.

Sreberny, Annabelle. 2001. Mediated Culture in the Middle East: Diffusion, Democracy, Difficulties. *Gazette* 62(2–3): 101–119.

Starrett, Gregory. 1998. *Putting Islam to Work: Education, Politics and Religious Trans-formation in Egypt*. Berkeley: University of California Press.

Stokes, Martin. 1994. Turkish Arabesk and the City: Urban Popular Culture as Spatial Practice. In *Islam, Globalization and Modernity*, ed. Akbar Ahmed and Hastings Donnan. Pp. 21–37. London: Routledge.

Thompson, Kenneth. 1998. *Moral Panics*. London: Routledge.

Topik, Steven, and William Gervase Clarence-Smith. 2003. Introduction: Coffee and Global Development. In *The Global Coffee Economy in Africa, Asia, and Latin America, 1500–1989*, ed. William Gervase Clarence-Smith and Steven Topik. Pp. 1–17. Cambridge: Cambridge University Press.

Toth, James. 1999. *Rural Labor Movements in Egypt and Their Impact on the State, 1961–1992*. Gainesville: University Press of Florida.

Traube, Elizabeth. 1989. Secrets of Success in Postmodern Society. *Cultural Anthropology* 3(4): 273–300.

Turner, Victor. 1995. *The Ritual Process: Structure and Antistructure*. New York: Aldine.

Urban, Greg. 2001. *Metaculture: How Culture Moves through the World*. Minneapolis: University of Minnesota Press.

Useem, John. 1963. The Community of Man: A Study in the Third Culture. *Centennial Review* 7: 481–498.

van Nieuwkerk, Karin. 1995. *"A Trade Like Any Other": Female Singers and Dancers in Egypt*. Austin: University of Texas Press.

———. 2007. From Repentance to Pious Performance. *ISIM Review* 20: 54–55.

van Velsen, J. 1967. The Extended Case Method and Situational Analysis. In *The Craft of Social Anthropology*, ed. A. L. Epstein. Pp. 129–149. London: Tavistock.

Wallerstein, Immanuel. 1974. *The Modern World System*. New York: Academic.

Warschauer, Mark, Ghada R. El Said, and Ayman Zohry. 2002. Language Choice Online: Globalization and Identity in Egypt. *Journal of Computer Mediated Communication* 7(4): http://jcmc.indiana.edu/vo17/issue4/warschauer.html (accessed Apr. 14, 2008).

Wassef, Nadia. 1999. Asserting Masculinities: FGM in Egypt Revisited. *Middle East Women's Studies Review* 14(3): 1–9.

Wassmann, Ingrid. 2004. Why Are We Running This Story? *Egypt Today* (Nov.): 88–93.

Watenpaugh, Keith David. 2006. *Being Modern in the Middle East: Revolution, Nationalism, Colonialism, and the Arab Middle Class*. Princeton, N.J.: Princeton University Press.

Watson, James L., ed. 1997. *Golden Arches East: McDonald's in East Asia*. Stanford, Calif.: Stanford University Press.

Werbner, Pnina. 1997. Afterword: Writing Multiculturalism and Politics in the New Europe. In *Debating Cultural Hybridity: Multicultural Identities and the Politics of Antiracism*, ed. Pnina Werbner and Tariq Modood. Pp. 261–267. London: Zed.

———. 1999. Global Pathways: Working Class Cosmopolitans and the Creation of Transnational Ethnic Worlds. *Social Anthropology* 7(1): 17–35.

Wikan, Unni. 1996. *Tomorrow, God Willing: Self-Made Destinies in Cairo*. Chicago: University of Chicago Press.

Wiktorowicz, Quintan. 2003. *Islamic Activism: A Social Movement Theory Approach*. Bloomington: Indiana University Press.

Wilk, Richard. 1990. Consumer Goods as Dialogue about Development. *Culture and History* 7: 79–100.

———. 1999. "Real Belizean Food": Building Local Identity in the Transnational Caribbean. *American Anthropologist* 101(2): 244–255.

Williams, Colin C. 2007. De-linking Enterprise Culture from Capitalism and Its Public Policy Implications. *Public Policy and Administration* 22: 461–474.

Williamson, John, ed. 1994. *The Political Economy of Policy Reform*. Washington, D.C.: Institute for International Economics.

Winegar, Jessica. 2006. *Creative Reckonings: The Politics of Art and Culture in Contemporary Egypt*. Stanford, Calif.: Stanford University Press.

Wise, Lindsay. 2003. "Words from the Heart": New Forms of Islamic Preaching in Egypt. M.Ph. thesis, Oxford University. http://users.ox.ac.uk/~metheses/Wise.pdf (accessed Sept. 10, 2008).

Woltering, Robbert. 2007. Egyptian Public Intellectuals and Their "Wests." *ISIM Review* 19: 42–43.

World Bank. 1998. *Egypt in the Global Economy: Strategic Choices for Savings, Investments, and Long-Term Growth*. Washington, D.C.: World Bank.

Wynn, Lisa L. 2009. *Pyramids and Nightclubs: A Travel Ethnography of Arab and Western Imaginations of Egypt, from King Tut and a Colony of Atlantis to Rumors of Sex Orgies, a Marauding Prince, and Blonde Belly Dancers*. Austin: University of Texas Press.

Yano, Christine. 2004. Panic Attacks: Anti-Pokémon Voices in Global Markets. In *Pikachu's Global Adventure: The Rise and Fall of Pokémon*, ed. Joseph Tobin. Pp. 108–138. Durham, N.C.: Duke University Press.

Younis, Wesam Mohamed Ibrahim. 2005. *Gated Cities in Greater Cairo*. Unpublished M.A. thesis, American University in Cairo.

Yuval-Davis, Nira. 1997. Ethnicity, Gender Relations and Multiculturalism. In *Debating Cultural Hybridity: Multicultural Identities and the Politics of Antiracism*, ed. Pnina Werbner and Tariq Modood. Pp. 193–208. London: Zed.

INDEX

Abaza, Mona, 17, 18, 22, 199–200, 225n5, 232nn1,2, 233n14, 237
Abdel-Moneim, Shearin, x, 229n6
Abdel-Rahim, Sha'ban, 197, 243
abjection, 140, 242
Abu Khalifa, 146, 220
Abu-Hashish, Shereen, x, 39, 227n18, 237
Abu-Lughod, Lila, 5, 22, 34, 67, 125, 151, 156
adab (manners), 104–108, 110, 230n9, 242
'Adl, Muhammad, 97
advertising, 6, 24, 31, 35, 42, 49, 50, 82, 135, 161, 182–187, 192–195, 196, 220, 223, 228n6, 242, 246
agency, 7, 21, 29, 34, 93, 129, 223; consumer, 201; definition, 55; moral, 230n16; redistribution of, 109, 110; state, 26
'ahwa, 20, 21, 26, 61, 141–147, 149–151, 153–160, 163–168, 220, 232n4
Ain Sukna, 205
Akbar al Yom, 30
Akhla' (good character), 104–108, 110
Al Akkad Mall, 151, 153, 156, 160
Al Arabi Alsaghir, 24, 31, 41, 43, 45–50, 52, 55, 59
Al Bayan, 228n6, 240
Al Riyad, 77, 246
al walad da akhla'a (a child with morals), 105
Alaa Eldin, 24, 31, 41–49, 52, 53, 59, 226n8, 227n15
Al-Ahram, 30, 43, 178, 179, 180, 192, 244, 250
Al-Ahram Beverage Company (ABC), 178

Al-Ahram Weekly, 30, 161, 196, 238
'Alam Simsim, 81
Al-Aqsa intifada, 48, 197
Al-Azhar University, 85, 166, 179, 197
Alexandria, 117, 186, 192, 201, 220, 232; university, 115
al-haya (reserve, restraint), 133
Allison, Anne, 69, 70, 237
al-Mu'allim (The boss), 196, 197
Al-Rubai, 75, 76, 237
Alshaya Group, 234n1
American Jewish Congress, 198
American School in Cairo (ASC), 5, 19, 25, 50, 97, 99, 100, 111, 113, 130, 134, 139, 175, 194, 228n14, 229nn5,6,7, 230nn10,18
American University in Cairo (AUC), 5, 12, 22, 82, 83, 97–99, 103, 105, 111–120, 125, 126, 128, 130–132, 140, 151, 154, 155, 163, 164, 172, 183, 204, 219–223, 225, 227n18, 229nn1,3,6, 230nn17–19, 231nn21–23, 232nn30–32
Amunah the Amazing, 48
amusement parks, 17, 51
Anderson, Benedict, 32, 34, 47, 52, 125, 238
Anderson, Jon W., 125, 231n28, 238
anime, 43
anti-Semitic, 98, 187, 229n2
Appadurai, Arjun, 9, 33, 34, 72, 99, 213, 238
Applbaum, Kalman, 182, 235n9, 238
Arab, 2, 15, 25, 38, 49, 59, 68, 99, 110, 118, 202, 209, 230n15; character, 75, 79; children, 24, 31, 47, 52, 53, 78, 86;

253

Mark Allen Peterson is Professor of Anthropology and International Studies at Miami University of Ohio. He is author of *Anthropology and Mass Communication: Media and Myth in the New Millennium* and co-author of *International Studies: An Interdisciplinary Approach to Global Issues.*